Common Core Reading Lessons

The Common Core is placing a heavier emphasis on nonfiction, but that doesn't mean you have to give up your literature lessons! In this book, English teachers Stacey O'Reilly and Angie Stooksbury describe how you can combine nonfiction with fiction to meet the standards and give students a deeper understanding of what they are reading. This practical book provides a variety of nonfiction reading strategies as well as ready-to-implement lesson plans and text pairing suggestions.

Special Features:

- Useful strategies to help students analyze nonfiction
- Sample units with step-by-step agendas and lesson plans
- Ready-to-use classroom handouts and rubrics for assessment
- Suggested text pairings across genres and time periods

Stacey O'Reilly and **Angie Stooksbury** are English teachers at Big Walnut Local Schools in Ohio. They frequently present at conferences on the topic of reading and the Common Core.

Common Core Reading Lessons

Pairing Literary and Nonfiction Texts to Promote Deeper Understanding

Stacey O'Reilly and Angie Stooksbury

Routledge
Taylor & Francis Group

NEW YORK AND LONDON

First published 2014
by Routledge
711 Third Avenue, New York, NY 10017

And by Routledge
2 Park Square, Milton Park, Abingdon, Oxon OX14 4RN

Routledge is an imprint of the Taylor & Francis Group, an informa business

Library of Congress Cataloging-in-Publication Data
O'Reilly, Stacey.
   Common core reading lessons : pairing literary and nonfiction texts to promote deeper understanding / Stacey O'Reilly, Angie Stooksbury.
      pages cm
   Includes bibliographical references and index.
   1. Language arts (Secondary)—Curricula—United States.   2. Language arts (Secondary)—Standards—United States.   3. Literature—Study and teaching (Secondary)—United States.   4. English language—Composition and exercises—Study and teaching (Secondary)   I. Stooksbury, Angie.   II. Title.
   LB1632.O74 2013
   428.4071'2—dc23
                                                                              2013037760

ISBN: 978-0-415-73467-7 (hbk)
ISBN: 978-0-415-73319-9 (pbk)
ISBN: 978-1-315-81983-9 (ebk)

Typeset in Optima
by Apex CoVantage, LLC

Printed and bound in the United States of America by Publishers Graphics, LLC on sustainably sourced paper.

Contents

Contents

Acknowledgments

From Stacey: To all my boys: My husband, Brian, and sons, Gavin and Rowan, I love you forever, always, and entirely! Thank you for your patience and for allowing me to see life from other perspectives. I would also like to send a shout out to the people who have most inspired my teaching. My 7th- and 8th-grade teacher, Mrs. Pabst, challenged me as a reader and writer, encouraging me to value all learning opportunities. Cathy Cikra, my mentor at Kent, who always made time for me, guided me, taught me, and loved me through those early years. I hope to be the teacher you are. And to my parents, who taught me how to play well with others, work hard, and live with passion. My last shout out goes to Angie Stooksbury, who helped me transition and inspired me to take this next professional leap. I look forward to many more travels and adventures ahead of us!

From Angie: I would like to thank my husband, Brent, and my three children, Justin, Brooke, and Lexi, for understanding all of the extra hours I put in at school with my students. I love you so much. For my family and friends, thanks for challenging me to push myself farther than I thought possible. I would also like to acknowledge all of the wonderful students I have had the privilege of teaching over the last 20 years—without you, this book wouldn't have been written. You have continued to inspire and influence my journey as a teacher. Lastly, thanks to the Big Walnut School district for supporting my ideas and passion for teaching and for hiring Stacey O'Reilly, who has reinvigorated my love for education. Our planning, collaborating, and life discussions have meant so much, and I look forward to the years ahead.

Meet the Authors

Stacey O'Reilly studied English and received her bachelor's degree from The Ohio State University. From there, she completed her master's degree in teaching at Kent State University. She worked for Kent City Schools for eight years. A job transfer brought both her and her husband back to the Columbus area where she took a job with the Big Walnut Local Schools. She has worked at Big Walnut High School for three years, which is where she met Angie and began the collaboration of planning, presenting, and writing.

Attending Kenyon College and Ohio Wesleyan University, **Angie Stooksbury** obtained her degree in English Education. She acquired her master's degree in Curriculum and Instruction at Ashland University. She has been an English teacher for the last 20 years at Big Walnut High School in Sunbury, Ohio. Over the course of those years, she has taught all grades and levels of students from freshman English to upper level literature courses. Recently presenting at the National Council of Teachers of English (NCTE) conference on the Common Core led to the writing of this book.

Introduction

How to Use This Book

We have organized this book according to common topics and the way we build our year. An important note is that every year is different depending upon our students' needs. Ultimately, what is happening in the world also shapes what we use and how we use it. These lessons and units can stand alone or be taught in sequence. We have structured the chapters according to Common Core standards emphasizing the fiction and nonfiction connections. Each chapter begins with an overview, time frame, and standards met according to grades 9–10 specifically. All lessons and units can readily be adapted for grades 11–12. We discuss the why behind the connections and give ample explanation as to how these ideas can be implemented in your classroom. Each chapter ends with agendas, lessons, handouts, rubrics, and often opportunities for extension. As teachers, we want practical, user-friendly materials that work. Our hope is that you can take them directly from the page and include them within your teaching.

The O'Reilly and Stooksbury Duo

When we were first approached about writing this book, we were excited about the opportunity to share with other educators our ideas and lesson plans for the Common Core. We aren't researchers; we aren't professors of education. We are, two determined, stubborn, excitable, passionate people who care about our students not just during the year we share with them but FOREVER. Let's take a minute to introduce ourselves and how we became educators.

More about Stacey O'Reilly

Even before I could read, I was a reader making up stories as I flipped through the pages. As I grew older, I could be found sitting sideways in a chair, swinging on the porch swing, sprawling across my bed, a book always by my side. Reading was important, and from my parents to my teachers, reading and writing were celebrated as strengths of mine. I liked the attention of being asked to read aloud in class or share a paper I had written. The person who most influenced my desire to be a teacher was someone who hated being asked to do these things—my younger brother. He struggled with learning disabilities. I wanted to help him, but at first was too little. By the time we were both in high school, I got my chance. Again, sitting in my bed, this time with my brother beside me, I would read to him *Of Mice and Men, The Great Gatsby, Night, To Kill a Mockingbird.* We would read and review, discuss and disagree, move on and get through it together. That's when I knew I wanted to be an English teacher.

More about Angie Stooksbury

When I was just 10 years old, my fourth-grade teacher asked me to help her be "teacher" for a day. That was all it took. From that day on, I knew my dream was to grow up and become a teacher. I didn't want to be just an average teacher—I wanted to be one of the great ones, a teacher remembered fondly by my students for years after graduation. I had several amazing elementary teachers who still stand out in my mind, and a favorite middle school teacher, but when it came to high school, no one inspired me like those earlier teachers. It was then that I decided I wanted to be a high school teacher who was as passionate and caring as my favorite teachers in my early years. It was decided: High school, here I come. And although I liked all subjects, my passion was reading. I love to read, and I value the necessity of speaking and writing effectively; thus, English was my destiny.

Living and Learning

So now you know a little bit about each of us—hopefully, we haven't scared you off. Individually, we are strong educators pushing ourselves to constantly revise and improve what we have to offer students. However, together we have grown even more by continually pushing each other farther—sometimes even butting heads. A true test of a professional, collaborative relationship is joining forces to publish a book. We ask our students to work collaboratively and learn from each other; it is only right that we do the same.

The writing of this book happened quite suddenly, though in reality we have worked on it for the whole of our careers. The entire thing began with a move to a new district, a newly formed collaboration, and a goal to present together at a national conference. It began for us as we sat down for the first time to go over common assessments and planning. We had a like mission and quickly realized that our philosophies meshed well together. With a year of collaboration under our belts, the Common Core was introduced in our district. It was coming whether we liked it or not. And although we saw the usefulness of some of the changes established in these standards, we never imagined our work on it would lead us to publishing a book.

We put this book together on the basis of what we have lived and learned through our interactions in the classroom. What we offer is practical knowledge that can be applied in its original form and used in your classroom. You have our permission to take any of the ideas present in this book and make them your own. One way to make these lessons your own is to modify the agendas—we sure do. Often we take more time than what our agendas outline because of the tangents we find ourselves and our students exploring. Allow yourselves and your students the time to do this. We always find ways to make up the time in other places. A second modification comes with grammar and vocabulary. We do more with grammar and vocabulary than what is shown throughout these units, but we decided to leave it up to you as to where and how you pull these aspects in. Keep what you know you are doing well, but please be open to integrating some new ideas and accepting opportunities for change.

That's what we have done. We have taken bits of information and knowledge collected and stored over the years and turned them into something meaningful for our students and ourselves professionally. If some of the statements sound familiar, again we have taken from the various movements in education and kept what we felt were the best parts, the parts we continue to teach by.

Our philosophy puts the students first. We believe in creating lifelong learners. We know—you've heard that one before. Our simple reply is that if we want our students to succeed, then we have to try our best to awaken and equip them with the skills necessary to develop their inherent drive to learn. When we are little, we are curious about anything and everything. Somewhere along the way, that curiosity gets pushed aside. It's not gone, but we become so busy doing what has to be done that we don't make the time to simply explore something because it's of interest to us. That's what the Common Core has brought back to the forefront for teachers: Pushing our students to learn not because they have to, but rather because their curiosity is piqued. We want them to seek out information because of a craving to know more. When students start coming into class with topics that they have researched on their own, without it being assigned work, then all students win—not just in high school, but for the rest of their lives.

We can't begin to tell you how many of our current assignments were modified by (and in some cases, actually originated with) a student coming in with an idea or topic. Being open to students' ideas is essential. We believe in creating a learning environment that encourages students to take the journey with us. Together we, teachers and students alike, explore and travel exciting paths of unexpected twists and turns full of possibilities. This is why we love our job.

Don't Fight the Common Core!

Frustrated and Frazzled

A bad taste remains in the mouths of many educators from the frustrating, impossible mandates of No Child Left Behind. Now Washington is sending something else our way—the Common Core. The ever-moving pendulum, swinging faster than ever, moves toward yet another mark as most states prepare to implement the Common Core State Standards. Questions abound in every school district across the United States from teachers who work tirelessly trying to engage students, preparing them to enter the world. Educators must imagine careers to fulfill a future need unlike anything we currently know—a truly daunting task.

Now we are being asked to consider if what we have been teaching is really what our students need to know for their future success. Teachers are pondering, What are these new standards? Are they really necessary and valuable for our students? Should we just pretend to adopt them while we continue teaching with our tried-and-true methods? Can we give up Shakespeare for a close reading of a technical document? The real questions are, What are the new standards actually asking of us? Will teaching these standards truly propel students to the next level?

To begin to address these questions, let's go back to the moment you were first told to align your current curriculum with the new standards. The idea of the 70/30 split prompted the catch for most English teachers. When you heard that the Common Core called for a 70/30 split, some of you began to plan your retirement; some of you indignantly vowed to teach the way you've always taught; some of you were too new to the profession, still grappling with the day-to-day routine; some of you were ready to tackle this head on—we were in this latter group. Knowing that we are effective, resourceful, and successful teachers, we were determined to reinvent our lessons according to the new standards.

Having a combined experience of more than 30 years, working in a district where we are asked to teach 6 periods a day, juggling up to 4 preps, differentiating instruction from remedial to advanced, accepting funding cuts and failed levies, you know the story; we live this story in the teaching profession. Don't get us wrong: The idea of incorporating so much nonfiction initially had us wondering what our courses would become, what our teaching style would look like, and what these changes would do to our students' learning and overall appreciation of literature. Our instinct as teachers is to protect and push our students. We know we are doing a good job, but as we've explored the Common Core, we've found we can do better.

The 1st Hurdle to Change

The first major hurdle to get out of the way is that no one likes or welcomes change. As teachers, we like to plan, organize, and bring order to chaos. Just as we ask students to revise their work, we like to reflect on and revise lessons, hoping to master delivery, sequence, content, and assessment. We are so focused on knowing our students and teaching those students according to what's in their best interests that we can sometimes close ourselves off to change required by forces outside of the classroom. It's in our nature to close our classroom doors and teach.

The Common Core is asking us to consider opening our doors to the possibility of integrating more nonfiction within a traditional classic literature–based English classroom. Notice we said classic literature must be a part of every English classroom. The Common Core does not mandate or even suggest abandoning a primary reason we went into teaching. In fact, if you give it a chance, the Common Core will actually help you further engage your students and foster that love of reading that we want everyone to possess. The Common Core encourages students and teachers to read across multiple genres. As teachers, our responsibility is to embrace the idea that we must be teachers of literacy. Literacy is not contained in merely reading a novel with students and guiding them through review of what they should have discovered between the lines. Literacy is helping students develop strategies to discern the significant details in everything from a painting to a technical document. Strengthening students' analytical and critical thinking skills required for success both in and outside of the classroom equips them with the tools to find what's below the surface for themselves. Additionally, the Common Core promotes reading in a genre that outside of the classroom students undoubtedly encounter in volume. Yes, the Common Core actually can be an English teacher's friend. Let's explore how in the second hurdle.

The 2nd Hurdle: 70/30 Split Means What?!?

The 70/30 split mandate in the Common Core State Standards has teachers of every discipline wondering what that means in their subject. What does it really demand from English teachers? Do we actually have to teach 70% nonfiction? The answer that most agree with is "no." The 70/30 split is throughout the school day across all disciplines; however, let's not kid ourselves into thinking that we are responsible only for the 30%. We are teachers of literature, both fiction and nonfiction. It is our job to make sure that we are helping students to succeed. We can make compromises in the traditional classroom to accommodate more nonfiction. We are not suggesting watering down the curriculum, but rather making it more meaningful to students by bringing in relevant nonfiction pairings with the traditional classics. If you have ever struggled to engage your students with the issues of George Orwell's *Animal Farm* or Jane Eyre's plight in Charlotte Brontë's titular novel, then you know that today's students are reluctant at times to find relevance in classic literature. We have found that by incorporating the nonfiction piece into the classroom, not as a biography or as a separate unit, but in combination with the traditional classics, it will bring relevance and interest to even the most unenthusiastic students—it's the big picture that students missed before.

Our Reading Realities

Consider how much time you spend reading newspaper or magazine articles. We do this without even thinking. Our students are so busy with all of their classes, sports, and extracurricular activities that they are not necessarily keeping up with current issues. They are not reading to be informed citizens about the world around them. If we require our students to do what comes naturally to us, to keep informed, then it will become natural for them. They will begin to seek out information, not because it's assigned, but because they want to know. They will see the relevance. If you agree with this, then you will appreciate the added depth the Common Core can bring to the traditional English classroom.

Benefits of Teacher Revision

We always add depth to learning through revision. We ask our students to revise again and again and again, yet as teachers we become accustomed to teaching certain texts the same way year after year. We know what works, but that doesn't mean a little change can't make it better. In fact, partnering nonfiction and fiction bridges a gap that we didn't realize even existed.

The revision process also encourages us to bridge our own gaps with department members. We ask students to peer edit and share their work, yet as educators we often create our best lessons and hide them away from our peers. Incorporating the Common Core gives teachers the perfect opportunity to collaborate. Bring your best ideas to the table, and leave the rest behind in the file.

Together we have built a bridge for our students that is stronger and more direct to their end destination. Honestly, the process wasn't easy but negotiation and compromise never are. We get it. You've earned your degree. You don't need help. But what you do need is collaboration. If you cannot locate a colleague for collaborative planning in your department, look outside your department. If you still cannot find someone, the Common Core gives you the perfect opportunity to look in another district; however, integrating the Common Core can be done alone.

Collaboration

We began our collaboration with one common assignment. Without realizing it, behind our closed doors, we were instructing students on debate techniques. Our principal connected the dots and asked us to meet with each other. From there we planned our first grade-wide debate. Currently, we are enjoying our third year of collaboration. Working together on this lesson, we began to recognize and appreciate each other's strengths. We want all students in the same grade gaining equal instruction of required standards. Delivery and style differ, but the outcomes are constant. And this is what the Common Core is providing on a national level—consistency. As a nation, it is time to come together and give students an equal opportunity for success. The Common Core levels the playing field in public education.

Fiction versus Nonfiction

The first step in successfully implementing the new Common Core standards is to rethink what your list of required readings in the English classroom will include. Many of you chose to teach English because of your love of getting lost in the story and the lives of its characters. We love to read. We want our students to experience the same joy as we do when they get their hands on a good book. We want students to stay up too late reading, unable to put down the book, rather than falling asleep while struggling through what we assigned for homework.

Think about it: Outside of your classroom, how much fiction versus nonfiction do you encounter on a daily basis? We don't have a specific number, but we don't need a specific number to acknowledge that the scale tips greatly toward nonfiction. We are inundated with nonfiction in the forms of newspapers, news programs, magazines, blogs, advertisements, radio broadcasts, or podcasts—you name it, the list goes on. As educated adults, we automatically keep apprised of current events. We understand the importance of making connections between what is going on and what has happened while making predictions about the future.

Before the Core

Before implementing the new Common Core State Standards, we emphasized the literature and the way the themes, characters, and dilemmas related to students on a personal level without helping them extend those connections to the world at large. At least, we didn't emphasize these connections as much as we could or should have. Students come to us expecting everything they read to entertain them. As lovers of literature, we anticipate that students will be enthralled by Boo Radley and Huck Finn, intimidated by Dracula and Tybalt, inspired by Katniss Everdeen and Boxer. And often, that's not the case. If students are not going to love all literature, then our task must be to demonstrate how to learn from it.

Guiding students to evaluate a work not for its entertainment value but for its educational value is the chore at hand. In the past, we've asked them to connect with the characters on a personal level, without providing them with the tools to make the connections both to themselves and to the real world possible. Students must understand that we are not reading these texts because their parents had to; we are not reading these texts because as teachers we lack the initiative to plan something different. We are reading these classics because they illuminate truths about who we are as human beings.

We can read John Howard Griffin's *Black Like Me* as a time capsule of what the South once was, but to do so is to deny and neglect the fight we still face in regard to discrimination and prejudice. All of this to say, students can't possibly get the most out of a text without seeing how the pieces fit together. Those pieces are supplemental nonfiction readings that enhance understanding and expose students to the bigger picture. We see this looking like the spokes of a wheel (Figure 1.1). Once you spin the students outside of their comfort zones and what they've been taught to expect from class-assigned readings, the opportunities for learning are unlimited.

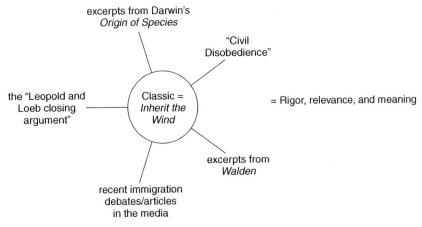

Figure 1.1 Promoting healthy eating

Tackling the Core through Research

Learning opportunities abound if time is carved out for research. In order for us to be able to facilitate the idea of students as researchers, we must first embrace the idea of the English teacher as researcher. We are all used to teaching and grading the "beloved" research paper, but we must take it a step, or maybe a leap, farther. We are accustomed to teaching the novel as a whole and possibly some lead-in background on the history of the time. We are not saying that this is wrong, but here is where we must make the leap.

The leap is thinking outside of the box, thinking about what was happening during the time the novel was written, but also what's happening during our time. It is our job to research and identify the clues, and set them before our students in a way that fosters independent critical thinking. It's their job to interpret and construct personal meaning from the clues. We are not spoon-feeding students. We are not telling them what to think, but rather showing them the steps that people take when educating themselves on a particular topic. For example, in teaching Erich Maria Remarque's classic novel *All Quiet on the Western Front,* the main character, Paul, laments the idea that he can no longer return to the life he once lived as a result of the effects of war. Because of what he has witnessed and lived through while so many others died, Paul is disconnected from civilian life. As a teacher, how do you go about getting a 15- or 16-year-old student to relate to a soldier's hopelessness, especially a soldier from World War I? We do this by asking our students what advancements we have made in a century to better transition our soldiers back into civilian life. This provides a good discussion on whether our understanding of post-traumatic stress disorder, treatment of soldiers wounded physically, emotionally, and socially, and other provisions offered to veterans is enough. Do we do enough for the men and women who volunteer to protect our country? After the initial discussion of what we know and how we have been affected personally, students set out to research the facts. By extension and contemporary connection, students better grasp what's happening in the novella as well as in their country. On a more personal level, they gain an awareness of a relative's experiences in war. In the beginning, we do the research, we find the clues, we narrow down the debate topic, but, ultimately, students will have the tools necessary to develop a well-researched conclusion and support it on any given topic.

The Core Benefits Writing, Too!

Although we have focused mainly on the reading, writing equally benefits from the analysis of nonfiction. Just as we consider the amount of nonfiction encountered throughout a day, students will be asked to write in a nonfiction structure far more often than a fiction format. Oftentimes in the English classroom, creative writing is emphasized primarily with fiction. The Common Core and its requirement of nonfiction reading bring about the opportunity to explore creative nonfiction. We learn by example. What better way to demonstrate quality nonfiction writing than to read, discuss, and emulate the crafted techniques and authors' works. Good nonfiction writing allows students to see outside the limits of a five-paragraph essay. By reading nonfiction essays, students examine different ways an author develops a thesis. If you're asking students to write a personal narrative, offer good examples of published personal narratives. If you're asking students to write a film review, require them to bring in three reviews from different sources on the same movie. If you are asking students to write a literary analysis, provide them with quality examples of how critics write about books. Students are sometimes surprised by how readable nonfiction can be (and so were we). Reading for voice and style, students gain a better understanding of the effects of figurative language and are more willing to experiment with it in their own writing.

Final Thoughts

A final point to keep in mind is that because the Common Core requires the nonfiction emphasis, as English teachers, we need to take the initiative in teaching students how to navigate nonfiction texts. The idea is that we are helping not only our students but also our colleagues as we implement the Common Core State Standards into all of our classrooms. An example of cross-discipline collaboration is the teaching of Rebecca Skloot's book *The Immortal Life of Henrietta Lacks*. Although the science teachers can readily handle the chapters dealing with anatomy and cell division, they might not be as comfortable dealing with the structure of the book or the moral and social issues that arise. In the real world, we don't move from science to social studies to history to lunch. We are not asked to look at one aspect of a problem. We are asked to solve the problem using our collective knowledge. The Common Core calls for us to pull our curriculum together as a means of providing students with real-world problem-solving skills.

Have we convinced you? Are you ready to fall in love with the Common Core? We don't blame you if your answer is still no! You've already been told by too many people that you *will* integrate the Common Core. If you're like us, you want to see *how* this works. The first step in understanding our thought process behind the balance between fiction and nonfiction is to review how we introduce it to our students. The following is a list of guided questions we use to approach everything we read.

Questions for Study

- How do we receive information? (Think verbal versus nonverbal; intention versus perception)
- How can we decipher the multifaceted messages in what we see and hear?

- How can we evaluate a theme as it relates to ourselves? To the greater world around us? (Moving beyond entertainment to education)

- How can critical thinking and reflection promote our well-being in the present and prepare us for our future?

- How is practical knowledge developed from studying both contemporary and classic literature, fiction and nonfiction, multigenres?

- How can we better arm ourselves with knowledge to combat life's obstacles?

So even if you aren't ready to profess your undying love for the Common Core just yet, stay with us. We aren't asking you to give up everything you love. When we first heard 70/30, our gut reaction was, "not in our classrooms." But now that we have taken the time to evaluate it for ourselves, test it out on students, and witness the gains in student learning, understanding, and ownership, we have embraced the enemy.

2 Choice Excerpts and Nonfiction Pairings

You Lose Some to Gain Some

Teachers build meaning with the classic texts, falling in love with characters and themes by teaching them year after year. Our students, tackling a text for the first time, need help building meaningful connections with the themes and characters. An exemplary method of providing students with opportunities for building connections lies in partnering classic works with contemporary nonfiction reading. Similarly, pairing contemporary or futuristic novels with historical documents and events mirroring the themes present in both empowers students with the knowledge to appreciate the big picture. In order for teachers and students to tackle the big picture, a teacher must accept the necessity of constructing knowledge through choice excerpts. By organizing lessons and units in this way, students are exposed to even more texts. This pacing and variety forces students to draw their own conclusions on the basis of personal comparisons, reading, and research rather than skimmed plot summaries. There are no shortcuts for students when critical thinking is the objective.

Common Core State Standards (in Our Own Words)

- RL.9–10.1. Cite strong and thorough textual evidence to support analysis of what the text says explicitly and implicitly. *Am I clear about what I just read?*

- RL.9–10.9. Analyze how two or more texts address a similar theme or topic in order to build knowledge. *How does an author impact my view?*

- RI.9–10.4. Interpret words and phrases in a text for connotative and figurative meanings, and analyze how those word choices shape meaning and tone. *Why did the author choose to say it this way?*

- W.9–10.1. Write an argument to support a claim using reasoning and textual evidence. *What's my purpose, and how do I develop and support it?*

- W.9–10.4. Produce clear, organized writing with purpose and audience in mind. *How do I write clearly to impact my audience?*

- W.9–10.8. Collect pertinent information from varied sources and mediums to deepen research while maintaining proper citation of those sources within writing. *How do I gather relevant information but maintain proper citation of the sources?*

- SL.9–10.4. Present information in an organized manner to engage listeners. *How do I say what I need to say to get my audience to understand and follow my presentation?*

- L.9–10.3. Make and apply effective choices for meaning or style in writing, and to comprehend more fully when listening or reading. *How do I apply the guidelines of MLA to write and edit my work?*

Relevance

Let's face it, change induces stress and requires additional work. But remember, implementing the new Common Core standards does not require you to change or abandon everything. Your basic scaffold for approaching a novel remains the same. The key is to make old texts relevant with new nonfiction connections. Classic literature has poignant truths about human nature, relationships, conflict, life, and loss. As teachers, we get excited about giving background information on the setting, the author, and the time period in which the book was written. We emphasize what was happening then; meanwhile, our students are thinking, "Wonderful. This took place in the 30s. That's like six decades before I was born. This should be exciting. . . ." Teachers build meaning with the classic texts, falling in love with characters and themes by teaching them year after year. Our students, tackling a text for the first time, need help building meaningful connections with the themes and characters. An exemplary method of providing students opportunities for building connections lies in partnering classic works with contemporary nonfiction reading. Similarly, pairing contemporary or futuristic novels with historical documents and events mirroring the themes present in both empowers students with the knowledge to appreciate the big picture. In order for teachers and students to tackle the big picture, a teacher must accept the necessity of constructing knowledge through choice excerpts. By organizing lessons and units in this way, students are exposed to even more texts. This pacing and variety forces students to draw their own conclusions based on personal comparisons, reading, and research rather than skimmed plot summaries. There are no short cuts for the students when critical thinking is the objective.

Consider the novels that you teach throughout the course of the year. Choose one. Whether you studied that novel in college or read it for the first time a month before you had to teach it, over time you developed an appreciation for the author's clever wording, plot twists, depth of the characters, revelations of human strengths and failings, and life's truths. Then you attempted to translate and foster that appreciation to reluctant readers. Depending on the grade level or on the year, there may have been tears (not necessarily theirs). Back at the drawing board, you reflect, revise, retry. Same novel, different approach, and different strategies equaled similar results. We are successful teachers, but if we are not reaching every kid then we need to find yet another approach. Believe it or not, the Common Core is that other approach.

Nonfiction Enhances the Learning

We understand that there is more to the Common Core than nonfiction. Adopting the new standards does not require eliminating literature analysis and appreciation from the curriculum. In fact, as we reflect on the new Common Core standards, we must admit that they are not that different from what we have always taught (at least in the state of Ohio). The nonfiction emphasis is the major difference. We still want our students to know and appreciate the classics; however, the hiccup is how to tie in the nonfiction aspect. When nonfiction and classic texts are partnered correctly, the learning is enhanced. Knowing that time is an issue, give yourself permission to pull excerpts from novels and blend them with nonfiction supplements. The idea is letting go. Consider the main objectives you originally focused on when teaching the novels. Yes, you will probably have to narrow the focus, but take comfort in the fact that you will reach greater depths in student learning and motivation.

Think about it: Authors write to illustrate some aspect of the human condition. We connect with literature because it is a reflection of life. Literature is life, and life is nonfiction. Hate, fear, forgive, celebrate—we live vicariously through the characters we most connect with. Once we are willing to accept that students must find that connection for themselves, the nonfiction possibilities are endless. Nonfiction is the essential element because it links current situations and happenings with situations and happenings in a novel. Partnering a recent article from the *New York Times* with an excerpt from classic literature generates interest and legitimizes texts that might otherwise be dismissed as outdated. Students relate when they hear about what you are reading outside of the 48-minute period you have them. Whether that's in the news or in a digital medium, it brings relevance and credibility to what's being studied.

Essential Excerpts and Choice

In order to bring relevance, we must find a way to engage all readers regardless of their levels with the same texts. When you are educating all, *all* means *all*. We can read the same things, though the approach should look different. Students deserve a common experience; we never want students to classify reading beyond or below their ability on the basis of what other classes are doing. Students must possess the confidence to tackle any text. As teachers, we empower our students by not limiting the options, forcing them to engage in their learning. We have to ask ourselves: What's the takeaway? Do we require these reluctant readers to struggle and suffer through some of the author's writing techniques that are beyond them? Or do students benefit even more from looking at condensed excerpts that establish the focus? Start with the main idea. Give students the overarching question that will be threaded throughout all texts. Again, we can't justify eliminating novels for these students, even though there were times we wanted to knock our heads against our desks, because of the pertinent themes and ties to today. Our students will feel better when administered the appropriate dose of a book. If given too much, all students feel sick; they will "black out" and refuse to take more of what made them sick the first time. The perfect dosage comes in partnering classic, contemporary, fiction, and nonfiction, allowing students to scaffold a more comprehensive understanding. Students take each piece representing a common element to build their personal understanding and perspective. A key piece has to be student choice.

For our purposes, that choice comes in the form of research. With all of these elements working together, students can't come back to us next year and say that they haven't read a single book that was assigned. More likely, students will come back and share additional discoveries relating to the topics studied.

An Example: *Frankenstein*

Let's walk through an example of using less to get more by carefully choosing the pairings. A popular text often taught at the high school level is Mary Shelley's *Frankenstein*. We taught this novel with multiple grades and ability levels. As with most things, our more advanced readers took ownership and responsibility of their learning, making it easy to explore all the nuances of the text. At the other end of the spectrum, our younger, more reluctant readers could not appreciate the story. They became lost in the frame narrative, complex sentence structures, and higher level vocabulary. We overdosed on *Frankenstein*. We asked ourselves: What's the focus when teaching this? The answer we came up with is another question; just because we can, should we? As Mary Shelley explored science through her character Victor Frankenstein's ability to bestow life, we ask our students to explore current scientific studies that can impact the lives they lead. Victor refused to take responsibility for what he created, abusing his knowledge, talents, and opportunities.

In terms of Mary Shelley's time period, scientifically what was once feared is now a real possibility. Contemporary companion texts that explore this idea include Daniel Keyes's *Flowers for Algernon*, Rebecca Skloot's *The Immortal Life of Henrietta Lacks*, and Neal Shusterman's *Unwind* and *UnWholly*. This is a great opportunity for differentiation. With *Flowers for Algernon*, teachers can choose between the short story, the film, or the novel. All three versions encompass the essential learning targets, but depending on time and student ability, one may better meet student needs. Another possibility is for high-level readers to study *The Immortal Life of Henrietta Lacks* in its entirety, or the more scientific chapters that can be more cumbersome, while struggling readers can be assigned chapters on background and ethical dilemmas. The way you bring the class together, whether it is through jigsaw presentations, Socratic seminars, or teacher-led discussions, is up to you. To tie in the high-interest teen novels *Unwind* and *UnWholly* will engage all readers. If you haven't read *UnWholly,* for example, there is an entire chapter comparing the genetically engineered creation of a main character by a corporation similar to that of Victor Frankenstein's creature. This comparison allows for a more thorough student understanding and appreciation of both texts. The influence of the classic on the contemporary strengthens the impact of both. The idea is to bring balance between the reading, writing, and research. An assignment we use to bring this unit full circle is one we endearingly call "Weird Science."

An Assignment: "Weird Science"

For this assignment, students must find two articles (from reliable sources) detailing current scientific research being conducted. This research can be controversial or conventional, but it must be timely; nothing occurring before the year 2000 is accepted. Once students find a topic of interest and two articles, they address the following questions:

- Who is conducting this research and under what *pretense*?
- What improvement or change are the researchers seeking?
- How is the research being conducted? Give a brief overview of the research practices.

- When and where in society has there been a need for such research?
- Should certain research be done just because it can?

Among the learning targets reached with this assignment are choosing and narrowing a topic, writing a researchable question, distinguishing credible and reliable sources, recognizing bias, organizing according to MLA, and developing a "so what?" conclusion.

Depending on the students' level, you can turn them loose to begin research or you might need to model for them. The research doesn't necessarily need to be groundbreaking, but it needs to be relevant to students. The topics have varied from dolphin communication to the latest treatment for stroke patients. Stacey's husband has a saltwater aquarium hobby, and after the death of a beloved puffer fish, some online research led to Rebecca Skloot's New York Times article titled "Fixing Nemo." The weird science modeled topic became fish veterinary medicine as a result. The online [my insertion] article became the perfect connection to teaching portions of The Immortal Life of Henrietta Lacks, also by Rebecca Skloot, because it was another example of this author's writing, and the topic was too quirky to be copied by our students. Again, we want a topic that is personally relatable—the attention grabber became a personal narrative describing at-home fish care that led to killing one's pet. First we explain how a real-life incident sparked curiosity and research. We then ask students to contemplate their own lives and interests. What do they need to know more about? The next step is giving students time to research. They must research what's out there to know what the possibilities are. After exploration of the topic, it's time for students to narrow the focus and write a researchable question. A teaching opportunity is revealed as students begin to recognize that there are discrepancies within the research. We can explain credible sources all we want in class, but it is through doing that students truly understand the amount of misleading information available to them online. And not only is misleading information discovered, but also the importance of reading for bias and perspective. Whether through student examples or examples offered in class, students decipher and determine purpose, pretense, and credibility. We want students to be able to master all of these skills, but ultimately we want to extend the learning by empowering students to be able to answer the "so what?" question. Students must be able to articulate: Why does this topic matter or not matter to me? If it doesn't matter to me, can I at least appreciate how it may matter to others? Establishing a standpoint for oneself but also being able to empathize with others' situations is vital.

Sometimes students' realization that the topic doesn't matter to them creates the perfect teachable moment to refocus and restart with something that does matter—creating student engagement. A student example involved the topic of cloning. The student chose this topic because it was controversial and interesting to her classmates; it also connected to class discussions of Frankenstein. As she began researching, she continued to hit dead ends. While there was an abundance of sources, she had no personal interest or buy-in. During a one-on-one conference, she showed no excitement about the topic. Knowing the student and her love of soccer, she could be redirected toward current research in sports medicine. As she began her research, she discovered articles pertaining to girls playing soccer and how to protect their knees. The point is that she is a girl who had witnessed teammates no longer able to play the sport they loved because of knee injuries. Now she is armed with research to combat on the field what she has learned in the classroom. What was once just an assignment was now daily practice. Relevance and rigor were created. There is practical application beyond an assignment. It is useful information that can be applied to daily life. Bringing the research full circle with the initial reading answers the question: Just because we can, should we?

The Rationale

As we ask our students to contemplate whether they should do something simply because they can, as teachers, we must turn the question on ourselves. Just because we can and have taught novels in their entirety in the past, is this the current best practice? If we are honest with ourselves, the answer is sometimes, but not always, yes. Excerpting some novels to make space for required nonfiction gives students a taste of that novel without them choking on it. The hope is that after a taste, they will want more. Additionally, students will leave our classrooms with a more extensive repertoire of titles and authors than they would have otherwise. More is not always more, but if balance is achieved, the pieces come together and less becomes more. Students are more well-rounded readers, writers, and researchers with balanced skill sets. Literature and the Common Core, balancing each other, address the needs of the 21st-century student.

Unit 1 and Sample Lesson Plans

Grade Levels: 9–10; adaptable to 11–12

Time Frame: 15 class periods

UNIT AGENDA:

Day 1   Just because we can . . . Should we???? Intro for *Flowers for Algernon*. Intro "Weird Science" assignment.

Days 2–3   Watch *Flowers for Algernon* and work on Weird Science project.

Day 4   Finish *Flowers for Algernon*. Intro *Frankenstein* and Frankenstein vocab. Would you rather have money or fame and glory?

Day 5   Draw your version of Frankenstein. What do you think of when you hear someone mention this character? (Write descriptive adjectives around your picture.) Other side of the paper—What is your biggest fear? Science and experiment discussion. Begin to introduce characters.

Day 6   Character intros and background ideas from novel

Day 7   Watch Boris Karloff *Frankenstein* movie. Why did Hollywood change the original so much?

Day 8   More *Frankenstein* background and characters

Day 9   More *Frankenstein* background and characters
HW: Read chapters 11–13

Day 10   Discussion and reward over chapters 11–13 HW: Read chapters 14–15

Day 11   Discussion and reward over chapters 14–15
HW: Read chapters 16–17

Day 12   Discussion and reward over chapters 16–17

Day 13   Tie up the loose ends.
HW: Weird Science presentations due tomorrow!

Day 14   Weird Science presentations

Victor Frankenstein and the scientist from *Flowers for Algernon* share a Common Core idea regarding science. After watching *Flowers for Algernon* and reading and annotating *Frankenstein,* address the following questions in a three-paragraph response:

- What do these characters think is the role or purpose of science?

- What do they think is the role of the scientist?

- How does each man view scientific advancement?

- Does either man think that there is anything wrong with his research or that he is "mad" for attempting to use science to alter life?

Remember, you must include quoted and paraphrased examples from both readings in your writings.

As a contemporary reader, be prepared to state clearly whether you agree or disagree with their views during class discussion. Considering when each piece was written and what you know about the time period, support your opinion with historical and modern examples.

Lesson 2
Frankenstein: Weird Science!

For this assignment, you must find two articles (from reliable sources) detailing current scientific research being conducted. This research can be controversial or conventional, but it must be timely; nothing occurring before the year 2000 will be accepted. Once you have found a topic of interest and two articles, address the following questions:

- Who is conducting this research and under what *pretense*?

- What improvement or change are the researchers seeking?

- How is the research being conducted? Give a brief overview of the research practices.

- When and where in society has there been a need for such research?

- Just because certain research can be done, in your opinion, should it be done?

Prepare a two-minute presentation on your findings. Note cards and/or an outline plus a typed bibliography must be turned in after your speech.

Presentation Rubric:
"Weird Science"

Name: _____

Personal Qualities +_____/20

- Confidence
- Eye contact
- Poised = few nervous movements
- Useful gestures and positive body language
- Note and respond to audience feedback

Preparation +_____/25

- Extremely familiar with what you are saying
- Able to answer reasonable questions
- Clear presentation of ideas
- Well-organized

Overall Presentation +_____/25

- A strong understanding of your topic was displayed
- The summary was complete and clearly stated
- Adequate explanation was given; *it is clear that you did your research*☺
- The presentation included a clear beginning and a distinct conclusion

Articles Attached to Outline or Note Cards +_____/30

- 2 articles from reliable sources
- Useful note cards or outline

Additional Comments:

Grade: +_____/100

Possible Extensions through Contemporary Young Adult Literature

As you know, a great way to get students reading the classics is to get them hooked on popular young adult books. Earlier in this chapter, we mentioned the novels *Unwind* and *UnWholly*, both written by Neal Shusterman, as ideal connectors. Another popular series to consider is The Birthmarked Trilogy by Caragh M. O'Brien. These books offer an interesting juxtaposition to the previous novels as well as to the classics. Rather than try to "advance" the human race, *Birthmarked* takes its readers into a possible future without the hospitals and luxuries we are accustomed to in our everyday lives. *Birthmarked*, the first novel in the series, introduces students to a society that has chosen to deal with genetic imperfections, medical mysteries, and technological failures by turning its back on the issues, opting to let nature take its course. This prospective future is a place where only the strong survive. Of course, that changes when the leaders realize that too many people are dying and they must figure out a way to prevent their demise.

The contemporary novels pose just the right questions and scenarios to get students thinking. While students are reading these books, have them research current trends and choices being made around the world today. A few examples are various studies being conducted on scientific advancement, as well as the legal battles being fought over parents' rights to withhold medical treatment from their children for religious beliefs. Encourage students to develop their own perspective on what is the right path to follow when it comes to who gets to decide what the future holds.

A possible culminating essay question for students to write pushes them to take a stand. Ask your students to consider where we have been and where we are going. From *Frankenstein* to *Flowers for Algernon* to *Unwind* to *Birthmarked*, what does our future hold? Are we moving in the right or wrong direction? How do we know?

Asking students to make the connections between what they are reading and the reality that they are living reinforces the importance of seeking to understand and make sense of the world. Having students study where we have been and where we are heading only lends support to the importance of getting involved with current issues and knowing where they stand on them. We want our students to appreciate the timeless, common themes in literature and how relevant these themes are to their lives.

Don't Forget the S.O.A.P.

Breaking It Down

This chapter outlines and examines the relevance of the **S**peaker, **O**ccasion, **A**udience, and **Pu**rpose within reading, writing, and speaking. Activities for student reading and exploration of nonfiction will be included. Building upon S.O.A.P., the rhetorical situation, and bias, this assignment transitions students from identifying the latter to demonstrating their understanding through analysis, synthesis, and application of these techniques. This section is one about discoveries, origins, and reception. A sample lesson involves students researching a mundane object and how it changed the world as the people of that time knew it. Not all discoveries are celebrated, so students must consider how society received the invention or discovery upon its introduction.

Common Core State Standards (in Our Own Words)

- RL.9–10.4. Determine meaning of words and their impact on purpose and tone. *Why does an author's word choice matter?*
- RI.9–10.6. Assess point of view and use of rhetoric and how it shapes perspective. *What do I know about the author's beliefs and values?*
- RI.9–10.8. Analyze and evaluate an argument or claim to determine validity and relevance. *Is the author reliable and credible?*
- SL.9–10.3. Evaluate a speaker's point of view and use of rhetoric. *How can I use multiple sources and perspectives to determine meaning?*
- SL.9–10.5. Make strategic use of digital media and visual displays to enhance a presentation. *How can I make my presentation effective?*
- SL.9–10.6. Demonstrate command of formal language to engage audience and meet expectations. *How do I say what I need to say to reach my audience and make it matter to them?*

English Taking Part

Initially, we found the idea of a 70/30 split daunting. But no matter how you break it down, nonfiction must become an integral part of every classroom. We get it. As English teachers, we could take this as a pass and say we are the 30—have fun, science, math, and history! However, realistically, we no longer work in an age where we all teach behind closed doors. We must come together and tackle this challenge by working together in the best interests of our students. Kids see five, six, or more teachers a day; we must be consistent and unified in our delivery and value of diverse ways information is offered. Supporting our students with the right strategies that can be applied across disciplines strengthens their skills. We must do more than simply throw in nonfiction. We must give students strategies and nonfiction that relates to their lives, enhancing the impact of the established curriculum. S.O.A.P. is that strategy.

S.O.A.P. Introduction

Once students grow accustomed to looking at texts for purpose and the reason behind our studying it, we ask them to break it down even further. We do this by instructing our students to "not forget the S.O.A.P." **S**peaker, **o**ccasion, **a**udience, and **p**urpose can and should be applied to any and all media both in and out of the classroom. By approaching texts in this way, bias is revealed. For example, if People for the Ethical Treatment of Animals proclaims that all commercial farmers abuse their animals, it is important to consider the source. Students must question and evaluate to avoid gullibility. We are instilling lifelong skills that protect the best interests of our students. So how do you go about teaching these concepts to students, especially younger students?

Advice

We begin by asking students to analyze the everyday, age-old advice from classic and contemporary writers. The importance of recognizing bias in an author's message can be introduced by tackling famous published advice. As adults, we understand the technique of listening to everyone but forming and adopting only the thoughts and ideas that keep us true to our values. Young people, bombarded by opinions and misinformation, must be taught to differentiate between the validity and credibility of multiple sources. An effective approach is beginning the year by asking students to analyze the advice they have received prior to starting the school year. Students are encouraged to evaluate what they believe and why. An introductory activity involves the following questions. These questions can take many forms; for example, teachers can pass them out prior to discussion and have students respond to questions on a handout or in a multipage reflection (depending on student level and how ready you are to grade volumes . . .). Teachers can also keep the questions for themselves to aid in guiding a class discussion. Take it or leave it.

Discussion Questions

- Think of one idea or belief you feel you would never waver on. Describe that belief in two or three sentences.
- Where did this idea or belief come from?
- Who else in your life shares this belief?

- Why is this belief so important?
- What experiences in your life have affirmed or challenged this belief?

We begin our study with advice because every student has experience receiving advice and has something to bring to the table. It is an elementary enough exercise that it allows students to safely explore S.O.A.P. Once students have discussed the advice they received, we start the process of considering who gave the advice and under what pretense. Did the student consider himself or herself an appropriate audience for the advice? Was the speaker too removed or not relatable enough for the advice to be worthwhile? For example, receiving dating advice from a grandparent might not always benefit the recipient. If a grandfather's frame of reference for dating includes sit-down dinners and ballroom dancing, then his advice on how to impress a lady is probably outdated in some ways. Grandpa does have some words of wisdom, but his expertise is not necessarily in this area. Students can more readily determine the worth of grandpa's advice because they share a relationship; we assume grandpa has the student's best interest at heart.

Speaker

- Do they know the speaker from any previous situations?
- Do they feel they can trust the speaker?
- What do they base that trust on?
- Is the speaker credible?
- What do they base that credibility on?

But, more often than not, advice comes from someone we don't personally know. Students are first asked to consider the speaker. Do they know the speaker from any previous situations? Do they feel they can trust the speaker? What do they base that trust on? Is the speaker credible? What do they base that credibility on?

After establishing the speaker's degree of significance, students must consider the occasion for which the advice was given. Is it a rite of passage, an opportunity to learn from past transgressions, or simply an opportunity to be heard?

Occasion

- What type of event?
- Time—Morning? Evening? Consider the social norms.
- Date? Month and time of year? Holiday?
- Setting? East Coast? Midwest? West Coast?

In terms of audience, students must ask themselves why them and why now? Teenagers are often inundated with people offering and forcing advice upon them. What part of their age opens them up to being advice magnets?

Audience

- What is the average age of the audience?
- Is the audience composed of a similar group (e.g., all men, all teachers, all inmates)?
- Large group? Intimate group?
- Is there a common belief or value set among the audience members?

Finally, students must dissect the purpose of the advice. Is the speaker getting anything in return for his or her words of wisdom? What outcome does the speaker intend with his or her words? It is by putting all of these components together that students can evaluate the meaningfulness of the message and the effectiveness of its delivery. This is the first small step in using S.O.A.P. for analysis. Taking what students already know is key to laying the foundation.

Purpose

- What is the reason for the event?
- What is the speaker's intention in speaking?
- Has the speaker established goals and/or objectives?

Expanding on the idea of advice, we analyze famous published works that make their own suggestions as to the way we should live. Robert Fulghum's *All I Really Need to Know I Learned in Kindergarten* can be compared with William Shakespeare's excerpt "Polonius' Advice to Laertes" from *Hamlet*. We build upon the previous battle between contemporary and classic by looking at an author who feels she is a timeless authority on manners and etiquette, the legendary Miss Manners. Points of interest for this author involve a closer examination of tone and diction as they relate to the overall message. Students either like her advice or hate it. This provides a great opportunity to discuss delivery, tone, bias, audience . . . a whole slew of terms and techniques.

Additional Advice Resources

An astounding number of poems about advice exist in the world; following you will find a few that we have used. This collection varies in degree of difficulty, allowing for differentiation in the classroom. These titles can be used independently or through a classroom jigsaw, please see the following:

- "Advice to a Girl" by Sara Teasdale
- "At Least" by Raymond Carver
- "Bandito" by Eleanor Lerman

- "Do Not Believe . . ." by Buddha
- "For a Girl I Know about to Be a Woman" by Miller Williams
- "If" by Rudyard Kipling
- "Do Not Go Gentle into that Good Night" by Dylan Thomas
- "Untitled" by Bruce Dethlefsen

An Assignment: "Inventions and Discoveries"

Building from a student's ability to identify S.O.A.P. for its meaningfulness and effectiveness, students are asked to apply this technique to their own work. We endearingly call this project "Inventions and Discoveries." This assignment is one about innovations, origins, and reception. We intentionally choose objects that are boring on a surface level. Examples of these objects include aerosol can, wallpaper, paper clip, frozen food, thermometer, windmill, and the flushing toilet. By researching mundane objects, students investigate the major discovery or invention and how it changed the world as the people of that time knew it. Not all discoveries are celebrated; students must consider how society received the invention or discovery upon its introduction. Did society feel it was a lifesaver or the root of all evil (or more likely something in between)? Students begin with research, keeping notes on their findings and sources. Their final product was to construct a presentation with thoughtful consideration of S.O.A.P., generating an intentional slant.

Be prepared to hear complaints about how boring these objects are. Don't break down and allow students to choose different objects. Part of what is being assessed is students' ability to bring purpose and perspective to their audience. They need to create the excitement. A student example that was particularly creative involved the elevator. Charismatic, vocal students protested their assigned object. The elevator is so commonplace that they were taking for granted that once upon a time it was new technology. Students had to find its original purpose. Once they became resigned to the fact that they were not going to be given a different object, they were forced to decide how they wanted their classmates to view the elevator . . . figuring out the S.O.A.P. As speakers, they were the keynote presenters for a Weight Watchers convention. The audience consisted of people wanting to lose weight. Their purpose was to educate the audience that one change can make a significant difference, and that change was to use the stairs rather than surrendering to laziness by taking the elevator. Students' ordinary object became extraordinary when they relied on the past to reeducate the present on their misuse of this invention.

Kids, Don't Forget the S.O.A.P.

S.O.A.P. is the logical starting place whether you teach 7th or 12th graders. It can be broken down for any level on the basis of the difficulty of the text it is being applied to. Teaching this tool early in the year is essential in helping students understand the implications of others' writing. S.O.A.P. gives students four easy ways to break down text to acquire meaning. Too often, students attempt to read a text without knowing where to begin. S.O.A.P. enables students to engage in the reading. Once students are able to break down other works, they begin to construct more thoughtful works of their own. Rather than merely responding to an assignment, students employ the S.O.A.P. strategy to more thoroughly approach both their reading and writing.

This skill is a real-world application that students must know and be able to effectively use day to day. As English teachers, we know there are all kinds of acronyms out there, but if we have to brainstorm the possible meanings despite our degrees, what chance do our students have of remembering them from year to year? Kids, get S.O.A.P. Kids, don't forget the S.O.A.P.

Unit 2 and Sample Lesson Plan

Grade Levels: 9–10; adaptable to 11–12

Time Frame: 7 or 8 days

UNIT AGENDA:

Day 1 4 Truths and a Lie activity; Fulghum's *All I Really Need to Know I Learned in Kindergarten*
HW: Letters and Shakespeare

Day 2 Discuss advice and Shakespeare; Cooke's "How Did You Die?"
HW: Miss Manners

Day 3 Manners discussion (tone, audience, motive/intention); "Hanging Fire"

Day 4 Further discussion of would you rather have money or fame and glory? Introduction of inventions and discoveries project

Day 5 Inventions and discoveries research day

Day 6 Final research day

Day 7 Presentations

Lesson 1
Inventions and Discoveries Across the Decades

This assignment is one about discoveries, origins, and reception. By researching the object fate has dealt you, I would like for you to research the major discovery or invention and how it changed the world as the people of that time knew it. Not all discoveries are celebrated, so I ask that you consider how society received the invention or discovery upon its introduction. Did society feel it was a lifesaver or the root of all evil (or more likely something in between)?

To complete this assignment, please tackle the following:

- Choose a partner
- Draw an object
- Research the object in the lab
- Keep notes on your findings and sources
- Construct a presentation with thoughtful consideration of S.O.A.P.
- Weave ethos, pathos, and logos throughout to appeal to your audience
- Generate an intentional slant
- Divide the speaking responsibilities with your partner
- PRACTICE
- Present with vigor and intelligence

Object: _____

Partner: _____

Presentation Tone:

_____

Facts:

Source #1

URL: _____

_____
_____
_____
_____
_____
_____
_____
_____

Source #2

URL: _____

_____

_____

_____

_____

_____

_____

_____

_____

Source #3

URL: _____

_____

_____

_____

_____

_____

_____

_____

_____

Inventions and Discoveries Objects

Air Conditioning	Barbed Wire
Bicycle	Soda
Chewing Gum	Defibrillator
Frozen Food	Lawn Mower
Pen	Piano
Razor	Safety Pin
Adhesive Tape	Seatbelt
Vacuum Cleaner	Wallpaper
Zipper	Aerosol Can
Aspirin	Hot Air Balloon
Cement	Elevator
Holograph	Plastic
Stethoscope	Windmill
Flushing Toilet	Tape Recorder
Thermometer	
Pneumatic Tire	

Presentation Rubric:
Inventions and Discoveries Across the Decades

Name: _____   Name: _____

Personal Qualities   +_____/10

- Confidence
- Eye contact
- Poised = few nervous movements
- Useful gestures and positive body language
- Note and respond to audience feedback

Preparation   +_____/15

- Extremely familiar with what you are saying
- Able to answer reasonable questions
- Evident examples of ethos, pathos, and logos
- Clear presentation of ideas
- Well-organized

Overall Presentation   +_____/25

- A strong understanding of your topic was displayed
- The summary was complete and clearly stated
- Adequate explanation was given; *it is clear that you did your research* ☺
- The presentation included a clear beginning and a distinct conclusion

Additional Comments:

Grade: +_____/50

Possible Extensions through Becoming an Inventor

If time permits, or the level of student demands a challenge, then follow up the Inventions and Discoveries project with students becoming the inventors. After students have researched an object or discovery that changed the world, it is time for them to change the world with their own invention or discovery. Empower students with the possibilities of fame, fortune, or altruism. Have them choose, or choose for them, a location around the world. Students should research the location and come up with a solution for a problem the area is currently facing. Students might study the food shortage in South Asia, the loss of habitat and resources in the deforestation of Brazil, or the discrepancy between the number of girls educated across the world compared with boys. The topics vary greatly, but the common denominator is that students are studying various cultures, acquiring knowledge on current issues, and then coming up with plausible and possible solutions. This extension emphasizes the standards, particularly the cultural and global aspects that are sometimes missed in the traditional teaching of the classics. Additionally, the critical thinking and problem-solving components students develop through this project are life skills required well beyond their high school years. Who knows? One of your students just might come up with the next discovery that changes the world.

Implementing Ethos, Pathos, and Logos

Reach 'em with Rhetoric

Ethos, pathos, and logos are essential tools in reaching an audience. This chapter illustrates how to define, recognize, and use the rhetorical situation in strengthening students' reading, writing, and speaking. Nonfiction sources will be evaluated. Grab bag practice lesson and advertisement project are included.

Common Core State Standards (in Our Own Words)

- SL.9–10.2. Evaluate sources and diverse media to identify purpose and convey information in proper format to audience. *How do I use diverse media formats to best relay information to an audience? Which format best suits my purpose?*

- SL.9–10.4. Present information in an organized manner to engage listeners. *How do I say what I need to say to get my audience to understand and follow my presentation?*

- L.9–10.1. Show evidence and command of the conventions of standard English grammar and usage when speaking or writing. *What does it take to speak effectively?*

- L.9–10.5. Demonstrate knowledge of and ability to use figurative language and nuances through word choice. *What is the best way to say what needs to be said?*

- W.9–10.10. Write often and for varied time periods, purposes, and audiences. *Why is it important to write?*

What's Rhetoric?

Rhetoric. Rhetoric? Simply defined, rhetoric is the way we use language to write or speak effectively. Convincing others and defending what we believe is an integral part of navigating daily life. Students must be taught to appreciate rhetoric and the many ways it can impact the outcome of getting what they want. Depending upon the age of the student and the previous exposure to rhetoric, you may find yourself beginning with the basic rhetorical question. Start by asking students some of the cliché questions that they may have heard and been too quick to answer. Some possibilities are "If your friend jumped off a bridge, would you jump too?" "How am I supposed to live without you?" "Aren't you ashamed of yourself?" "What business is it of yours?" "Why me?" Students may laugh, but many will admit to getting into trouble for answering these questions or for "talking back." Teaching students that some questions are not meant to be answered verbally introduces them to the idea that rhetoric forces them to play a game. Questions are used to promote thought and emphasize points. Part of the art of rhetoric is listening to what is being said and how it is being said in order to understand your next move.

Rhetoric

Rhetoric is the way we use language to write or speak effectively.

Ethos, Pathos, and Logos

We acknowledge the importance of rhetoric but can find ourselves, and our students, overwhelmed by the endless possibilities. To achieve a small, capable plan of attack we approach rhetoric through ethos, pathos, and logos. Ethos is the credibility, character, and competence of the speaker. Pathos is the emotional appeal of the speaker. Logos is the facts, statistics, and logical appeals the speaker makes. Ethos, pathos, and logos are essential tools in reaching an audience when woven together in the right doses based upon the composition of the audience.

Ethos, Pathos, and Logos

Ethos is the credibility, character, and competence of the speaker.
Pathos is the emotional appeal of the speaker.
Logos is the facts, statistics, and logical appeals the speaker makes.

An Example of Breaking It Down

Ethos

Let's break it down. Students must consider where the information is coming from and adequately evaluate the source. There is no magic formula for calculating ethos here; a list of initials following a name does not always make a person credible. For example, a doctor of sociology speaking at a symposium to raise awareness on issues plaguing the homeless population in the

United States will have studied, gathered research, and interpreted the data, perhaps even spent years detailing his conclusions in writing. Based upon our reflection of his credentials and life's work, we find him to be a credible resource. Another speaker at the symposium is a former homeless transient with a general equivalency diploma (GED) who spent more than 20 years living on the streets across the United States. At first glance, the audience might admire his ability to turn his life around while overlooking his credibility. But, if you think about it, he has lived the life that the researcher has only studied. His experience is no less valid than that of the doctor, and his brings an aspect that the doctor can't provide. Students need to see that both of these men are essential to the program because combined they provide the scope and depth to truly understand the issue.

Pathos

Pathos is the fun one. It is tricky because the audience alone determines the success of the speaker's appeal. Too much or too little and you've lost your audience, but it's the one appeal you must have; it's the most used appeal for a reason. Pathos humanizes the speaker and the topic. Let's take another look at the doctor and the former homeless man. If the doctor can't connect with the audience on an emotional level, the audience will question why homelessness is his life's work. If he doesn't appear to care, then why should they? Without living a life of homelessness, how does he connect? As a speaker, the doctor needs to relate his facts with pictures, witness accounts, and personal anecdotes. In contrast, the homeless man has the advantage in pathos if he can provide the details of his experiences without losing his audience by evoking too much pity. He needs to be able to paint a clear picture of the homeless experience from his perspective, keeping in balance his own experiences without losing his purpose; his purpose is not to construct a tale of woe but to illustrate the truths of homelessness. Again, both speakers must generate pathos, but the methods they use to accomplish this must be authentic.

Logos

Logos is the most straightforward of the three appeals. Students of all ages quickly recognize the strength of the research or lack thereof. The key is for students to realize that not all research is equal. Just because there are numbers or sources cited doesn't mean that the material effectively supports the claim. Going back to our symposium on homelessness, we haven't addressed the purpose of the conference. It is easy to jump to conclusions on the purpose of a conference on homelessness; however, there are two sides to every story. One topic might be to provide awareness, assistance and resources, job support, and health services to the homeless population. Another possible topic is to address the negative impact of homelessness on tourism and small businesses across the United States. Clearly, the research needs to differ vastly depending on the forum. Students must always question the purpose or intent of the speaker and the occasion. Not all research should be treated equally. Facts and figures do not always deliver validation.

Appeals in Advertising

Once students appreciate the way ethos, pathos, and logos work together to sway the audience's opinions, it's time to show students how advertisers use these appeals on them. Even though students may be unaware of the power that advertisers wield, a quick introductory activity leaves them with no doubt. Begin with a discussion or handout of the most common jingles and slogans not only from today but also from prior decades; inevitably, students are surprised by how many they know. As teachers, your surprise may come in another form. We battle year to year to get students to recall and use their prior knowledge of our subject matter, yet they quickly recite any number of slogans from before they were even born. A few examples we use to kick things off include "I'm lovin' it," "Just do it," "Where's the beef?," "Think outside the bun," "Like a rock," and "Good to the last drop." Notice how we start with slogans for items that students currently use and lead into products that they are less likely to purchase or consume. You will find it doesn't matter; they know them all. After this brief introduction, ask students to dig deeper by considering the following questions.

Discussion Questions

- Why do these slogans stay with you while last year's history class is long forgotten?
- What is common among these slogans? For example, consider sentence structure, sounds of words, and diction.
- Where and when do you hear these? Could the reader's mood affect the ability to remember?
- For the aforementioned slogans, jot down any images that come to mind. How does the advertiser connect the slogan with an image?
- Are there any sounds that accompany the slogan? For example, type of voice used, certain sound effects, or music?
- What feeling or emotional response do you often have after hearing or seeing a slogan? Why do we react more to some than to others?
- Why is the subject of certain commercials or ads left vague? Outside of celebrity endorsements, why don't we have a specific speaker or group identified?

Finding Evidence by Selecting Advertisements

The Car Example

You have the questions, now you need to pick a common item and collect a variety of advertisements, both print and televised. An item that offers a wealth of possibilities is a car. Most everyone purchases a car, and depending upon the age group you are working with, students (particularly middle and high school aged) love to dream about their future vehicles. The car market attempts to attract a wide variety of people ranging in age, socioeconomic background, gender, and purpose. Cars are perfect because a car is an item that is both a need and a want. No matter if you are listening to the radio, watching television, or flipping through a magazine, automobile advertisements are everywhere. These ads promote various lifestyles depending on the vehicle that is being sold. For example, a minivan will never be targeted to the young and single crowd. Similarly, the two-seater sports car ad will never contain the image of a father pushing a double stroller and carrying a diaper bag while leaving a trail of toys behind him.

In looking at rhetoric beyond bandwagon appeal, generalizations, snob appeal, weasel words, and colloquialisms, students can find greater meaning by approaching the advertisements through ethos, pathos, and logos. Considering our car example again, students must be asked to look at the way the sales pitch changes depending upon the intended audience. We know the purpose; they want to sell us a car. The important factor that students need to understand, identify, and use for themselves is how the company develops the sales technique. Students must be able to recognize the ethos, pathos, and logos as well as the speaker and audience portions of S.O.A.P. For example, if you are marketing a car towards a mother, then she will want name-brand recognition; is this a company she can trust? These are a couple of the aspects addressing ethos.

Delving into pathos, what type of emotion would a mother associate with a car? What feelings does the ad need to evoke to get her to choose this vehicle over another? Here the advertisement must convey the car as more than a mode of transportation. The car must become a place where memories are made. It is a home away from home for the family to interact and share everything from the experiences of their day-to-day lives to road trips and family holidays. The car means so much more when there are stories attached rather than just lists of facts and figures about engine size, miles per gallon, and available options.

But those facts and figures can't be overlooked. Here is where logos plays its role. The mother shopping for a car wants to make sure her family is safe while traveling down a busy city street or cruising along the open highway. What safety features come standard on the vehicle? Which ones are optional? Safety is a priority, but she also concerns herself with being frugal in regard to the family budget. What is the base price of the vehicle compared with the price of the one advertised loaded with all available options? How does the base price and standard options of this vehicle compare with other vehicles in its class? Logos pulls together the rhetorical situation and completes the sales pitch.

All of this is accomplished by looking at a single item with many possibilities. The mother can be looking at minivans, crossovers, SUVs, or any number of family-sized vehicles. The differences are established from the varying makes and models. Even though all of these vehicles will serve the same basic purpose, their companies pride themselves on the various features, styles, roominess, or fuel efficiency.

Allow us to save you some time. Over the years, we have developed this unit and gathered a wide variety of car print and commercial advertisements. Some of our favorites include those created for the Toyota Prius, the Volkswagen Jetta and Beetle (Bug), the Cadillac line, Chrysler, and Dodge trucks. We like the Prius advertisements because, first of all, they are hitting on a current trendy topic of environmental awareness and "going green." These advertisements also attempt to appeal to a broader audience with their different models within the same car family. Volkswagen is also a smaller car that boasts good fuel efficiency. We enjoy this particular company because of the way it pokes fun at itself within its own advertisements while pulling in pop culture allusions such as *Star Wars*. The three U.S. car companies offer contrasting perspectives, focusing less on going green and more on American spirit, identity, and luxury. The Dodge Ram commercial "So God Made a Farmer" illustrates a perfect example of American spirit. Using the late Paul Harvey as the voice for the American farmer, Dodge defines what it means to work hard and complete your work with compassion and integrity, making your life worthwhile. Chrysler specifically chose as its spokesperson the controversial rapper Eminem, a Detroit native. Clearly a risky move, but this choice is one worth discussing, especially with what Chrysler is trying to say about the car being "imported" from Detroit. Chrysler's emphasis on developing identity is the essential element impor-tant to breaking down and understanding the meaningfulness of this commercial. The idea of who you are versus how others view you before they know you is all part of that identity and the compa-ny's attempt to redefine their company's image. Cadillac's image is all about luxury. People say "This is the Cadillac of . . ." because Cadillac is known for being top of the line, setting the standard for American luxury. Cadillac relies on its name and reputation more so than celebrity endorsements. An everyday need such as a car can become a want based on the way it is marketed by companies.

The Credit Card Example

The next challenge to give students is composed of advertisements that feature the same product from the same company but that are geared toward different audiences.

Consider an ad for a credit card. The same credit card company must appeal to a baby boomer as well as to a college student. How does this company change its pitch to grab the attention of completely different generations? The marketing group must move beyond interest rates and annual fees to target specific potential customers. In this example, the logos is going to remain the same, but the ethos and pathos will vary drastically according to age and financial circumstances. In terms of ethos, celebrity endorsements can range from the current number one pop artist performing on stage to a Fortune 500 executive boarding a private jet with briefcase in hand. Obviously the previous examples illustrate ethos by the selection of celebrity endorsers; celebrity endorsers lend their credibility to a product or brand based on the consumers' per-ceptions. However, pathos is also evident in the activities that endorsers are engaging in. Who doesn't want to know the feeling of performing on stage when one is in college? Who doesn't want to imagine being so successful that after years of hard work one can travel aboard one's own private jet?

Cars and credit cards are two very different items, but at the same time very common posses-sions in U.S. society. Students have buy-in because these are products that they will be shopping for and using in the near future. Even a kid doesn't want to be taken advantage of, so by exposing the manipulation used by marketers, students understand the real-world connection between rhetoric and consumerism. Not only do we highlight the rhetoric employed in manipulation, but we also make known the fact that teenagers are the number one targeted group by advertisers in the United States. Teenagers like to believe that they are trendsetters and seek out the latest products. They are a perfect group for marketers to target because of their perceived control of the family's discretionary income.

Advertising in Schools

Students often feel overlooked or ignored because of their age, so learning that millions of dol-lars are being spent trying to figure out the teenage brain excites them. This provides a perfect transition to introduce the latest battle of whether to permit advertising in schools. Bringing in nonfiction articles on the subject establishes the debate among students in your classroom. We start the examination of the topic by offering an article on each side of the issue. As students evaluate the role of advertisements currently in their school, the search can be as basic as which soda company holds the rights to the school's concession stands. Students research and find support for their position while keeping in mind the credibility and reliability of the sources. This provides great opportunities for class discussion, debate, and persuasive writing.

The Assignment: "Make Me Buy"

Once students learn how they are being manipulated, it's time for them to become the manipulators. We learn by doing. In this case, the doing is creating an advertisement to sell a product to the targeted audience—their classmates. Students are asked to choose a product and to develop a marketing strategy. Just as we looked at color layout and design in print ads, they must create a visual highlighting the best features of their product while targeting the intended audience. Students are asked to do a lot with very little. In preparation of this assignment, we review figurative language, ethos, pathos, logos, and S.O.A.P. All of these techniques must be present in the finished product, but the catch is that students are allotted only 10–15 sentences in which to achieve the desired effect. Some students choose to design an elaborate tri-fold poster board; others design an online web catalog, while still others create a replica of their product with specifically designed labeling. The second catch is that this assignment asks students to deliver a persuasive project without speaking. Their words must speak for them and be enough to entice others to buy their product.

Image Grammar

And for their words to speak for them, we require students to use Harry Noden's five basic brushstrokes as found in *Image Grammar: Using Grammatical Structures to Teach Writing*. We find that this structure is a practical way of developing grammar awareness within student writing. The five basic brushstrokes emphasize varying sentence structures and specific word choice to create more powerful effective writing. This is grammar made easy for students who can take the basic structures and make them their own again and again throughout various writing assignments. We have found that this is truly a way for students to "show" rather than "tell" in their writing. You will find an adapted explanation of the five brushstrokes in the lesson handouts with this chapter.

The use of *Image Grammar* should help students formulate better concise, descriptive writing, and perhaps the "Make Me Buy" assignment will seem deceivingly simple. However, it covers every technique that students must know to be able to demonstrate their understanding of rhetoric. An additional component accomplished through this project is forcing students to rely solely on their words and visual appeal. We all know those students who are full of charisma, who can talk their way out of a Saturday school before the slip can be written. When a speech is assigned, their grade reflects their confidence and personal draw. Likewise, we all know those kids who are quietly hoping never to be called on. They avoid eye contact with the teacher and struggle to keep from shaking and stuttering during an in-class presentation. This assignment is the great equalizer. The students with the great charisma often times find their words fall flat when they aren't permitted to breathe life into them. In contrast, the quiet student whose words lose their zest when softly delivered finds success in the persuasive power of the writing.

Presenting the Project

The process of presenting this project looks quite different from other projects students present throughout the year. For this project, the emphasis must be silence. On the day of the presentations, have students enter the classroom and select a "choice" area of the room to set up their display. Beside the display, students should place a blank sheet of notebook paper on which peers can comment on why they have chosen to purchase or pass on the product being sold. Each student is also given a set amount of play money to spend discriminately; all money is to be spent before the end of the class period. Again, remind students to spend their money on the basis of the writing, the design, and overall appeal established by the project—not on friendships. The final piece is to come to class the following day to discuss and reflect on what aspects worked and why. We also look at areas where there are opportunities for improvement with individual projects. Ultimately, this project is a fun and competitive way for all students to acquire the skills necessary in making an impact on an audience.

Rhetoric: A Weapon

Before this unit, very few students would have realized the importance of rhetoric not just in writing but in how it is a necessary weapon to combat poor decision making in their daily lives. If you have ever wanted to get in your students' heads; if you have ever wanted students to remember what you've taught as much as they remember those slogans from decades ago; if you have ever wanted to protect their well-being, then here is where the Common Core and its nonfiction element makes it happen. There is life after high school. By teaching students the art of rhetoric and how to detect and employ ethos, pathos, and logos, we are giving them a weapon to wield. We always say that instead of being manipulated, we want our students to be the manipulators. We can only hope they use their newfound power for good.

Unit 3 and Sample Lesson Plans

Grade Levels: 9–10; adaptable to 11–12

Time Frame: 2 or 3 weeks

UNIT AGENDA:

Day 1 Intro Image Grammar and Rhetorical Devices

HW: Choose any object and try to "sell" it. Use a minimum of three rhetorical devices and at least one sentence using image grammar. *Be looking for an ad that speaks to you*

Day 2 More on rhetorical devices, figurative language, and image grammar. Use an Action Shot to practice.

HW: Write a paragraph selling your least favorite thing in the entire world. *Be looking for an ad that speaks to you*

Day 3 Paragraph discussion, Critical Consumerism, and "Gotta Have It": What does it prove?

HW: Find an ad that speaks to you (ethos, pathos, logos)

Day 4 Start with an ad on projector. Students discuss for appeal. Concept Review. Dove Evolution Video. Partner work on ads w/ two-sided critique handout number 2.

HW: Read *Time* magazine article "I Feel Pretty" by Joel Stein.

Day 5 Discuss "I Feel Pretty" for use of rhetoric and ethos, pathos, and logos. Review ad appeal.

Read "The Selling of Our Schools: Advertising in the Classroom" by Glori Chaika for *Education World*.

HW: Write a paragraph focusing on the way ethos, pathos, and logos is used in the article.

Day 6 Discuss "The Selling of Our Schools: Advertising in the Classroom" responses. Read and discuss "Schools for Sale" by Michael Winerip from the *New York Times*.

Intro "Make Me Buy" projects
HW: Outline for project

Day 7 Socratic seminar on advertising in schools

Day 8 Work day on "Make Me Buy" project

Day 9 In-class presentations and "purchases"

Day 10 Follow-up discussion
HW: Complete part 3 of the project, the reflection piece

Lesson 1
Critical Consumerism

1. Think of a time when you wanted to convince your parent to let you do something. What did you do to persuade him or her?

2. Were you successful in getting what you wanted? If so, why? If not, what would you do differently to get your way?

3. What is currently popular? Some might say this is what is "cool" right now. List objects and ideas that are "cool."

4. How do you define "cool"? Who decides "coolness" (celebrities, athletes, other groups)? When and why does something cease being "cool"?

5. What was "cool" last year in school? What is considered "cool" this year in school? Why do some things remain "cool" while others become "uncool"?

6. Analyze this statement: Ads sell ideas, not products.

Heading of Advertisement: _____

1. **Audience:** Think gender, age group, income (socioeconomic status), and location (trends and lifestyle of East coast, West coast, urban, suburban, etc.).

2. **Purpose:** Ads want to get you thinking a certain way beyond simply "buy this product."

   - **What is the company's intended perception for audiences?**

   - **What are the company's actual intentions? Again, we know they want to sell you something; dig deeper.**

3. **Ethos, Pathos, Logos:** Where does this ad hit you and why?

4. **Persuasive Techniques:** What techniques are employed? Review your notes on bandwagon, weasel words, idioms, and so on.

5. **Advertisement Design:** Think about color, images, people featured, layout, bold/italicized/pulled-out words, and so on.

Lesson 3

"Put it before them briefly so they will read it, clearly so they will appreciate it, picturesquely so they will remember it and, above all, accurately so they will be guided by its light."

—Joseph Pulitzer

A Short Guide to Basic Brush Strokes
Taken from Harry Noden's *Image Grammar*

Core Sentence: The puppy was jumping into the lake.

Your Core Sentence: _____

_____

Absolutes

Technical Definition: A noun and a participle
Grammar Made Easy: noun **+** -ing word

Example: Ears flapping, tongue lolling, the puppy was jumping into the lake.

You try: _____

_____

Appositives

Technical Definition: A noun followed by another noun. The second noun renames
                                      the first or adds new information.
Grammar Made Easy: noun **+** noun

Example: The puppy, a gray ghost, was jumping into the lake.

You try: _____

_____

Participle Phrases

Technical Definition: A verb form ending in –ing or –ed.
Grammar Made Easy: -ing word or –ing phrase(s); –ed word or –ed phrases

Example: Sliding on the edge of the bow, the puppy was jumping into the lake.

You try: _____

_____

Adjectives Out of Order

> Technical Definition: Adjectives describe or modify a noun or pronoun. Adjectives are typically placed before the word they modify. Example: Black cat
>
> Grammar Made Easy: noun, adjective and adjective . . .

Example: The puppy, spontaneous and adventurous, was jumping into the lake.

You try: _____

_____

Active Words

> Technical Definition: Indicates that subject of the verb is acting or doing something
>
> Grammar Made Easy: No "be" verbs. Example: am

Example: The puppy plunged into the lake.

You try: _____

_____

Lesson 4
Make Me Buy!

Product Project

Initial Considerations:

- What is the product you will market?
- Who is your intended audience? Define this group of people by offering three to five distinct characteristics as you see them.

_____

_____

_____

For this Assignment:

Part One:

Using your item of choice as inspiration, create a product description directed toward your intended audience. This description should comprise **10–15 sentences**, including but not limited to **two examples of image grammar** and **two examples of figures of speech**. Choose a price for your product based on your words. How much are your words worth? **Your price range is between $10–$100, $101–$300, and $301–$500.**

Part Two:

Considering your intended audience and product, create a visual for your product as a continuance of your words. What environment or background could you place your product in to highlight its best features? How might you target a specific consumer? Can you sell a particular lifestyle? Sketch, photograph, generate with a computer, or use any other tool available to create this portion of your project.

Part Three:

In a paragraph, analyze your product description and visual. What choices have you made regarding diction, figures of speech, rhetoric, and sensory details? What role did your visual play? Reflect on the effectiveness of your overall campaign to sell this product.

Lesson 5
Make Me Buy! A Brainstorming Activity

The product you are interested in marketing:

(Example: Nail Polish)

_____

A more interesting name for the product:

(Example: Tempting Talon Tints)

_____

List five adjectives describing your product:

1._____   2._____   3._____

4._____   5._____

List five verbs to provide action for your product:

1._____   2._____   3._____

4._____   5._____

Provide two figures of speech for your product:

1._____   2._____

Use an example of image grammar to describe your product.

1._____

Understanding that only a minimum number of words can be used, write a three-sentence teaser of <u>who</u> could use this product and <u>how</u> they can use it to add to their lives. Simply, why consumers <u>cannot</u> live without this item.

_____

_____

_____

_____

Presentation Rubric: Product Project

1. Attention-grabbing opening/hook

    _____/5

2. Audience and purpose of the product acknowledged

    _____/5

3. Convincing sales pitch; tone and purpose appropriate

    _____/5

4. Adequate support was given for purchasing the product

    _____/15

5. The product write-up included a clear beginning and a distinct conclusion

    _____/10

6. Attempted to persuade audience rather than just inform

    _____/10

7. Two examples of figures of speech are underlined

    _____/5

8. Two examples of image grammar are underlined

    _____/5

9. Thoughtful choices of color, format, images, and creative design

    _____/10

10. An apparent appeal to ethos, pathos, and/or logos has been made

    _____/10

11. Final has been proofread and corrected (punctuation, spelling, organization, capitalization, sentence structure, etc.)

    _____/10

12. The overall effect of final product persuades buyers to purchase

    _____/10

    points _____**/100**

A Possible Extension through Pop Art

Throughout our studies, the goal is to combine as many genres as possible to provide a well-rounded approach to understanding a topic. As we study persuasion, and advertising specifically, a unique perspective is realized through incorporating analysis of pop art. We study the appeal and power marketers possess over the average person; the extension of pop art interpretation allows students to explore and marvel at an artist's ability to reinvent and take ownership of the everyday, yet highly crafted medium. This acts not only as a means to teach students how to read art, but also as a way to read meaning into a piece. Messages, words, ideas—communication in all forms is taken out of context daily. An exercise in evaluating pop art enables students to use the context clues as well as prior knowledge to construct meaning for a new visual piece; students can better put into words their interpretation because they already know something about the piece because of the way the artist has relied on popular slogans and/or images to relay a new message. What was Andy Warhol saying with his Campbell's soup cans? Or Roy Lichtenstein with his use of comic strips and newspaper advertisements? Again, though the premise seems simple, students must take the reading skills and practice them in a visual medium, making sense of the artist's satire. They are reading in a new way. Obviously, some art can be controversial or not appropriate for the grade you teach. There is plenty of pop art to choose from; don't be deterred if the first few pieces you search contain some innuendo that if used in the classroom will produce some voicemails from angry parents. Just keep looking—you will find student-friendly pieces.

Using art in the classroom increases literacy and cultural awareness. Pop art, specifically, shows students a genre of art they can understand and appreciate; this may not be the definition of art they expected. As we study allusion and the various voices that take ownership of an event by providing a personal meaning or interpretation, Pop art is a clear illustration of how all genres are interrelated and work with and off of each other.

5

Looking at History through Multiple Genres

Pulling It Together and Constructing Meaning

Using the students' recent exploration of ethos, pathos, logos, and S.O.A.P., it is now time to take the leap into the way authors employ these devices to construct meaning and to develop purpose and tone in their work. This unit is also an opportunity for students to explore the relationship between real-world experiences and their influence on written and spoken expression. Credible resources, reading for fact rather than just for effect, reading strategies for tone and purpose, diction and semantics, and developing the individual perspective based on a variety of sources are the learning targets. Lessons walk through chronicling the events of September 11, 2001, and the Kent State University shootings of May 4, 1970. Within these activities, students will listen to Crosby, Stills, Nash, and Young's song "Ohio," look at Pulitzer prize–winning photography from the event, and read the *New York Times* article "4 Kent State Students Killed by Troops" by John Kifner.

Common Core State Standards (in Our Own Words)

- RL.9–10.1. Cite strong and thorough textual evidence to support analysis of what the text says explicitly and implicitly. *Am I clear about what I just read?*

- RL.9–10.2. Define the theme or central idea of a text and show the details that shape and reveal a message. *How do I know what I just read?*

- RL.9–10.5. Examine the ways an author creates effects like surprise, suspense, and anger in a text. *Why does structure matter?*

- RL.9–10.6. Analyze a point of view or cultural experience in a work of literature from outside the United States. *How does point of view or cultural experience impact the writing? What insight can I gain about other cultures through literature?*

- RL.9–10.7. Analyze the representation of a subject in two different mediums. *How does creative choice matter? How do various mediums impact an audience?*

- RI.9–10.2. Determine the theme or central idea of a text and how it is developed and shaped by the author's choice of details and structure. *Can I explain and support what I just read?*

- RI.9–10.3. Explore the methods the author uses to unfold a series of events and the connections that are drawn between them. *What are the key points being developed, and how do they relate to the overall purpose?*

- RI.9–10.4. Interpret words and phrases in a text, including figurative and connotative meanings. Analyze the overall impact of choices and diction on meaning and tone. *What aspects of the author's writing are most effective?*

- RI.9–10.5. Analyze the structure of a text and the way the author develops ideas and claims. *Why does word choice matter? How are claims developed?*

- RI.9–10.6. Determine an author's point of view or purpose in a text and analyze how an author uses rhetoric to advance that point of view or purpose. *Author's choice: Why does it matter? This is the key standard in this section.*

- RI.9–10.9. Analyze seminal U.S. documents and how they address related themes. *How does time period and point of view affect theme? Who is the author, and why does it matter?*

- L.9–10.4. Clarify and establish the meaning of unknown and multiple-meaning words through various strategies and methods. *When I don't know a word or it doesn't make sense, what do I do?*

- L.9–10.5. Demonstrate knowledge of and ability to use figurative language and nuances through word choice. *What is the best way to say what needs to be said?*

Current Events

Think about your high school years. Chances are, there is a significant national or world event that shapes your memory of that time. Were you driving down the road when you heard news of Elvis's death on the radio? Perhaps you were excitedly watching the launch of the Space Shuttle Challenger when tragedy struck. Or, maybe, you were in a doctor's office looking down at the cover of *Time* magazine when you saw for the first time a picture of Dolly, the cloned sheep. So what event did you choose? Can you remember where you were, who you were with, what you were doing? More than likely, a number of events spring to mind. At the time these events took place you may not have grasped the cultural and historical importance. However, as the event unfolded and new information came in, your feelings and understanding about what happened began to form a personal impact. The news was no longer just something that happened, but rather something that happened personally to you, your country, and your world. Discussing the events with others, watching news feeds, reading articles, listening to radio broadcasts, or viewing photographs or film taken of the event molds an unforgettable connection that is forever engrained in our memory.

Unlike the hours we have spent outlining facts and dates in a darkened classroom, finding those facts and dates on our own builds memory and relevance. We all like a good story, but how do you create meaning? Part of meaning is created through discussions and retellings of important events that happen to us and others in our lives. Going back to your high school decade, odds are you had multiple encounters with the topic and essential and nonessential facts in different forms. The role different people played in your processing of that information can't be underestimated. For example, when Elvis died you may have been too young to grasp why your grandmother and mother reacted like they did. The response of others gave you pause on an event that you may have just glanced over. Sometimes we obtain knowledge so that we are in the know, so that we can attempt to appreciate why the news matters so much to others.

Relatable Materials Create Meaning for Students

Giving students material they can relate to also creates meaning. For example, many of us teach about the Holocaust. If we throw around numbers like 6 million, students find it difficult to wrap their minds around the tragedy. They know it's horrific. They understand they are supposed to acknowledge the massive loss. They are shocked that people went along with Hitler's plan. But when they come back to the number 6 million, it holds little meaning. They can't conceptualize what that represents. When you attach a single story of individual survival and loss, the facts and statistics come to life. Without the human connection, 6 million remains a number and significance is lost.

Too often we rush to a finish, losing significance because we haven't given students time to allow the information to sink in. Stacking standard upon standard, throwing in a little background on the author and time period without giving students an opportunity to make connections that will allow authentic learning to take place is regrettable. In our current state of education, with large classes containing varied learning abilities, we are asked to accomplish so much with so little. Though it seems like an impossible task to meet every objective, bringing opportunities for individual associations provides the essential link between what's required and what's relevant. It's not that what is required isn't relevant; it's that kids can't find the relevance without our help. For us, it comes back to showing students that what was written in the past still holds essential truths to what we value now.

Go back to the event you chose from the decade in which you graduated. That event holds meaning because you received the information firsthand; you didn't study the event in a single paragraph out of a history book; read a single short story or novel; hear a bit of news in passing. The event is momentous because you have constructed meaning by sifting through information and reflecting with others. So often in school, as we attempt to meet standards within time constraints, we prepare simple summaries for students of what they should take away versus promoting students to construct their own meaning from the information about a topic. Part of this is time, but another part is trust. You have to trust that students will dig in. Trust that students will work independently and skillfully to understand and achieve the knowledge we want them to possess. As teachers, we think students can never know what we want them to know unless we directly deliver the message.

Textbooks and lesson plans are model examples of moving directly to the point; the path to learning is linear without many opportunities to stray. Although we all appreciate the opportunity to check one more item off our list of learning targets for the year, the check mark is premature. Yes, students tested well. They master the game of memorizing and regurgitating information to get the grade. But how much do they really know? What can they really apply and do? If we are honest with ourselves, students are not capable of as much as is required to be successful in the future.

Tackling the Time Barriers

Some of you are shaking your heads right now, thinking about how you cram that last unit in every single year. You are becoming frustrated contemplating how you have barely enough time to cover what you need to now, much less add materials that take you off that linear path. Take a breath. Let's look at the standards and targets. Some are easier than others. We can check off a percentage at the beginning of the year because students have been working on certain objectives, in varying degrees, for a number of grades. However, the new Common Core demands that we take a closer look at everyday literacy.

Everyday Literacy

Everyday literacy is the student's ability to synthesize the information received and take ownership while establishing meaning. Students can't accomplish this goal if we have already done the work for them. Delivery of the message is no longer the goal; rather, guiding students to discover the message on their own is the outcome sought. We repeat; you can't do this for everything. You need to pick a couple of targets and make time to model how you find meaning and then summarize the essential parts. You will be surprised by how quickly students will begin to add to the discussion by bringing in outside resources on their own. Students appreciate the opportunity to contribute value to the dialogue beyond the surface-level comprehension responses. Once we take the time in the beginning of the year to give students the tools to participate in this way, students take more ownership of their learning. We can cover more topics with more depth. We don't have to continually review concepts because students have gained a genuine understanding rather than a surface-level awareness.

Flexibility Is Key

The tricky part to this approach is being accepting of multiple answers and views. Students and teachers alike must appreciate that there is no single right answer. Constructing meaning is a messy business. If you are going off the linear path, you must also be ready to go off the script. You won't always know the answer—that's OK. This is a great opportunity to model for students how we go about finding answers to questions or problems when we don't have all the facts or answers to share. We understand that this is a risk for some teachers. Taking risks makes people uncomfortable. It is uncomfortable for some students as well because they just want us to tell them the right answer so they can move on with the lesson and get their A. If everyone is a little uncomfortable, then we are all on our toes as thinkers and learners. We all become teachers. We all become learners. Wading through the mess together, we settle on an understanding of the topic and bring order to the information uncovered.

September 11th and the Kent State Shootings

In our classrooms, we ask students to explore the events of September 11th and the Kent State University May 4th shootings to demonstrate the importance of flexibility and open-mindedness necessary for everyday literacy. We chose September 11th because the event is a recent piece of history, spoken of and remembered yearly in the media, and one that offers a multimedia retelling. We chose the Kent State University shootings not only because it exemplifies a local tragedy as it's viewed from a national lens, but also because for many of our students, college is the beginning of their American Dream. We ask our students: How can innocent students losing their lives by the actions of the United States National Guard on their home campus coexist with our definition of the American Dream?

When establishing an understanding of the American Dream, we must look to the seminal documents of the United States as a means of exploring the ideals of those who hoped and fought for their dreams before us. What was their vision for the country? Have we reached the potential they envisioned? Have we exceeded it?

We can start to uncover the dreams others imagined for the country by looking at Winthrop's 1630 text "A Model of Christian Charity" where he strives toward a "shining city upon a hill." What did Winthrop have to say in 1630 that President Ronald Reagan thought relevant to bring back in the 1980s? Throughout this unit, we like to investigate how the past has influenced the present.

The Declaration of Independence and the Preamble to the Constitution show the official beginnings of what the United States was to become and specifically outlines the dream of equality; all men are created equal with unalienable rights. When the definition of "men" changed, so did the Constitution. Slavery was abolished; the right to vote was granted to all citizens regardless of gender and race. Looking at these amendments contributes to the dream and how the dream changes and evolves to include contemporary needs.

Franklin Delano Roosevelt's "Four Freedoms" speech reminds Americans of a country whose fundamental ideas are worth fighting for. While Elie Wiesel's "Hope, Despair and Memory" speech and Martin Luther King, Jr.'s "Letter from the Birmingham Jail" were written in different times and for other reasons, all share a core belief that we as human beings can and must rise against injustice. Again, we focus on words becoming actions and dreams becoming realities.

What are some current issues and ideas that were beyond what the founding fathers could imagine? How do we deal with these contemporary issues in light of the American Dream and progression of our country? The legalization of gay marriage, abortion, medical marijuana—these battles were beyond the scope and vocabulary of the United States outlined in the past by the founding fathers in the seminal documents. How will the leaders of today write to these changes?

After study of the seminal documents and the defining of the American Dream, we ask students to learn from the history of the Kent State University shootings and events of September 11th. Students can readily research the event and find ample material as well as dialogue with parents to gain a better understanding of the impact of these historical times. We find significance in students connecting with these histories because, although they are recent, current students are too young to remember and feel the impact. Much like the 6 million statistic when it comes to the Holocaust, students understand that the events of September 11th and Kent State are horrendous, but they lack the connection that brings personal relevance.

Just as we've said before, we don't want students forming their opinion of an event based on a single summary, a single source. We know that through examining various sources, conversing with other people, and the passing of time, we generate conclusions and a broader scope of understanding. We may not have the luxury of the passage of time, but we can offer students various credible sources and the opportunity to have a dialogue with others.

Credible Sources

As we begin our discussions on credible sources, we give students articles from well-known newspapers and magazines such as the *New York Times,* the *Los Angeles Times,* the *Smithsonian,* and *Time* magazine to name a few; we also look at local newspapers for the community perspective. By examining these various sources, we create a perfect opportunity to discuss that certain magazines, newspapers, and news programs, despite having a reputation for being credible, can contain slant and bias. Comparing the various perspectives of a number of media outlets exposes students to the individual slants, allowing students to better assess where the truth lies within the information they are receiving.

We also appreciate that all of these resources have amazing online archives for students to access. Most districts struggle financially, but by asking students to use the Internet we encourage technology awareness and skill development without requiring any additional dollars to purchase class copies. Examining these various articles gives students a chance to practice their analysis based on S.O.A.P. When looking at the aforementioned list of included newspapers and magazines, you might have noticed that we include both East and West coast perspectives. Our local perspective covers the Midwestern view. The idea behind this is variety. We don't want our students to be limited with the information they receive based on where they live. We emphasize the importance of finding sources with various perspectives from diverse places. We need to educate ourselves on what people are saying, particularly when that perspective might differ from our own. Students are encouraged to gather numerous sources to construct a well-rounded body of opinions. Students form their own perspective based on the educated opinions found.

Bias

You can't gather opinions from so many diverse perspectives without tackling bias. Bias isn't always a bad thing. We want students to decipher bias based on feeling rather than bias that goes beyond feeling and skews facts. S.O.A.P. gives us a tool by which to judge our sources. Again, who is the speaker? Do we know that speaker from any other occasion? What is that occasion? Is the occasion sponsored by a credible agency or organization? Who is the audience? Would students consider themselves part of that intended audience? What is the purpose? The purpose is pulled together after examination of the first three.

Diction

As we continue to deconstruct a text, we must ask students to pull out specific diction. Upon second reading, students must be asked to mark and identify specific words and phrases that strike them or could hold multiple meanings. This is where denotation versus connotation comes into play. An example is the word *retard.* Many of you reading that word took pause. Why would English teachers of all people think it appropriate to include that word in their book? Clearly, denotation versus connotation matters. *Retard* literally means to slow down, but you don't take pause because of the original intention of the word. You pause because of the unfortunate connotations the word now exudes, not to mention the tone it establishes. Tone can be tough for students, especially high school students. They find it easy to establish tone when hearing something verbalized, but often become confused or misread an author's tone when it's left entirely up to their detective skills. As a reading strategy, have students identify specific words and phrases that seem to matter before they try to summarize the author's overall main point or identify the piece's tone. Ask students to consider what words an author chose to lead them to a particular understanding. All too often, students rush to deliver their understanding of what an author meant without taking the time to find the essential support necessary to prove they are correct in their assumptions.

A Return to Ethos, Pathos, and Logos

A continuation of this line of thinking is ethos, pathos, and logos, which allows students to break the reading down to yet another level. Pathos is the easiest of the three for teenagers to comprehend. Asking students to describe their feelings when reading about a topic is a good starting point when looking at the rhetorical situation. The next element of the rhetorical situation is ethos. Part of ethos is showing and reviewing the necessity of credible sources. For example, students must acknowledge why the *New York Times* is a more credible source than an anonymous blog spot. When researching online, is an author included? Does the site itself embody a certain credibility? Consider PBS.org compared with random-guy-living-in-his-mother's-basement.com. Which would you trust? Hopefully, for the sake of young people everywhere, you chose the former. But those young people aren't finished yet. Additionally, students should comb the article for testimonies from experts and reliable quotations from notable personalities in that field.

Completing the rhetorical triangle is logos. Logos is important because it encourages students to read for fact rather than just effect. Students need to be reminded to examine the logos, because as human beings we can become so caught up in the emotion of the situation that we can easily be swayed from the credibility of the facts. What are those facts, dates, percentages? Are these figures consistent with the figures found in other sources? Students struggle sometimes at the redundancy of information from one source to the next. Reassure them that this redundancy supports accuracy, and it's actually a good thing.

A Need for Redundancy

We are looking for redundancy between articles, but we must take a multimedia approach. Some genres lend themselves more appropriately to ethos, pathos, or logos. Only by looking at different outlooks and comparing them do we gain a complete picture of the situation. A poem may grab our attention initially and prompt us to seek out a newspaper article. That newspaper article could lead us to a documentary that introduces us to a book. Discovery of information is circuitous. We hunt for it, making it that much more exciting when we find the pieces that allow us to more fully understand the situation. When you see a situation from multiple angles and perspectives, you can more completely grasp the big picture. We require our students to diversify their sources. They are never permitted to have only online sources, only print sources, only film sources.

Pulling it together, please feel free to use the following lesson plans and examples to start the process with your students. We consider these the first steps in encouraging students to take ownership of finding information and analyzing information in order to construct personal meaning. Some students will come ready to accept this challenge, while others will need to be gently led. This is a change for both you and for your students. Give yourselves time and permission to change what follows and make it your own.

Unit 4 and Sample Lesson Plans

Grade Levels: 9–10; adaptable to 11–12

Time Frame: At least 8–10 class periods

UNIT AGENDA:

Day 1 Research the events of September 11th and complete guided questions.

Day 2 Discussion and review of guided question research (see lesson #1).

HW: Read "Of Altruism, Heroism and Evolution's Gifts" by Natalie Angier

Day 3 In-class writing (see lesson #2)

Day 4 Read "A Day of Terror: An Assessment; When an Open Society Is Wielded as a Weapon Against Itself," by Michael R. Gordon, and complete lesson #3.

HW: September 11th——"Leap," poem and videos

Day 5 Discussion of lesson #5.

HW: Respond to the prereading questions (see lesson #6a)

Day 6 Whole-class discussion of questions. Read Margaret Atwood's "A Letter to America."

HW: Complete accompanying questions (see lesson #6b)

Day 7 Research day to prepare for lesson #7

Day 8 Found Poems (see lesson #7)

Day 9 Share poems and review rhetorical situation.

Day 10 Close unit with a comparison of images of July 4th and September 11th; discuss S.O.A.P. regarding each date, keeping ethos, pathos, and logos in mind. What impact does the passing of time have on our awareness and emotional perspective regarding history? (Note to teachers: You will find humorous adaptations of July 4th that offer a strong contrast to the serious nature of September 11th portrayals. This provides a great opportunity to explore tone and purpose.)

1. What events led up to the attacks of September 11th, 2001?

2. Who were the victims?

3. Who were the perpetrators?

4. What was the aftermath in the United States?

5. What was the world response to this event?

6. How did the U.S. government respond? Consider the Homeland Security Act and the Patriot Act specifically.

7. Summarize one conspiracy theory resulting in the investigations following the attacks.

Lesson 2
Defining Altruism

Begin by reading "Of Altruism, Heroism and Evolution's Gifts" by Natalie Angier. Create a working definition of "altruism" as it's presented in the article. After reading and annotating, respond to the following quotations:

> "'For every 50 people making bomb threats now to mosques,' he [Dr. James J. Moore, a professor of anthropology at the University of California at San Diego] said, 'there are 500,000 people around the world behaving just the way we hoped they would, with empathy and expressions of grief. We are amazingly civilized.'
>
> True, death-defying acts of heroism may be the province of the few. For the rest of us, simple humanity will do."

Does this conclusion hold true today? What evidence is there to support your position? Consider current events in society as a means of comparison.

Identify the following as you read the article "A Day of Terror: An Assessment; When an Open Society Is Wielded as a Weapon Against Itself" by Michael R. Gordon.

Speaker:

_____

Occasion:

_____

Audience:

_____

Purpose:

_____

Now, please consider the following. First, quote the line and then identify the function of that line within the context of the article. Is your chosen line an example used to inform, persuade, illustrate? Label accordingly.

Ethos:

_____

_____

Pathos:

_____

_____

Logos:

_____

_____

Lesson 4
Can You Feel the Pathos?

For the following section, teachers should select age-appropriate videos from YouTube. These videos should be shown prior to reading the following pieces as a means of emphasizing the pathos.

- "Photograph from September 11" by Wisława Szymborska
- "Leap" by Brian Doyle
- "I Saw You Walking" by Deborah Garrison
- "When the Towers Fell" by Galway Kinnell

Lesson 5
Defining the American Dream

1. What was the American Dream to the founding fathers of the United States of America? Why do you think that was their dream?

2. What is the American Dream today? Has it changed much from the dream the founding fathers imagined?

3. What are the basic principles/values encompassed by the American Dream?

4. Is the American dream the same for a natural born citizen as it is for an immigrant? Explain.

5. Why is the American Dream common knowledge? What is its purpose? Its effect?

6. Is the "dream" a reality for most citizens? Is it still achievable? Has it become cliché?

1. Write a paragraph on how we define ourselves as Americans. Consider both the positives and negatives.

2. Some common stereotypes of Americans are that we are fat, uneducated, and racist people. Dispel these untruths in a well-constructed, thoughtful paragraph.

Lesson 6b
Read and Annotate

Read and annotate Margaret Atwood's "A Letter to America." After reading, respond to the following:

1. Write a paragraph on how Atwood, a Canadian author, defines America. Consider both the positives and negatives.

2. Choose two allusions that Atwood uses to define America. Research the history and significance of each. Develop a paragraph explaining the relevance of each allusion. Consider why Atwood would choose these examples to illustrate/define America. How do these choice examples set us apart from the rest of the world?

3. Atwood writes, "This is a difficult letter to write, because I'm no longer sure who you are." After reading her letter, please explain the **tone** in which this is said. What is she trying to get across with her tone?

4. What is Atwood's **purpose** for writing this essay? Please use specific examples from the essay to support your argument.

5. Atwood ends with, "You, too, have great spirits of the past you may call upon: men and women of courage, of conscience, of prescience. Summon them now, to stand with you, to inspire you, to defend the best in you. You need them." Is this a **call to action**? Explain.

Lesson 7
Word Search

Take a day in the computer lab to complete research on the events of September 11th. Look specifically at articles from U.S. newspapers and magazines. What was being written days, months, and years after the event? Choose three articles encompassing each of the latter times. Keep track of your search by recording the publication names and dates as well as the article titles and authors. Highlight telling, inspiring, shocking, frightening, illuminating lines from these articles. Basically, look for lines that strike you in some way. Remember ethos, pathos, and logos. This genre of writing typically relies on ethos and logos, and yet, is it possible to write about such tragedies without pathos?

Once your lines are chosen, create a Found Poem. Using the words and phrases that are most significant, construct a poem by providing links that connect the ideas. As the poet, you must make a point or illicit an emotional response. Remember, you do not need to use entire lines. You may also change word forms (i.e., endings and tenses). Feel free to add your own words and punctuation to create emphasis and meaning. Include citations beneath your poem giving credit to the original writers who made your Found Poem possible.

Examples

Terrorists slam jet planes into the towers
The terrified scramble down
Hand in hand, they reached for each other
Survival
The New York firefighters charge upward
Never to be seen again

People falling in flames,
Falling from the sky
Something of themselves to the hearts of the wounded
Whisper prayers for the sudden dead
The heart of us all beats against the void

Rallying and surprising even ourselves
His hand and her hand nestled
Greatness and holiness
Within them like seeds
A spirit of cooperation will arise

Believe against evil
Love is why we are here

We are amazingly civilized
Simple humanity will do

Extraordinary ordinary
Stunning simple
Love

Borrowings from:
"Of Altruism, Heroism and Evolution's Gifts"
By Natalie Angier
Published: September 18, 2001
And
"Leap"
By Brian Doyle
Published: March, 2002

Example 2: "Choices" by Angie Stooksbury

Terrorists
Slam jet planes into the towers
Harrowed humanity scrambles
At two hundred miles an hour
Falling so far and so fast
They struck the pavement
Pink mist in the air

Terrorists
Advance toward an unknown
Passengers together plot resistance
Plane fails to reach its target
The indomitable spirit of a rock-solid America
The heart of us all——
Beating against the void

Human Beings
Like seeds that only open under great fires
Have greatness
Climbing over the rubble
There's a grandness in the human species
True death-defying acts of heroism
Perfect simple ferocious love
Individual choice

Borrowings from:
"Of Altruism, Heroism and Evolution's Gifts"
By Natalie Angier
Published: September 18, 2001
And
"Leap"
By Brian Doyle
Published: March, 2002

Opportunities for Extension

Using the book *American Ground: Unbuilding the World Trade Center* by William Langewiesche, break the class into small, diverse, learning groups of 4 or 5 students. Assign each group a chapter to read and annotate. After students have a working knowledge of their chapter, they will create a presentation for their classmates. The point is for the entire class to have an understanding of the book as a whole, based on each group's presentation. (Note to teachers: The structure for these presentations can take on many forms depending on time and resources.)

Another possibility, if time is a factor, is to include the children's book *Fireboat: The Heroic Adventures of the John J. Harvey* by Maira Kalman with the September 11th lessons. This colorful, creative, short nonfiction work introduces New York City in 1931 and follows the journey of a fireboat, the *John J. Harvey*, from when it was first put on active duty through its retirement and its return to active duty on September 11, 2001. Students will appreciate its message while gaining further insight into the events of September 11th. We like this lesson and the manner in which it highlights the history of the fireboat and its ongoing usefulness despite being auctioned at one point in its past for scrap. As teachers, we continually argue the relevance and present day meaningfulness of the classics; just because something is old doesn't mean it's outdated and worthless. The *John J. Harvey* was considered by most people to be a heap of junk; however, the 1931 vessel completed a job in 2001 that nothing else could accomplish. Additional nonfiction reading and research is always an option; what other John J. Harvey–type stories are there?

Numerous articles on and pictures of this historic ship exist, including the following articles and video:

- "A Shining Light in Our Darkest Hour" by Richard O. Aichele
- "Born-Again Hero" by Roy Attaway
- Jessica DuLong and Fireboat *John J. Harvey* on CBS Sunday Morning, as archived on YouTube

6 Writing with Spin to Rewrite History

When Words Matter

Fact: History is rewritten. Why can't our students be the ones to rewrite it? The best way for students to understand "the tricks of the trade" is to test out their honed "manipulation" skills on their peers. What better way for students to try out their own manipulation skills than to put their own personal spin on history? After spending time figuring out how other writers interpret and retell history, we want students to try their hand at these techniques. Students are assigned a decade to research through multiple genres and perspectives. Students must write their own history, bringing to the forefront a unique bias and perspective as it relates to a contemporary audience. A nonfiction model is William Lutz's "No One Died in Tiananmen Square," which is available online. The nonfiction writing and research stems from reading dystopian novels such as Aldous Huxley's *Brave New World*, Suzanne Collins's *The Hunger Games,* Cory Doctorow's *Little Brother,* George Orwell's *1984,* and Katie Kacvinsky's *Awaken*. In all of these novels, history is rewritten.

Common Core State Standards (in Our Own Words)

- RL.9–10.3. Study and evaluate how multilayered characters develop throughout a text, progress plot, and relate with other characters. *How are characters developed? What can I tell about each character based on the way they interact with each other? How do a character's actions and thoughts develop and contribute to the theme?*

- RL.9–10.7. Analyze the representation of a subject in two different mediums. *How does creative choice matter? How do various mediums impact an audience?*

- RI.9–10.7. Analyze various accounts of the same subject told in various mediums. *In what ways does an author's creative choice impact an audience?*

- W.9–10.4. Construct clear and sound writing that engages the audience with desired style that achieves purpose appropriate to assignment. *What goes into creating a well-developed, engaging piece of writing?*

- W.9–10.7. Carry out research assignments of various lengths to solve problems and investigate diverse subjects to gain understanding. *What does it take to be a good researcher?*

- W.9–10.8. Collect pertinent information from varied sources and mediums to deepen research while maintaining proper citation of those sources within writing. *How do I gather relevant information but maintain proper citation of the sources?*

- SL.9–10.2. Evaluate sources and diverse media to identify purpose and convey information in proper format to audience. *How do I use diverse media formats to best relay information to an audience? Which format best suits my purpose?*

- SL.9–10.5. Make strategic use of digital media and visual displays to enhance a presentation. *How can I make my presentation effective?*

- L.9–10.1. Show evidence and command of the conventions of standard English grammar and usage when speaking or writing. *What does it take to speak effectively?*

Some Love for Dystopian Novels

We all have read them. Maybe you even had a phase where you read nothing but dystopian novels. These supposedly perfect worlds, stringently structured to attain stability, where one hero or a group of revolutionaries sets out to enlighten the submissive people and end the suffocating dominance of the government. Everything coming from the government must be questioned. Nothing is as it seems. You are told you are always happy, and if you are not you are given another dose of pain killer; you are told that you must fight for your life in an effort to atone for past revolutions; you are told you have committed crimes against the government when your only fault was skipping school and playing an online game; you are told you are at war with a new enemy when you remember just yesterday that enemy was your ally; you are told that online school is what's best for you even though you desire to experience what the outside world has to offer. An obvious theme threaded throughout these examples is that of control. One way that control is exerted throughout all of these dystopian novels is through media and the rewriting and distortion of news and history. So much time has passed that the average citizen doesn't even know what's true anymore. Citizens are so focused on getting through the everyday mandates the government forces upon them that they lack the motivation, time, and voice to seek the truth that leads to change.

We need to ask ourselves, why do our students love this type of novel? What about the aforementioned situations draws them in and compels them to read further? As teens, students experience the desire to be out on their own and be responsible for themselves without anyone telling them what to do, controlling their every move. Teens are aware and notice changes that could be made to improve society, but lack the time as they bounce between activity and study. Much like their dystopian counterparts, their busy lives dictate that they keep moving forward without pause and time to orchestrate change. When teens do come forward with an innovative idea, far too often they are told they have not lived enough life yet to know what to change or how to institute that change. They know they have something to say and contribute but do not necessarily have the audience to hear it.

Bias Control as History Is Rewritten

On May 4, 1970, students at Kent State University in Ohio had something to say, but the U.S. government didn't want to hear their message. Protesting against the Vietnam War, students congregated in mass facing the lines of National Guardsmen sent in by the government to control the crowd. To this day, no one knows why the first shot was fired into that crowd, but what followed involved U.S. soldiers wounding and killing a number of college students. Already some of you might be forming a bias based on what you know of this event or the few lines you have read here. Either way, when you read about soldiers firing upon civilians, it is difficult to remain impartial. If you lived through it, then you have already formed your own opinion on the basis of your experiences. For those of you hearing about this event for the first time, perhaps you are distraught over U.S. soldiers killing college-aged U.S. men and women. You can't get over the fact that our government would condone shooting our youth. What if we add to this information by telling you that the youth burned down a campus building a few days before, precipitating the need for military presence? We hope that what becomes obvious is that you need more information to accurately form an opinion.

In the previous paragraph, you more than likely noticed your bias swaying from one side to the other as new information was introduced. We can attempt to control that bias on the basis of how we word the information presented. If we had called the event a tragedy, then we would have framed your thinking in a certain direction. Another deliberate choice was to emphasize the actions of the soldiers and to mention the arson committed by the students only later. Obviously the facts are the same, but the order in which they are introduced can shape an audience's viewpoint or bias. As adults and as teachers, we use these skills daily to get students to do what they need to do. Unbeknownst to students, they can be equally adept at building their arguments in convincing their parents why they should receive certain privileges. In a continuation of the work shown in the previous chapter with September 11th, we give students the Kent State University shootings because more than likely they have no previous knowledge to color the event.

Multimedia Perspectives

The Kent State lesson gives us the opportunity to continue the discussion of how multimedia perspectives influence personal understanding and bias. Through a song, an article, and photographs taken at the time, students explore the meaningfulness of the author's message and the chosen format of delivery. Some of the initial questions for this example are, How can a song compete with a newspaper article in establishing a message? Can a picture truly speak a thousand words? What is the purpose of the piece? What advantage does the chosen medium have in accomplishing its purpose? To illustrate, consider the purpose of the newspaper article versus the purpose of the song. Likewise, consider the intended audience of each. The song that we have chosen is meant to rally support and mobilize America's youth to take a stand against the actions and choices of the government. Because young people are often found listening to music, it might be more difficult to reach them through a print medium such as the newspaper. A song is catchy and to the point, and they would be exposed to it multiple times throughout the day. On the contrary, a newspaper article has a single run, and in 1970 (aside from going into the archives in a library), once it's gone, it's gone.

With all of that said, once you introduce photographs of the event for consideration, students are able to form for themselves an understanding of how various findings on the same topic can be blended to lead an audience toward an intentional bias. Once the foundation has been established on how to deconstruct the messages offered through various mediums, students are ready to construct and spin events around their personal slant aimed at a chosen audience.

An Assignment: "The Decade Project"

This is where the decade project comes in. It's not so much about change as it is about giving power to students' voices, ideas, and interpretations. In a nutshell, the decade project relies on students interpreting for themselves the facts of a historical event, rewriting that event to contain their own personal bias, and powerfully delivering their version to their classmates. Let's crack the shell and find out the details of this project.

Basic Differentiation for the Project

We know that we can assign upper level and honor students practically anything and they will run with it. Unlike the honor students, the lower level students, who we assume will require too much class time and assistance to make the project worthwhile, are given an alternative assignment. Again, there is so much to do with so little time that we consider this an inevitable cut. No more than we would want them to underestimate themselves, we need to stop underestimating them. As teachers of both honors and inclusion classrooms, we have realized that with specific modifications all students can meet the learning targets. Our task is to figure out how to get them there.

Sometimes we begin in the middle, focusing on the needs of the average student in our lesson creation. Other times, we look at the end goal and work backward. For the decades project, we knew where we wanted the students to end up; we also knew that we wanted all of our students to take part in this project. Once that lesson is established for the average learner, modifications are made to meet the needs of the struggling students as well as the advanced students. Where can we take this average lesson in terms of enrichment versus modifications to best support students' success?

Student success begins by acknowledging that we learn by doing. For some of our struggling readers who have a tough time deciphering tone, diction, theme, and bias, they will learn by creating rather than by simply labeling as they have done in the past. Giving these students the opportunity to pull apart information to form new perspectives better defines some of these standard characteristics that we want students to glean from their reading assignments. We strive to provide all of our students with similar learning opportunities. Sometimes we come up with good ideas for an honors class but talk ourselves out of even attempting to modify the lesson for a lower level class.

We want to challenge all of our students but feel overwhelmed by surrendering so much instructional time to one project. We realize that our lower level classes require more face time and one-on-one guidance initially to be successful in this type of learning opportunity. Without laying the proper foundation in the beginning, students can become lost and frustrated if too much is required as outside homework. If structured suitably and presented appropriately, all levels of students will reach the desired learning targets and some students will even go beyond.

Depending upon the grade level and ability of the students, how much prep you've done for this type of assignment, and the time available to complete the project, the initial prompt may take many different forms. Our recommendations would be as follows:

- **Upper level or honors classes:** Assign students a decade and a continent to research. Through their research, students must narrow the focus, choosing a single historically significant event to learn more about. Out of everything from that decade and on that continent, students must choose something that they feel they can bring a unique perspective to. In choosing this event, students also must consider their classmates as the audience, shaping the final product to impact their peers' learning. Our main stipulation with the upper level or honors students is that they choose a stance that is contrary to popular belief or opinion.

- **Mid-level or college preparatory classes:** Give students the choice of three major events from a particular decade and continent. Provide the basic background on those events in order to help them narrow the focus and be more successful in choosing an event best suited to their interests. Once students choose their high interest–level event, they must develop the opposite opinion than what is typically presented.

- **Lower level or inclusion classes:** Provide students with two major events from a particular decade and continent. Some of you might find it advantageous to select events students have had prior exposure to in history or science classes. This way, students will have a basic working knowledge they can build upon through their own research. Others might find it more worthwhile for students to explore a wholly unknown event. The choice is yours. However, you will want to assign a specific lens for the students to use as a focus for their research. For example, a group of students could be assigned North America as their continent. Possible major events offered for their selected topic include the Vietnam War, the Patriot Act, and First Lady Michelle Obama's Let's Move! Initiative. Students may be assigned a progovernment slant on the events of Vietnam; an antigovernment slant on the Patriot Act; a neutral informational position on the Let's Move! Initiative.

Empower Student Writing through Choice

Notice that no matter the students' level, the key is to empower their learning and the writing through choice. To review the aforementioned choices, let's take a closer look at the topics and stances. For the Vietnam War, we know students will find ample evidence against the U.S. government and the draft. Thus, we make them present on the opposite position. When investigating the Patriot Act, students will find that in the beginning citizens were all too willing to give up personal freedoms regarding privacy in order to find the terrorists responsible for the September 11th attacks on our country. Recently, however, U.S. citizens are questioning what they are willing to give up and wondering if the government should be limited in its access to private information and communication. Again, we ask students to take the less popular position. In comparison, First Lady Michelle Obama's Let's Move! Initiative seems trivial. The reality is that students are faced with the mandates of this initiative daily when they enter their school's cafeteria. This is a contemporary battle that holds a high level of interest; students find it difficult not to have an opinion because of their firsthand experience with restricted lunch choices. We have noticed a dislike of this initiative, which is why our students must present from a neutral stance. In choosing the topics and stances, we hope to challenge students to explore the other side. By doing this, students gain an awareness of how difficult it is to change an audience's perspective from a traditionally held opinion.

Choice Does Matter

All students benefit from the same objectives within the assignment; the scaffolding used to get students there is what looks different. The final products, depending upon the level of student, will employ the use of different mediums. As teachers, we encourage students of various learning abilities to implement a medium on the basis of their need for individualized practice or extension. We also use the choice of medium to foster students' talents in music, photography, art, poetry, storytelling, and so on. We all have those students who are in a garage band looking for any opportunity to share their music with a captive audience. Maybe you have a secret poet in the classroom who has shared poetry with you but needs that nudge and reason to share the talent with peers. The possibilities and choices are endless. Words matter when students' opinions and choices are valued.

Unit 5 and Sample Lesson Plans

Grade Levels: 9–10; adaptable to 11–12

Time Frame: 9–15 class periods

UNIT AGENDA: (Note: The decades project should take place after the Kent State lesson and during the dystopian novel unit. Remember, depending upon the amount of time you have, the type of students in your classroom, and the technology and resources available, the time frame will vary greatly for this unit.)

Day 1 Introduce decade project and discuss possibilities; assign or allow students to choose partners.
HW: Begin research on your time, place, and possibly events in history.

Day 2 In-class group time to discuss and make a plan of action (assign research topics and roles)
HW: Research, research, research

Day 3 Read, annotate, and organize research findings; group work at end of the period
HW: Continue research

Day 4 Group discussion of events and acknowledgment of questionable details surrounding the events. Begin to brainstorm your group's chosen perspective and slant.

Day 5 Group drafting of presentation for event(s)
HW: Continue to write personally assigned role

Day 6 Work Day

Day 7 Work Day

Day 8 Presentations

Day 9 Presentations

Lesson 1
Are You the Hero of *Your* Story?
Opportunities and Choices Begin Here
Be Informed; Be Involved; Take a Side; Take a Stand!

Let's travel through time! You are about to go on a journey, a journey across time and location. Your task is to complete research on an assigned continent and decade. Using your group's research, generate a multimedia/genre analysis of your chosen historical event—the event your group feels lends itself to bias and a chosen slant to best exemplify that time and place. Keep in mind what we have studied in regard to motive, diction, style, juxtaposition, genre, euphemism, metonymy . . . these are just some of the special effects that will aid you in creating a presentation that stands out.

Your group will draw a time period and a continent from one of the following. Your first step is to gather as much information as you can on the various notable occurrences from that time and place. Keep in mind that not everything in the news is newsworthy. Not everything you read or find will be relevant for your purposes. For example, although we might be interested in the alleged Loch Ness Monster in Europe, for our purposes, "Nessie" really doesn't meet the criteria for a European event that impacts the world. Take notice of major wars, leaders, revolutions, diseases, and technological breakthroughs and discoveries, but by no means let these limit your own findings and interests.

This is your project. The key is figuring out what matters to you and your intended audience if delivered with an appropriate slant. Have fun rewriting history and making your own version.

Topics for Consideration

North America

1900s–1930s

40s–70s

80s–2010

South America

1900s–1930s

40s–70s

80s–2010

Asia

1900s–1930s

40s–70s

80s–2010

Europe

1900s–1930s

40s–70s

80s–2010

Australia

1900s–1930s

40s–70s

80s–2010

Africa

1900s–1930s

40s–70s

80s–2010

1. Create a brief timeline of events/occurrences.

2. More specifically, who started it? Who finished it? Why does it matter?

3. Are there good guys and bad guys as you interpret them from what you have researched? Consider the sources as well as intended bias.

4. Who was affected at the local, national, and world level?

5. Why are the events remembered? What earns them a place in history? For example, what was impacted, destroyed, changed, improved, lost, rediscovered?

Lesson 3
Bringin' the Bias

1. Consider all of the research your group has completed. What is your chosen event and why? Be sure to include the specific place and time it occurred.

2. Who is your intended audience and why?

3. List two or three specific details of the event that lend themselves to your chosen bias.

4. What mediums will best convey your biased message to your audience? Remember, your group must incorporate a minimum of five different mediums during your final presentation.

5. Develop an outline with effective and smooth transitions as to how your chosen mediums will flow together during your presentation for optimal impact on your audience.

Presentation Rubric: The Decades Project

Name(s): _____

Personal Qualities   +_____/20   +_____/20   +_____/20

- Confidence
- Eye contact
- Poised = few nervous movements
- Useful gestures and positive body language
- Note and respond to audience feedback

Preparation   +_____/25

- Extremely familiar with what you are saying
- Able to answer reasonable questions
- Clear presentation of ideas
- Well-organized

Visuals   +_____/30

- Readable
- Appealing and eye-catching; draws the audience's attention
- Careful consideration of layout and organization
- Seamless transitions
- Complementary blend of words and images

Persuasion and Bias   +_____/30

- Obvious and appropriate slant (but cleverly conveyed without being overwhelming)
- Thorough construction of bias throughout *entire* presentation
- Bias of speakers clearly and strongly delivered to audience

Special Effects   +_____/20

- Intentional use of literary devices and figurative language
- Well-chosen placement
- Techniques woven throughout presentation
- Special effects were purposeful and effective—not thrown in randomly

Overall Presentation   +_____/25

- A strong understanding of your group's event was displayed
- The summary was complete and bias clearly demonstrated

- Adequate explanation was given; *it is clear that you made history your own* ☺
- The presentation included a clear beginning and a distinct conclusion

Additional Comments:

Grade: +_____/150

Group Event: _____

Time and Place: _____

1. What is your understanding of the event? Give a brief summary of what you think happened based on the group's presentation.

2. As an audience member, who were you supposed to be? Did it work for you? Why or why not?

3. What was the bias? Were you swayed to accept the group's stance? Explain.

4. Was the chosen topic meaningful? Should it have been chosen as the topic to represent the continent and decade?

5. What were some of the strengths of the group's use of multimedia? Where could it improve?

    Circle your grade for this group: A   B   C   D

Opportunity for Extension:
Utopian versus Dystopian Project

With dystopian literature being trendy, a chance to partner a classic with something contemporary lies within combining the old with the new. Have students choose whether they would like to create a dystopia or utopia on the basis of what they have read in the classic and contemporary novels. This project provides a chance for students to envision various future scenarios while keeping in mind the necessary elements of this genre.

On the following pages are some of the different ways we have introduced these ideas to students.

Dystopia Project
Dystopia

noun

A society characterized by human misery, as squalor, oppression, disease, and overcrowding.

A dystopia is the idea of a society in a repressive and controlled state, often under the guise of being a utopia. Dystopian societies feature different kinds of repressive social control systems, various forms of active and passive coercion. Ideas and works about dystopian societies often explore the concept of humans abusing technology and humans individually and collectively coping, or not being able to properly cope with technology that has progressed far more rapidly than humanity's spiritual evolution. Dystopian societies are often imagined as police states, with unlimited power over the citizens.

Many people have attempted to create utopias—a perfect place for all people to cohabitate in a state of bliss; however, all utopias to date have failed. I am not going to ask you to attempt to create something that is doomed for failure. To the contrary, I want you to experience success. Thus, I want you to create the perfect DYSTOPIA. In order to complete this task successfully, please consider the following:

- What makes the perfect dystopia?
- What do the leaders of the dystopia gain?
- How can you create an atmosphere in which people want to follow your rules?
- Consider the initial reactions of the citizens; anticipate resistance.
- Outline the plan for your city. Include a slogan to rally and brainwash.
- How do you maintain authority? How would you govern?
- You must create a world where people see the need for control.
- Keep a narrow focus—magnify a current flaw with society (free speech, authority, free thought, free information, intelligence, genetics, age, race, energy, etc.).

Prepare a presentation that will convince the class that your dystopia is the one that would be the best (worst) for it. You will need to be detailed and creative to persuade/force people to follow your new order. Your project will look different from that of your peers. It should. I want unique projects and presentations. Please go beyond mere posters and PowerPoints. Consider all aspects of life and how to modify them to exemplify your dystopian society. Think way outside the box. You are limited only by your imagination—impress me.☺

My Dystopia Outline

City Name: _____

Year of Creation: _____

What is the problem that led to the creation of the new city? _____

_____

_____

As a result of this problem, what lasting effects are your citizens trying to cope with? (these effects are why they need your help)

What do you have to offer the people in your city? Why do they need you?

Outline of your city: business, housing, jobs, food supply, recreation, prisons, schools, etc. How are these operated? How do you control them? How do you decide who gets what?

City's Slogan/Catch Phrase:

City's Symbol(s):

Map of City:

Presentation Rubric:
Dystopia Project

1. You have identified the problem that led to the creation of the new city/world.

    _____/10

2. You have identified the lasting effects your citizens are trying to cope with and are using these to convince them that they need your help. (Family, education, transportation, property and wealth, government, media, elderly, religion, healthcare . . .)

    _____/30

3. You have established a slogan that defines your world and rallies/controls your citizens.

    _____/10

4. You have a developed plan for takeover. You have clearly mapped out why citizens should follow you and your leadership.

    _____/20

5. You have thoroughly mapped out an outline of your city and how it will function. You have prepared for all aspects of life.

    _____/30

6. You have presented strategies for addressing potential problems in your city—ways you will handle civil disobedience, crime . . .

    _____/30

7. Organization is original and logical.

    _____/30

8. Presentation is clear and concise, addressing all requirements set forth by the assignment.

    _____/30

9. Able to answer all questions from peers and persuasively defend your city.

    _____/10

Total _____/200

Another Brave New World:
The Creation of a Utopia

"We live in the best of all possible worlds."

Dr. Pangloss from Voltaire's *Candide*

By reading Aldous Huxley's *Brave New World,* we have explored the effects of certain ideologies on the future state of our world. For this assignment, imagine your "ideal" world. Create, through writing, a utopian society. Use what you have learned from reading *Brave New World* to guide your exploration. A warning: As a class, we will attempt to turn your utopia into a dystopia. What unintended consequences can be anticipated given the choices you make for your perfect world?

To help you get started, consider the following categories. Don't worry about what is possible; just imagine what you feel would be ideal.

1. Family units and child-rearing responsibilities
2. Education
3. Transportation
4. Distribution of property and wealth
5. Government
6. Media
7. Sports and leisure
8. Care for the elderly
9. Religion
10. Healthcare

Finally, utopias uphold a strong slogan for the people to rally around. What will the slogan of your world be?

The format for this project can take many shapes, but I would like to avoid having just a poster or just a PowerPoint. Think creatively and originally. Create a "Classified" folder for your utopia as if you are an outsider discovering this place for the first time. Your task, then, is to take your finding home to present to people within your "world." Imagine what sort of items you might collect and what those items would illustrate about the new world. This should be a multigenre project with endless possibilities. Some suggested items for your project include:

- Symbols and signs
- Slogans
- Rules
- Letters

- Interviews
- Film footage
- Interviews
- Speeches
- Photographs
- Field notes
- Advertisements
- Schedules
- Memos
- Agendas
- Whatever else you can imagine☺

Again, don't be limited by what is possible in our present world; rather, focus on your imagined "best of all possible worlds."

Presentation Rubric:
"A Brave New World . . .?"

Name: _____

Personal Qualities   +_____/15

- Confidence
- Eye contact
- Poised = few nervous movements
- Useful gestures and positive body language
- Note and respond to audience feedback

Preparation   +_____/35

- Extremely familiar with what you are saying; each person in the group plays a part
- Creative and thoughtful utopia design
- Able to answer reasonable questions
- Clear presentation
- Well-organized
- Ability to defend utopia

Visual Component   +_____/25

- Creative approach
- Contributes to what has been said
- Neat and appropriate
- Presented with clear explanation

Overall Presentation   +_____/25

- A strong understanding of your topic was displayed
- The summary was complete and clearly stated
- Adequate explanation was given; it is clear that you thoroughly thought about what your ideal world would be like
- The presentation included a clear beginning and a distinct conclusion

Grade: +_____/100

7 The Debate

Words that Win

Once students understand how authors, companies, politicians—the world—targets them, the debate unit brings it all together by asking students to develop complete, well-supported arguments. Viewing sample debates and reading complete arguments (both past and present), students then prepare for a grade-wide debate. In continuing with constructing and analyzing effective arguments, this chapter will scaffold *Inherit the Wind, The Great Debaters, Antigone,* and *12 Angry Men* as each connects to the overall guiding questions. Excerpts from "Civil Disobedience" and *Walden,* the closing argument from the Leopold and Loeb trial, and Atticus Finch's closing from *To Kill a Mockingbird* are among the samples used to guide student writing.

Common Core State Standards (in Our Own Words)

- RL.9–10.9. Analyze how two or more texts/authors address similar topics or themes. *In what ways does an author's choice impact an audience?*

- RI.9–10.1. Cite strong and thorough textual evidence to support an argument and make inferences drawn from the text. *How do I know what I just read?*

- RI.9–10.6. Assess point of view and use of rhetoric and how it shapes perspective. *What do I know about the author's beliefs and values?*

- RI.9–10.7. Analyze various accounts of the same subject told in various mediums. *In what ways does an author's creative choice impact an audience?*

- W.9–10.1. Write arguments to support claims using valid reasoning and sufficient, credible evidence. *What do I want to prove, and how do I support it?*

- W.9–10.2. Write texts that inform/explain a topic clearly showing complex ideas in an organized, well-developed analysis. *How do I write to clearly communicate my purpose and inform an audience?*

- W.9–10.4. Construct clear and sound writing that engages the audience with style. *What goes into creating a well-developed, engaging piece of writing?*

- W.9.–10.5. Rewriting and editing as needed to develop specific purpose and engage the audience. *What needs to be changed to make this paper better? How is the audience best reached? What is the purpose of this writing?*

- W.9–10.6. Use the Internet and technology to produce writing as well as to interact and collaborate with others. *How does working with peers strengthen my writing?*

- W.9–10.7. Carry out research assignments of various lengths to solve problems and investigate diverse subjects to gain understanding. *What does it take to be a good researcher?*

- W.9–10.8. Collect pertinent information from varied sources and mediums to deepen research while maintaining proper citation of those sources within writing. *How do I gather relevant information but maintain proper citation of the sources?*

- W.9–10.9. Obtain textual evidence to support claim/position. *How do I gather the best support for my position?*

- W.9–10.10. Write often and for varied time periods, purposes, and audiences. *Why is it important to write?*

- SL.9–10.1. Prepare for and participate in collaborative discussions with varied partners on a variety of topics. *How do I work effectively with others to build a solid argument?*

- L.9–10.1. Show evidence and command of the conventions of standard English grammar and usage when speaking or writing. *What does it take to speak effectively?*

- L.9–10.6. Attain and correctly use vocabulary appropriate to context and purpose that demonstrates college and career readiness. *What do I do if I don't know a word? Why does word choice matter?*

Taking a Side and Taking a Stand

Who doesn't like a good argument? The feeling you get when verbally sparring; the exhilaration sparked by passionate views; the glint in the eye when you have your opponent cornered. Everyone loves to voice an opinion during a debate; the key is being able to back it up. What is better than a good argument? Winning the argument. Whether we are trying to decide which football team is better, where to go for lunch, which political candidate has the best policies, or how to solve world hunger, the art of supporting an argument, taking a side and taking a stand, is essential.

Taking a side and taking a stand is exactly what we want our kids to do. In order for students to achieve active participation, we encourage them to realize that they must first be informed and involved in today's issues. If it doesn't matter in the outside world, then why should it matter in the classroom? Students need to see why what they are learning matters now, as well as how it connects with what they will be faced with in the future. So often students feel like they keep learning random terms, facts, formulas, and other abstract bits—it seems so trivial. The fact is that 10 years down the road our students are NOT going to have some kind of epiphany where they realize the key piece of a mystery has laid dormant in their brains since ninth-grade English.

Now don't get us wrong. Outside of being a contestant on Jeopardy, most of our students will not need to know the name of the Scottish poet that John Steinbeck alluded to when naming his classic novel *Of Mice and Men*. However, that doesn't mean we don't want our students to have an appreciation and awareness of this knowledge. We teach these pieces and connections for a reason. Nothing excites us more than when we see the connectedness of what's happening outside of school walls with what we are teaching. Essentially, though, nothing matters without students making the connections for themselves.

Let's go back to that Scottish poet, Robert Burns. In 1785, he commented on the injustice and lack of harmony between a mouse and a man. Obviously, it is not that simple, but what a great starting point for students to draw connections concerning conservation and the balance necessary between progress and the needs of other species. And that, ladies and gentlemen, goes beyond Jeopardy.

Demonstrating Persuasion

Just as our ability to acquire knowledge and our techniques for applying that knowledge evolve, so does our demonstration of persuasion. When we are little, we quickly learn that temper tantrums sometimes help us to get our way. As we get a little older, sometimes we were able to convince others to give in to our wishes with tears. However, the older we get, the less tantrums and tears work. We begin to change our methods without even knowing it. Instead of immediately stomping our feet and pouting, we move on to making demands. If a student asks to leave the classroom for a drink of water and the teacher asks "Why?", the student will not be permitted to go when the answer given is "Because." Answering the question "Why?" with "Because" doesn't hold up in an argument. We learn that we must be able to support our decisions and desires with plausible reasons. We recognize the value of backing up our opinions and views with substance—in the English classroom, we call this textual evidence. Our students need guidance in making a solid argument through textual evidence so that they can get what they want without resorting to tears and tantrums. Students learn to support why they need a drink of water. A student coming from physical education, where an intense game of dodge ball was fought, requires hydration in order to focus on the English lesson. With an argument like this, that kid receives the pass to get a drink.

The Debate Process

Choosing a Topic

On a larger scale, research, reason, formulation, and articulation of a sound argument are the core components of the debate process. Throughout our year, we lead up to the debate unit. By the middle of the year, students are familiar with techniques that good writers and speakers use to engage an audience, but they have not been given a formal stage to employ these strategies. To bring relevance and rigor, we recommend a grade-wide debate. Although this can be more time-consuming, we suggest that the debate topic change every year to remain timely and of interest to students. Students should hear about the topic outside of the classroom through various media outlets.

For example, one year we planned to debate the effectiveness of digital education or online schooling versus traditional public education. After a tragic school shooting hit the news, this topic seemed less significant than the more pressing issue of school safety. As safety measures were put in place in our school district as well as school districts across the United States, students had varied opinions, staunch views, and a definite interest. The missing factors were the knowledge, facts, and information to support their opinions and views—more or less sway anyone's thinking. Because we are open to and in tune with our students' interests, our flexibility paid off when switching topics at the last minute. Although the topic of online education is relevant, we couldn't pass up the timeliness and readily available information in all media concerning school safety. We can save the original topic for another year; what can't be saved is student energy and enthusiasm for a current topic affecting each and every student now.

Practice, Practice, Practice!

Once you've settled on a topic to debate—wait. Be patient. Save the best for last by introducing a practice topic or two. Let students become familiar with research; review ethos, pathos, and logos; establish debate jargon and structure; practice writing contentions; and demonstrate an expressive impactful delivery. This is complicated; we are asking a lot of our students. They need freedom to practice and make mistakes without negative consequences. Learning comes from trial and error. Students must practice working collaboratively and understand that the strength of their team is only as good as the preparedness of each person. We don't want this realization to come in front of their entire grade. Having a few smaller in-class debates establishes what is required for them to be successful debaters.

Smaller Debates

What's a smaller debate, you might be asking? Once we have introduced and covered what a debate is, then we spend three class days per smaller debate. Ideally, we prefer to divide students into teams that have an opener, a closer, and three interactive debaters. The first debate practice round is the shortest in length. We give the openers and closers 2 or 3 minutes. The interactive debaters, who are also given a total of 3 minutes to complete their portion of the debate, must each have one contention and one refutation to clearly present their argument. In the beginning, students will have no concept of time. They will feel that they are more than adequately prepared for the time period; however, once they see how slowly the stopwatch ticks away when standing in front of their peers, they will be better practiced with more research and depth for their position in the next round. Therefore, in the second round of debates, we add approximately 2 minutes to each role. By the second round practice, everyone in the classroom takes on and practices a number of different roles. Students begin to recognize their personal strengths as well as compensate for their weaknesses by choosing teammates of varying talents.

Teammates' talents are revealed in a small classroom setting in which teacher and students can provide constructive feedback in a timely manner. Along the way, we find ourselves stopping the first smaller debates to provide guidance and suggestions. Throughout this process, students are asked to take on multiple roles and to be flexible in switching from opener to closer to debater. Again, we want all students to have exposure to each of the roles available and the skills that each entails. Students often surprise themselves (and us) by finding their niche in a role opposite of one they originally set out to win through auditions for the final grade-wide debate. Without the "required" opportunity to try on different roles, many students would never know where their true strength lies.

Finding Strengths and Working Collaboratively

Realizing and using their individual strengths, students also appreciate the benefit of collaboration. How often do we ask our students to research and write collaboratively? This type of work allows students to realize that regardless of how strong individual members are, without transitions and cohesiveness between contentions, the overall product can be weak. Proof of true teamwork comes when students are able to transition seamlessly from one contention to the next because of their collaborative research and writing. Writing in isolation will not bring success in this type of assignment. Perhaps even more important for our students, collaborative writing and teamwork are required more and more in the work world.

Preparing our students for their future careers is exciting. Studies show that an increasing number of the jobs that our current students will eventually be working haven't even been created yet. The debate project brings in so many different facets of learning. We are changing the rules of the game and finally bending it to our will. Students soar toward futures where anything is possible because they have mastered the skills necessary to take a side and take a stand in their lives.

Where the Classics Fit In

While working on their side and the stand they are taking in the debates, students are also busy reading and studying classic literature. Plays such as *Inherit the Wind, Antigone,* and *12 Angry Men* serve to illustrate the importance of taking a stand in life. In all three of these examples, the protagonists feel they must stand against popular opinion to defend what they believe to be morally correct and imperative. This principle, the ability to know and fight for what you believe in, is our life goal for our students. We want it to become a compulsion; a need that must be met in order for them to feel they are leading full lives. Lofty, right? For some students, they readily take this in high school, for others, it is laying the foundation that will become more firm as they mature. Again, we don't want students to be Don Quixote out there fighting windmills all the time; however, we do want them to be equipped with the skills to tackle real obstacles that get in their paths.

Antigone and *12 Angry Men*

Let's begin with shorter works of *Antigone* and *12 Angry Men*. Depending upon the time available, both plays work really well with this unit. The play *Antigone* can be read and discussed over three or four 50-minute class periods. Antigone couldn't overlook the dishonor brought upon her brother when King Creon decreed her brother a traitor unworthy of burial. We ask students to consider the following overarching questions while reading: Are we obligated to follow laws that we disagree with? What happens when average citizens take the law into their own hands? Can you think of a time when breaking a law is justified?

12 *Angry Men* can be read or watched in two or three class periods. The moral dilemma can be conquered only if all 12 jurors look past personal prejudices and stereotypes in reviewing the facts of the case in order to seek the truth. One man must stand alone to put the pressure on the other jurors in demanding a fair trial process for the accused, thus providing a perfect example of what we want our students to do. Juror 8 illustrates the important balance of listening and hanging back until it is the right time to step forward and pose leading questions that force the other jurors to reevaluate their initial conclusions. Juror 8's example of open-mindedness is also something we want for our students. Don't just jump to conclusions. Take a second to step back and take into consideration all of the information coming in. A few overarching questions for this play are as follows: How do people form opinions? In other words, what do they base those opinions on? How do you find balance between listening and gathering the facts and stepping forward with your opinion? What do various communication styles look and sound like—nonverbal versus verbal? How do you firmly articulate your opinion without losing your audience? What are your moral boundaries?

A Couple of Nonfiction Connections

A nonfiction tie-in to taking a stand for moral reasons is found in Clarence Darrow's closing on the infamous Leopold and Loeb case. Darrow's moral boundaries were drawn against capital punishment. Even though there was no doubt that these teenagers were guilty of murder, Darrow saw fit to fight against the death penalty not just in this case but in all instances of capital punishment. The question becomes, What are you willing to tolerate and overlook versus what do you have to fight for? A fitting fiction connection is with Atticus Finch's closing in Harper Lee's classic novel *To Kill a Mockingbird*. Both the real-life man on which Atticus Finch is based and the fictional character have clear boundaries that they are unwilling to cross and are driven to take a stand against the majority opinion.

A nonfiction connection with *Antigone* is Henry David Thoreau's "Civil Disobedience." Antigone harms no one in breaking the law. She civilly disagrees with the law the king established. Without hurting anyone or resorting to physical violence, she does what she believes is right by honoring and burying her brother. The conflict is between gods' law versus man's law, providing a perfect transition into Robert E. Lee and Jerome Lawrence's *Inherit the Wind*.

Inherit the Wind

Inherit the Wind is our favorite lead-in to the debate unit because it provides the perfect outlined argument illustrated by the face-off between Henry Drummond and Matthew Harrison Brady, based on real-life figures Clarence Darrow and William Jennings Bryan. The play dramatizes the historical Scopes Trial, which became known as the "Monkey Trial." Just as Antigone fought for gods' law versus man's law, the Scopes Trial examined Biblical teachings on the origin of man versus scientific teachings on evolution. After reading newspaper articles, analyzing political cartoons, and watching documentary footage on the event, students are then able to compare and contrast the nonfiction and the historical fiction of the play. This offers an ideal opportunity for discussion regarding S.O.A.P.

Additional *Inherit the Wind* discussion questions include the following: What benefits are there to a school system that supports separation of church and state? What drawbacks are there to this separation? How do you differentiate between personal beliefs and universal human rights? Furthermore, how do you separate the two? For example, throughout the play there is a question as to whether Henry Drummond is an agnostic or an atheist. Ultimately, his personal beliefs on this subject don't matter as much as his belief that everyone should be guaranteed freedom of thought and the right to express those thoughts.

Another question of relevance concerns the influence the judge receives before determining Bertram Cates's sentence. The judge clearly shows his Christian support and bias throughout the proceedings; however, at the end of the trial, with a timely reminder from the mayor, the judge appears less biased in order to gain reelection in November. This is an example of the bias crucial for our students to recognize not only in others but also in themselves. The character E. K. Hornbeck represents the real-life journalist H.L. Mencken, who is an extremely biased participant in this media event. In that this is the first court case historically to be opened to the media, it is important for students to recognize the slant of his writing as well as its impact on a nationwide audience. Students need to be able to determine this bias in the readings we provide as well as in the research materials they are finding while preparing for the debates. Bias is everywhere and within everyone. The critical aspect for our students is that they identify bias and discern how it is impacting the truth.

The following lessons are ones that we use to help our students take a side and take a stand in the game we call life. You will find some lessons to be very specific as we walk our students through the debate process. Other lessons are more open ended to permit the students more flexibility with their research. All lessons can be modified depending on time and class size.

Unit 6 and Sample Lesson Plans

Grade Levels: 9–10; adaptable to 11–12

Time Frame: Up to 30 class periods

UNIT AGENDA:

Day 1   Impromptu debates: Each team draws a silly topic to debate

Day 2   Discussion of successes and opportunities for improvement; basic notes on debate process

Day 3   Additional notes on debate process and terms

HW: Prereading questions on *Antigone* and find one source for assigned small debate topic

Day 4   Discussion of *Antigone* questions; in-class reading of *Antigone*

HW: Find two additional sources for small debate and begin reading and annotating sources

Day 5   Continue reading *Antigone*; class time for debate prep and source share

HW: Find sources to fill void discovered in group work

Day 6   Finish reading *Antigone;* final discussion questions pulling together major themes of the play and character comparisons

HW: Write intro draft for small debate

Day 7   Group work for small debate prep

HW: Draft claims for small debate

Day 8   Group work for small debates; begin watching the 1957 classic film *12 Angry Men* starring Henry Fonda

HW: Draft closing for small debate

Day 9   Group work for small debates; continue watching the 1957 classic film *12 Angry Men* starring Henry Fonda

HW: Practice and time individual parts for small debates

Day 10   Finish watching *12 Angry Men* and discuss; if time remains, final group work for small debates

HW: Practice and time individual parts for small debates

Day 11   Small debates; feedback received from class and teacher. (If additional practice is needed, please build into your agenda time for a second debate. We usually follow through with the second debate as noted in the chapter.)

Day 12   Intro *Inherit the Wind* with creationism and evolution definitions handout

Day 13   Discuss handout; writing of class definitions of both terms

HW: Write a response on personal stance on the topic

Day 14   Four Corner Debate Activity

Day 15   Intro grade-wide debate topic and assign sides

HW: Research stance and gather credible sources

Day 16   Begin reading *Inherit the Wind;* 20-minute debate group meeting

HW: H.L. Mencken quotes, handout 9

Day 17   Continue reading and discussing *Inherit the Wind*

HW: Continue finding additional research and gathering credible sources to integrate into your assigned debate role

Day 18   Continue reading and discussing *Inherit the Wind;* group time for debate prep

HW: Draft of your assigned debate role

Day 19   Continue reading and discussing *Inherit the Wind;* group time for debate prep

HW: Revise, practice, and time debate role

Day 20   Finish reading and discussing *Inherit the Wind;* assign Quotation and Themes Analysis, handout 8

HW: Finish handout and prepare for in-class essay

Day 21   In-class essay about *Inherit the Wind*

Day 22   Debate group work

HW: Read Henry David Thoreau's "Civil Disobedience" excerpts and practice debate role

Day 23   Discuss Thoreau and final group work for debate

Day 24   Debates

Day 25   Debates

HW: Read excerpts from Clarence Darrow's closing in the Leopold and Loeb trial

Day 26   Discussion of successes and opportunities for improvement in the debate as well as discussion of persuasive techniques used by Darrow; a call for students to sign up for grade-wide debate auditions

Days 27–30 Watch the 2007 film *The Great Debaters,* directed by and starring Denzel Washington, while those auditioning for grade-wide debate practice for their choice roles. (Auditions are held after school. No other time is given for debate prep in class. After teams are selected, it is their responsibility to meet and prepare. Time keepers, moderators, and judges can be chosen at the teacher's discretion.)

Lesson 1
The Debate! Plan of Action

● **Topic:**

_____

● **Your Position:**

_____

Key facts of the topic:

_____

_____

_____

_____

_____

_____

_____

_____

_____

Evidence in support of your position:

_____

_____

_____

_____

_____

_____

_____

_____

_____

_____

_____

_____

Evidence predicted to be used against your position:

_____

_____

_____

_____

_____

_____

_____

_____

_____

Essential questions to ask during the interactive portion of the debate:

Question: _____

Question: _____

Question: _____

Question: _____

Question: _____

Question: _____

Anticipated questions to discredit your claim asked by the opposing team:

Question: _____

Question: _____

Question: _____

Question: _____

Question: _____

Question: _____

Lesson 2
Claims and How to Write Them

A claim persuades, argues, convinces, proves, or provocatively suggests something to a reader who may or may not initially agree with you.

Opinion vs. Arguable Claim

Opinion:

*Dogs are the best pets.

*I like country music.

*I think Shakespeare is better than Poe.

Arguable Claim:

*Dogs make better pets because of their obedience, their personality, and their loyalty.

*Country music has become popular for reasons other than music quality, such as the message in the music, the family-friendly lyrics, and the tempo of the songs.

*William Shakespeare is a more powerful writer than Edgar Allan Poe because Shakespeare's themes relate to all readers.

What are the differences?

*An Argument/Claim is supported by evidence that can be debated or challenged. An opinion is simply supported by more opinion.

*A claim can be supported with research/textual evidence/testimony/reasoning.

*A good claim addresses the "so what?" question!

*Remember, not all claims are equal. Choose wisely!

Counterclaims

Counterclaim = Opposing argument

*Remember, in proving your claim, you should always consider what your opponent may argue. Be prepared not only to argue on the offensive (claim) but also on the defensive (counterclaim).

Position:_____

_____

_____

Claim:_____

_____

_____

Data/Research:_____

_____

_____

Warrant/Connector:_____

_____

_____

Data/Research:_____

_____

_____

Warrant/Connector:_____

_____

_____

Counterclaim:_____

_____

_____

Rebuttal:_____

_____

_____

Lesson 3
Opening Statements and Closing Arguments: Preparation for the Debate

Opening Statements

Purpose: To inform the audience and the judge(s) of the facts of the debate from your team's point of view. Opening Statements should be detailed but concise; remember, you do not want to exhaust or confuse the audience. This is not the appropriate time to argue a point but rather to simply and clearly state the facts.

Closing Arguments

Purpose: To persuade the judge in favor of your team's opinion. This is your final attempt to argue/persuade why your side should win.

Style: Choose a style you are comfortable with. Should you be loud and strong or calm with friendly persuasion?

Tips for Writing the Opening Statement:

1. Create a theme. Use a story with a moral or that focuses on a specific value.

2. Start with a strong appeal to the audience's emotions. Concisely tell everything about your side's position.

3. Explain what you are going to prove. The judge and audience need to know what to look for during the debate.

4. Even though it's a beginning, don't forget it needs an ending. End big! Speak confidently about your claim, assuring the judge and audience why they will find it easy to side in favor of your team.

5. Use simple language.

6. Write it and deliver it like you believe it!

7. Use logical organization.

Tips for Writing the Closing Argument:

1. Prepare a message of thanks to those in attendance.

2. Summarize the entire argument briefly. Organize your closing as if you are telling a story, including key points and evidence for your position.

3. Refer to arguments you think your opponent might make. You want to be prepared to challenge your opponent's closing.

4. Use simple language.

5. Write it and deliver it like you believe it!

Tips for Presenting:

1. Memorize or use minimal notes
2. Make eye contact with judge and audience
3. Stand up straight; do not sway or fidget

Lesson 4
Opening Statement—Will Stricter Safety
Measures Make School Safe?

The following is meant to be merely an outline! You must change the order, in some cases, and expand on the information for impact. Don't think that you are required only to fill the lines provided; feel free to attach a page. Upon completion, number each section to indicate the order in which each will be presented. Consider where in the opening each piece will create the greatest effect.

Statement of Position:

_____

_____

_____

_____

Attention Grabber: _____

_____

_____

_____

_____

_____

1. Fact or Statistic (Logos and Ethos): _____

_____

_____

_____

_____

Explanation and Relevance of Fact or Statistic:

_____

_____

_____

_____

_____

2. Fact or Statistic (Logos and Ethos): _____

_____

_____

_____

_____

Explanation and Relevance of Fact or Statistic: _____

_____

_____

_____

_____

3. Fact or Statistic (Logos and Ethos): _____

_____

_____

_____

_____

Explanation and Relevance of Fact or Statistic: _____

_____

_____

_____

_____

Claim with Subtopics:

_____

_____

_____

_____

Pathos (Remember, there is heightened pathos in the opening!):

1. _____

_____

_____

_____

2. _____

_____

_____

_____

Rubric 1: First Debate

Introduction has an effective hook/attention getter   /10

Introduction creates an image/idea in listeners' minds

Statement of your position is clear and well developed   _____/10

Contentions are chosen that best support position   _____/10

Contentions contain ample and credible support

Cross examination is focused, persuasive, and targets   _____/10

opposition's main points (refutation)

Closing effectively sums up all main points   _____/10

Overall effect is persuasive, impactful, and leaves   _____/10

little room for disagreement

Intro_____ Middle_____,

_____, _____ Closing_____

Self-Assessment: Based on my understanding of the assignment, I will get _____

_____

Please explain your rationale for the grade you have given yourself. _____

_____

_____

_____

_____

_____

Handout 1: Sample Time Table for Debate

Debate Assembly

12:25	Students Called to Auditorium and Seated
12:30	Welcome
12:35	Introduction of the Debaters
12:45	Explanation of Debate Process and Acknowledgment of Judges
12:49	Moderators will Begin Debate with Affirmative Introduction
12:50	Affirmative Introduction
1:00	Opposition (Negative) Introduction
1:10	Debate
1:25	Audience Questions
1:45	Opposition (Negative) Closing
1:55	Affirmative Closing
2:05	Judges Confer and Decide Debate Outcome
2:10	Closure
2:15	Dismiss to Buses

Time Keepers:

Coded Time Reminders:

Handout 2: Judge's Sheet for Debate
Grade-wide Debate

Debate Question: _____

Thank you very much for agreeing to participate in this important debate as a judge. Your role is vital to the success of this project. The students have worked extremely hard in their preparation for today. Please make sure that you do your best to listen to all the information presented before making a decision. The following rubric is meant to aid you in making a fair judgment. Please feel free to write notes as the debate takes place. Again, thanks for your help in making this a learning experience for everyone involved.

PLEASE CONSIDER THE FOLLOWING:

Introduction has an effective hook/attention getter. It creates an image in the listeners' minds. The introduction has a cohesiveness/flow that is well developed and leads to a clear position/thesis.

Affirmative: _____

_____

_____

_____

_____

Opposition: _____

_____

_____

Contentions/arguments are chosen that best support the team's position. Each contention contains ample and credible support.

Affirmative: _____

_____

_____

Opposition: _____

_____

_____

Cross-examination is focused, persuasive, and targets opposition's main points (refutation).

Affirmative: _____

_____

_____

_____

Opposition: _____

_____

_____

_____

Closing effectively sums up all main points.

Affirmative: _____

_____

_____

_____

Opposition: _____

_____

_____

_____

Overall effect of debate is persuasive, impactful, and leaves little room for disagreement.

Affirmative: _____

_____

_____

_____

Opposition: _____

_____

_____

_____

_____

Winner of the debate is:

_____

_____

Rubric 2: Final Debate

Introduction has an effective hook/attention getter	_____/10
Introduction creates an image/idea in listeners' minds	_____/20
Statement of position is clear and well developed	_____/20
Contentions are chosen that best support position	_____/10
Contentions contain ample and credible support	_____/20
Cross-examination is focused, persuasive, and targets opposition's main points (refutation)	_____/20
Closing effectively sums up all main points	_____/30
Overall presentation is persuasive, impactful, and leaves little room for disagreement	_____/20

Opener ____/50

Middle _____/50   **Middle** _____/50   **Middle** _____/50

Closer _____/50

Comments: _____

_____

_____

_____

_____

1. In your own words, jot down your understanding of the following words:

   Evolution:

   Creationism:

2. What are some interesting ideas shared by your classmates for these two words? Write down some of the differences between your definition and what the class presents.

3. Class definitions:

   Evolution:

   Creationism:

Lesson 6
Where Do You Stand? *Inherit the Wind*

On the issue of whether public schools should teach evolution, creationism, a combination, or neither, where do you stand? In a thoughtful paragraph, state your opinion and provide at least three reasons to support your position. In writing this paragraph, consider your audience and purpose. You should strongly state your opinion, just as we have during the debates, but remember to be sensitive to your audience, who will likely have a variety of thoughts on the subject. You don't want to offend anyone or make anyone feel disrespected. Your goal is to present your side while respecting the unique beliefs and personalities within our classroom community.

Lesson 7
Four Corner Debate—Teacher Guidelines

- After students have written their response to lesson 6, begin the next class period with introducing the Four Corner Debate.

- Label four corners of your classroom with the following words: *CREATIONISM, EVOLUTION, BOTH, NEITHER.*

- Explain to students that these words represent the various positions that can be taken when debating the question of how the origin of man should be taught in a public school setting. Creationism and evolution strictly adhere to the singular notion of each idea; only that idea in isolation will be presented in the classroom. Choosing "both" indicates that students believe public schools should introduce the concepts of creationism and evolution as theories. The choice "neither" represents the philosophy that the subject should be overlooked entirely in the public schools setting, leaving it to the parent/guardian and religious institution for guidance and education.

- Begin with a reminder that this is a heated topic and to be mindful of other students' beliefs and opinions. Everyone should have the opportunity to share and be heard. As we have been focusing on all along, support is essential. Remind students that when voicing their opinion, they must be able to back up that opinion with credible points.

- **Step One:** Ask students to silently move to the corner representing the position they have written about for homework.

- **Step Two:** Once students reach their corner, have students discuss within their group their reasons behind their choice. As a group, students should be able to decide on their best arguments in favor of their side.

- **Step Three:** Have each corner present in an orderly manner. (At this time, ask students if anyone would like to change position and move to another corner based on the arguments that they have heard.)

- **Step Four:** Open the discussion up for cross-corner, whole-class debate.

Lesson 8
Inherit the Wind: Quotations and Themes Analysis

Read the following quotations and consider the context in which each was said. Explain the significance of FIVE of the following quotes in relation to the entire play and to our daily lives. Identify the speaker(s) of the quote. Please write thoughtful, detailed responses in complete sentences. Each response should be a minimum of five sentences.

1. "You murder a wife, it isn't nearly as bad as murdering an old wives' tale. Kill one of their fairy-tale notions, and they call down the wrath of God, Brady, and the state legislature" (50).

2. "The man who has everything figured out is probably a fool. College examinations notwithstanding, it takes a very smart fella to say, 'I don't know the answer!'" (55).

3. "But it is possible to be overzealous, to destroy that which you hope to save—so there is nothing left but emptiness. Remember the wisdom of Solomon in the Book of Proverbs— 'He that troubleth his own house . . . shall inherit the wind'" (67).

4. With all respect to the bench, I hold that the right to think is very much on trial! It is fearfully in danger in the proceedings of this court!" (72).

5. "The individual human mind. In a child's power to master the multiplication table there is more sanctity than in all your shouted 'Amens!' 'Holy, Holies!' and 'Hosannahs!' An idea is a greater monument than a cathedral. And the advance of a man's knowledge is more of a miracle than any sticks turned to snakes, or the parting of waters!" (93).

6. "Bert, whenever you see something bright, shining, perfect-seeming—all gold, with purple spots—look behind the paint! And if it's a lie—show it up for what it really is!" (110).

7. "A thought is like a child inside our body. It has to be born. If it dies inside you, part of you dies, too! . . . The ideas have to come out—like children. Some of 'em healthy as a bean plant, some sickly. I think the sickly ideas die mostly, don't you, Bert?" (125).

8. "Because I refuse to erase a man's lifetime? I tell you Brady had the same right as Cates: the right to be wrong!" (127).

9. "A giant once lived in that body. But Matt Brady got lost. Because he was looking for God too high up and too far away" (128). *Make sure to address where the speaker is suggesting God lives in regard to Mr. Brady.*

10. "He picks up the Bible in his other hand; he looks from one volume to the other, balancing them thoughtfully, as if his hands were scales" (129).

Lesson 9
H. L. Mencken and the Scopes Trial Quotation Reflection

Mencken was an infamous (**why infamous instead of famous?**) journalist who was considered by many to be brilliant but cynical. He reported on the Scopes Trial with a biting wit unsurpassed during his time. For this assignment, get to know this renowned American through his words, specifically the following selected notable quotations. Choose one quotation and openly respond to it with your understanding, interpretation, and opinion of his words. There is not one correct answer to this assignment; instead, I'm interested in seeing your thought process clearly and thoroughly illustrated.

The Choices:

- "Any man who afflicts the human race with ideas must be prepared to see them misunderstood."
- "Injustice is relatively easy to bear; what stings is justice."
- "Conscience is the inner voice that warns us somebody may be looking."
- "A society made up of individuals who were all capable of original thought would probably be unendurable."

Life is about *perspective*. Perspective forms opinions and beliefs, and it is what drives humanity to act or not to act. How much power and influence does the individual have to change society's perspective? Consider the following:

- Cates/Scopes vs. Evolution
- Drummond/Darrow vs. Evolution
- Darrow vs. Death Penalty
- Brady/Bryan vs. Evolution
- Cates/Scopes vs. Dayton, Tennessee and Creationism

Please make sure to respond in a fully developed literary analysis essay. You may use your copy of the play and handouts as well as all the articles we have discussed. Each body paragraph must contain at least **one quote** and **one example** for support.

8

A Reflective Writing Assignment

We Come Full Circle

This chapter delves into an assignment that both begins and ends the year with our students. The assignment encourages reflection as well as authentic connections with an intended audience while requiring students to integrate multiple types of writing.

Common Core State Standards (in Our Own Words)

- W.9–10.3. Write effective narratives to develop experiences through effective writing techniques. *How do I develop a story that keeps the reader engaged?*

- W.9–10.4. Construct clear and sound writing that engages the audience with style. *What goes into creating a well-developed, engaging story?*

- W.9.–10.5. Rewriting and editing as needed to develop specific purpose and engage the audience. *What needs to be changed to make this paper better? How is the audience best reached? What is the purpose of this writing?*

- W.9–10.10. Write often and for varied time periods, purposes, and audiences. *Why is it important to write?*

- L.9–10.1. Show evidence and command of the conventions of standard English grammar and usage when speaking or writing. *What does it take to speak effectively?*

- L.9–10.2. Use appropriate punctuation and spelling when writing. *What does it take to write well?*

- L.9–10.3. Make and apply effective choices for meaning or style in writing, and to comprehend more fully when listening or reading. *How does the author's choice impact the reader?*

The Letter

It seems so simple: A letter, something we have all written and received since we were first taught to read and write. A letter to incoming freshmen offering advice on how to survive their first year; on how to make friends and avoid enemies with peers and teachers alike; on how to build a G.P.A. that will allow them entrance to the college of their dreams; on how not to give in to the anxiety and pressure of a new place; on how to make the most of change and experience all that is high school. Who wouldn't want this for their final exam?

Our students find that what seems so simple is far more complex than it first appears. Writing a letter seems easy until they begin to think about how they want their words to be taken seriously and how their intended audience is unknown. Chance, maybe even fate, is what will deliver their letter to its recipient.

The Steps Involved in Writing the Letter

The first step for students is to reflect and self-assess their own year of school. Admitting failure is difficult to say the least, and for some students acknowledging success is even more difficult. Self-reflection and self-assessment are crucial life skills. Students need to be able to accurately and informatively evaluate their strengths and weaknesses.

Once students have a handle on their own experiences, their second task is to translate those experiences into worthwhile advice. Students must figure out what they have to say and how they are going to say it. At this point in the year, they know that in order to be effective they must employ ethos, pathos, and logos in their writing.

Always Bringing It Back to Ethos, Pathos, Logos

Ethos is probably the most challenging for students because it requires establishing an authentic voice. Students must come across in their writing like they know what they are talking about while still appealing and relating to a peer. They are all experts on their individual experiences, but they must compel their reader to accept them as the expert. This is a final opportunity to encourage students to recognize their own bias and to not permit that bias to color their writing. For example, saying that everyone struggles with arriving to class on time because of the brief minutes between periods is an overstatement. Rather, students need to offer advice on making the most out of the time available. The latter takes it from a complaint to a sound piece of advice. The purpose of the letter is to offer these types of solutions, not to give into biased rants or praises. The idea is to achieve a balanced, credible view—nothing will ever be as good or as bad as someone thinks.

Retaining the balance is a direct reflection on students' ability to use pathos. We want students to grab and maintain their reader's attention by using pathos—emotion gets you. What we don't want is to read a sob story or a too-good-to-be-true tale of what it's like to be in high school. The writer must admit equally to both positive and negative experiences in order to appeal to and gain the trust of their reader. An emotionally honest reflection on the year creates a connection between the writer and the reader without which the purpose of the letter is lost. Advice will not be accepted as truthful guidance to follow.

You might be asking yourself, where does logos fit into a letter to incoming freshmen? The answer is everywhere. Wouldn't you want to know the location of the freshman lockers? Where the location of the cleanest bathroom with all of its stall doors intact is in the building? How much extra money is needed to hit the vending machines if school lunch doesn't appeal to you? How to generate an equation that factors class order with book weight to equal the number of locker stops necessary during a school day? Yeah, logos matters.

The third step in this process is for students to deliver advice beyond the essential day-to-day survival guidelines. This advice isn't as much about classes and how to navigate the building but more about how to remain true to oneself and avoid the little pitfalls of high school. Keeping word choice and tone in mind is critical during this stage of writing to maintain the connection with the reader. Students shouldn't sound like the obsessive stalker girlfriend or the dumb jock, but they should offer pertinent, personal advice that will help their reader avoid potential high school drama.

The Quotation

The final component of the letter is a well-chosen quotation. Throughout the year, we establish that words matter. Not only do the words matter, but also their placement within the piece needs to be appropriate and strong. Don't just stick a quotation in there because you are supposed to; make the words matter. Remind students to give credit where credit is due. After all, they might have the opportunity to introduce their reader to their favorite author, artist, or songwriter. Consequently, when looking up the source of their favorite quote, students might come across information that leads them to a new song, book, or painting they never knew existed.

Lesson 1
You Say Goodbye, and They Say Hello!

As you approach the end of the year, I want you to reflect on the experiences and lessons you encountered over the past nine months. What do you know now about high school, extra-curricular activities, lunchroom etiquette, and so on that you wish someone would have clued you in on before? What worried you that, after a few days of being at school, seemed silly?

For this final exam, I want you to write a letter in your natural voice (which, of course, is an intelligent, sophisticated, witty one) welcoming the newcomers while offering them insider information they won't hear from anyone else about what they should expect. You've survived this year of school; this is your opportunity to help someone else survive.

Paragraph 1   Introduce yourself and your topic

Paragraph 2   Compare/Contrast the major similarities of middle and high school

Paragraph 3   Compare/Contrast the major differences of middle and high school

Paragraph 4   Advice for the new freshman

Paragraph 5   Close

As you write:

- Be yourself!
- Realize that you are an expert on this topic.
- Allow your creative energy to take over; make the writing interesting and reader worthy through any tricks and special effects imaginable.
- Introduce who you are and what the year was like for you.
- Be genuine!
- Check your grammar and spelling; you want to make a good impression.
- Use letter format.
- Be truthful but not mean. This isn't your moment to seek retribution for a wrong committed by one of your teachers (all of whom I'm sure are wonderful!).
- Remember: Your objective (an assigned one that will be graded) is to provide comfort and not to inspire fear!

- Add a quote that you find inspiring; what words can they live by during the opening days of school?

- Finally, think about decorations; how will you make your letter the one they all fight over on the first day? How will you make sure your letter lands in the right hands? Does your letter offer advice specifically for a guy or a girl? If so, decorate accordingly.

These are the requirements, but realize that beyond this list you can make this as grand as you please. As always, I wish you a happy, inspired writing. I can't wait to learn something from you about what it's like to be a student at this high school!

Room to Brainstorm:

Rubric

1. The introduction of the paper acquaints readers with yourself and your topic. Remember, you need to grab the reader's attention, establish your voice, and prepare the reader for the letter's purpose. Be yourself while keeping in mind you want this person to trust you as the expert in this situation; you must establish credibility from the beginning.

_____/20

2. The body of the paper is fully developed with examples. You must compare and contrast the major similarities and differences of middle and high school with a minimum of three points for each. Offer advice for the new freshman that is varied and specific.

_____/35

3. The organization of the paper is logical and reflects the structure suggested in the introduction. Each paragraph also has a clear topic sentence, transition, and a concise paragraph closing.

_____/15

4. The conclusion of the paper is effective and strengthens or reflects the main idea stated in the introduction. You have added a quote that you find inspiring; these are words incoming freshmen can live by during the opening days of school. Remember, you want to end with your own words, not someone else's. Find an appropriate place to tie in the quotation. You have given credit to the quotation's author.

_____/20

5. The paper is free from most distracting errors in spelling, punctuation, capitalization, word choice, sentence structure, and other grammar. Are there small errors in the final copy that could have been avoided by proofreading?

_____/10

Total: +_____/100

A *Romeo and Juliet* Assignment

True Love and Its Letters

A staple in most English classrooms, *Romeo and Juliet* is a classic with themes of love, loss, and tragedy. Adding a focus on real-life romance and heartbreaking pairings brings in the nonfiction aspect of the Core while helping students appreciate the timelessness of love and its possible shortcomings.

Common Core State Standards (in Our Own Words)

- RI.9–10.3. Explore the methods the author uses to unfold a series of events and the connections that are drawn between them. *What are the key points being developed, and how do they relate to the overall purpose?*
- W.9–10.7. Carry out research assignments of various lengths to solve problems and investigate diverse subjects to gain understanding. *What does it take to be a good researcher?*
- SL.9–10.1. Prepare for and participate in collaborative discussions with varied partners on a variety of topics. *How do I work effectively with others to build a solid argument?*
- L.9–10.6. Attain and correctly use vocabulary appropriate to context and purpose that demonstrates college and career readiness. *What do I do if I don't know a word? Why does word choice matter?*

Shakespeare

What is a year of English without varying degrees of exposure to Shakespeare? Not a good one, that's for sure (by our standards). The continued pressure for teachers to accomplish more with our students without additional time and tools is frustrating. However, one thing we can all agree on is that Shakespeare stays in the English classroom. With that being said, there is also room to enhance students' appreciation for his writing. We have all taught the bard's questionable background, the Globe Theatre, the Elizabethan era; but what about love letters? Yes, that's right—love letters. Romance is a topic that fascinates young and old alike. True love letters and stories give teachers a chance to expose students to the good, the bad, and the turmoil that is love while exposing them to another genre of nonfiction writing. These letters also lend themselves to yet another historical exploration.

When to Use the Love Letters

Whether you choose to use the letters to help introduce *Romeo and Juliet* or you incorporate them within or at the end of the play is up to you. However, students will gain a deeper appreciation of the timelessness of the themes present in the play when they see how universal those themes are. Perhaps an even more worthwhile result is that students gain a better understanding of the importance of making good decisions versus acting rashly when it comes to love. We like to ask our students this question: Is *Romeo and Juliet* the greatest love story of all time? Or perhaps we have all been fooled, and it is the greatest cautionary tale of all time. Kids come to class believing that they know all about the play because of the numerous renditions they've seen played out in sitcoms, movies, and music. This question establishes what we want students to look for as they read. We all want the greatest love story ever told, but, as teachers, we want students to question what love is and understand the consequences of rash choices.

Voltaire's Love Letter to Olympe

The first "love" story possibility is that of Voltaire and Olympe. It is believed that because of parental disapproval of their relationship, Voltaire was imprisoned. Voltaire reportedly risked death to be with the woman he loved. See the similarity to the story of Romeo and Juliet already? Olympe and Voltaire's relationship provides an ideal connection with Shakespeare and the idea that love is worth risking everything for—or is it? Just as Olympe isn't Voltaire's last love affair, Rosaline wasn't Romeo's last either. A copy of the famous love letter is included with the assignment.

Sid Vicious and the Love of His Life

Another "love" story belongs to punk rocker Sid Vicious and his girlfriend, Nancy Spungen. An article to introduce the students to this infamous star-crossed couple is "Punk Rock Romeo and Juliet: Sid Vicious and Nancy Spungen" by Anthony Bruno. There are many sources online where students can see handwritten love letters from Sid to Nancy. Also, another medium that is of interest to students is Sid's music. There are various lyrics and videos available online for students to explore. Students oftentimes listen to music for the beat and rhythm without fully grasping what the lyrics are trying to convey. This is a good opportunity to analyze lyrics and word choice and why they are so powerful.

The previous couples are just two interesting ideas to get you started. Please feel free to permit students time to make their own discoveries.

Lesson 1
True Love or Foolishness?

Famous love stories and love letters can be found everywhere if we look for them. An interesting example is Voltaire's love letter to Olympe Dunover. Now why, you might ask, is this one so interesting? Well, I'll tell you. Voltaire was in prison because he fell in love with a young girl. He was willing to do whatever it took to escape so that he might be with his true love—even if it meant death. Now the story changes depending on who is telling it. Some say it was Voltaire's father who was opposed to the relationship; some say it was Olympe's mother. The fact is that parents stood in the way of love—sound familiar?

Read the following love letter written by Voltaire to his love, Olympe. While reading, consider this question: Should love be followed no matter the cost? Write a well-developed paragraph supporting your position.

Love Letter—Voltaire to Olympe Dunover

The Hague 1713

I am a prisoner here in the name of the King; they can take my life, but not the love that I feel for you. Yes, my adorable mistress, to-night I shall see you, and if I had to put my head on the block to do it.

For heaven's sake, do not speak to me in such disastrous terms as you write; you must live and be cautious; beware of Madame your mother as of your worst enemy. What do I say? Beware of everybody; trust no one; keep yourself in readiness, as soon as the moon is visible; I shall leave the hotel incognito, take a carriage or a chaise, we shall drive like the wind to Sheveningen; I shall take paper and ink with me; we shall write our letters.

If you love me, reassure yourself; and call all your strength and presence of mind to your aid; do not let your mother notice anything, try to have your pictures, and be assured that the menace of the greatest tortures will not prevent me to serve you. No, nothing has the power to part me from you; our love is based upon virtue, and will last as long as our lives. Adieu, there is nothing that I will not brave for your sake; you deserve much more than that. Adieu, my dear heart!

Arout (Voltaire)

"I'll die before I'm 25, and when I do I'll have lived the way I wanted to."

—Sid Vicious

1. From your prior knowledge of Shakespeare's classic love story *Romeo and Juliet,* what aspects of Sid and Nancy's tale make them the "punk Romeo and Juliet"? Be specific and include textual evidence to support your argument.

2. In *Romeo and Juliet,* some readers blame the parents, some blame the friar, while still other readers blame Romeo and Juliet themselves. Who is to blame in the tragedy of Sid and Nancy? Support your answer.

3. "Punk was the **antithesis** of civilized middle-class values." Please explain why punk is the antithesis here. Show that you understand what *antithesis* means.

4. "Doing drugs, wearing tattered clothes and safety pins in facial piercings, living in squalor, and never paying more than a dollar for anything were not just lifestyle choices, they were part of the punk **ethos.**" What is "punk ethos"?

An *Animal Farm* Assignment

The New Rebellion Begins

From middle school to high school, *Animal Farm* is found on syllabi in classrooms across the United States. Just as the pigs overtake the Joneses' farm, students relish the opportunity to take over your classroom. This assignment gives students the opportunity to hone their newfound persuasive skills by taking what they've read about on the page and putting it into action.

Common Core State Standards (in Our Own Words)

- SL.9–10.1. Prepare for and participate in collaborative discussions with varied partners on a variety of topics. *How do I work effectively with others to build a solid argument?*
- SL.9–10.4. Present information in an organized manner to engage listeners. *How do I say what I need to say to get my audience to understand and follow my presentation?*
- SL.9–10.5. Make strategic use of digital media and visual displays to enhance a presentation. *How can I make my presentation effective?*
- SL.9–10.6. Demonstrate command of formal language to engage audience and meet expectations. *How do I say what I need to say to reach my audience and make it matter to them?*
- L.9–10.5. Demonstrate knowledge of and ability to use figurative language and nuances through word choice. *What is the best way to say what needs to be said?*

Taking Over the World

Who hasn't dreamed of taking over the world? George Orwell warns readers of the possible corruption in government. Those persons in positions of leadership, although we hope they have chosen this career path to improve conditions, create and maintain agencies for those in need, and to foster the overall well-being of the citizens, can oftentimes become just as corrupt and harmful as an enemy.

Animal Farm Then

For years we have "covered" the novel—the Russian Revolution, literary terms such as *allegory* and *propaganda*, symbols and themes. These aspects still coincide with the Common Core but can be rejuvenated by infusing the unit with additional opportunities for student choice and ownership.

Animal Farm Now

To make the reading relevant, students need the chance to put their own spin on the lessons learned from reading the novel. This project asks students to question and detect areas where genuine change is needed in their school. Students will surprise you with the areas they feel require improvement. We ask students to make a list of changes necessary as well as detailed explanations for each change. Students will cover everything from adding escalators to maintain traffic flow to school lunch additions to make their day brighter. We've had students go as far as looking at the challenges facing our school in a scientific manner. A group began by weighing a backpack loaded with a typical day's textbooks. From there, the group ran trials based on their various class schedules, taking into consideration the distances traveled while wearing their loaded backpacks, timing the route from one end of the building to the other to prove the need for longer time between class periods. Weighing the backpack was also followed by a study about the harm to young children's developing bodies after carrying heavy loads. After doing extensive trial runs and research, the group requested that the principal attend their class presentation in order to review their findings. They had an audience outside of their classmates. They felt heard.

Be aware that you will also hear plenty . . . because this assignment's major component relies on the effective use of fear as a manipulator, pull on your thick skin. You will be targeted as their dictator, arch nemesis, antagonist. The goal of the project requires students to convince their peers of the necessity of getting rid of their teacher and current leadership. Don't be too sensitive. Have fun with this; the kids do.

Animal Farm **Project**

Attention students: You need to plan your agenda. You are going to attempt to take over this class. Yes, that's right. You are going to try to become the leaders of this classroom. The first big decision is whether to work alone or with a partner. After making this extremely important decision, here's what you need to do.

1st—Think about the things that would make your school and this class better.

2nd—Make a list of everything that is wrong.

3rd—Make a list of new rules and policies. **Remember—even though this is a takeover, you must be realistic.** Your new rules must be within reason so that the school can continue to function. Think about changes that **could** be made to create a better school district. You still have to come to school and hopefully learn something. Your goal is to come up with ideas that would be beneficial to learning.

4th—You must type a list of what's wrong and how you are going to fix the problems.

5th—You will prepare a written speech and visual aid (poster, pamphlet, etc.) to promote your thoughts and ideas. Remember, you can bribe your fellow classmates with things Anything is fair during election time. **PROPAGANDA**

6th—You will present your detailed plan in front of the class.

7th—Make sure that you come up with a slogan or catch phrase. Think of a gimmick that will help everyone remember you.

8th—You must create an ad (video) using fear as the primary device to sway people to your side. You will play this at some point during your presentation. Make sure that you plan accordingly in order to really make the ad effective. Seamless transitions are important here.

You will be graded on the content of your rules, the organization and delivery of your speech, and the creativity of your visual, slogan, and video. Have fun with these. After everyone presents, the class will vote. The winning person or pair will get bonus points.

50 = Typed, well-developed list of rules and rule changes with rationale

50 = Content and delivery of speech

50 = Visual aid, etc.

50 = Video   200-point project:

Presentation Rubric:
Takeover Project

Name(s): _____

Personal Qualities +_____/15 +_____/15

- Confidence
- Eye contact
- Poised and polished = few nervous movements
- Interaction with audience

Preparation +_____/15

- Well rehearsed with appropriate audience targeted
- Able to interact with audience and gain its interest
- Clear presentation of changes needed
- Obvious attempt at swaying audience's vote
- Slogan was catchy and readily apparent

Overall Speech Portion +_____/20

- Careful consideration and use of rhetoric, bias, persuasion, and propaganda techniques
- Clearly demonstrates why you should be the next leader(s)
- A strong understanding of learning targets was displayed
- The presentation had a clear beginning, a distinct conclusion, and all of the various requirements were effectively woven in the speech

Visuals +_____/50

- Readable
- Appealing and eye catching; draws audience's attention
- Careful consideration to layout and organization
- Appropriate flow within presentation
- Complemented goal of project

Video +_____/50

- Careful planning was evident
- Video unequivocally used fear to persuade audience to listen
- Figurative language was well chosen and woven throughout video
- Images were well chosen and placed effectively for desired impact
- Seamless transitions
- Video had a creative and clear beginning, middle, and end

Typed Rules +_____/50

- Careful thought to current issues was apparent
- Rationale behind changes was well developed
- Clear benefits to the school were evident
- Target audience was obvious
- Changes and modifications to the school building, personnel, and general way of doing business were addressed with thoughtful explanation and care to improving the quality of education

Additional Comments:

+_____/200

Appendix

Nonfiction Resources Used in This Book

Advertising Resources/Make Me Buy Project

Advertising in Schools Becoming More Common

By Trevor Hughes, USA TODAY

http://usatoday30.usatoday.com/news/education/story/2012-06-03/advertising-in-schools/55366346/1

Resources: Marketing To Kids

By Christine Lagorio

www.cbsnews.com/8301-500823_162-2798401.html

Alpha Girls for Advertising

www.cbsnews.com/video/watch/?id=2796977n%3e%2520%3cimg%2520src=

Dove Evolution of Beauty

http://youtu.be/hibyAJOSW8U

Joel Stein and His Manly Makeup (Note: Without a *Time* subscription, you may not have access to the actual article)

www.time.com/time/video/player/0,32068,636417635001_2025701,00.html

Greatest Movie Ever Sold clip

http://youtu.be/92fOw-bQ12Y

Car Advertisements

Volkswagen Dog Example #1

http://www.youtube.com/watch?v=KqBfZ6vXPS8

Darth Vader Volkswagen

http://youtu.be/R55e-uHQna0

Saint Bernard Volkswagen Dog Example #2

www.youtube.com/watch?v=VX0vLERX63k

Chrysler and Eminem

http://youtu.be/SKL254Y_jtc

Ram Truck: Farmer

www.youtube.com/watch?v=AMpZ0TGjbWE

Cadillac and Kate Walsh: Does Your Car Turn you On?

www.youtube.com/watch?v=jkEw1rsBUak

Other Fun Examples

Orbitz

http://youtu.be/WEJJUGJZxpU

Surface

www.youtube.com/watch?v=iB5txqll8jQ

Debates

Sample of a Debate Gone Wrong . . .

http://youtu.be/cUixOwWcDpQ

Weird Science

Rebecca Skloot's "Fixing Nemo"

www.nytimes.com/2004/05/02/magazine/fixing-nemo.html?pagewanted=all&src=pm

Megan Gambino's "Creating a New Kind of Night Light: Glow-in-the-Dark Trees"

www.smithsonianmag.com/ideas-innovations/Creating-a-New-Kind-of-Night-Light-Glow-in-the-Dark-Trees-215077381.html

Advice

Robert Fulghum's "All I Really Need to Know I Learned in Kindergarten"

www.ccsf.edu/Resources/VOICE/instructorslessonplans/personaldevelo/missionstatement/mstatement2/text.pdf

Miss Manners Archive

www.washingtonpost.com/lifestyle/advice

William Shakespeare's Hamlet: "Polonius' Advice to Laertes"

www.readwritethink.org/files/resources/lesson_images/lesson372/PoloniusExcerpt.pdf

Edmund Vance Cooke's "How Did You Die"

http://allpoetry.com/poem/8619995-How_Did_You_Die_-by-Edmund_Vance_Cooke_

Audre Lorde's "Hanging Fire"

www.poetryfoundation.org/poem/171288

Smithsonian Article on Miss Manners Q and A with Miss Manners by Arcynta Ali Childs

www.smithsonianmag.com/arts-culture/Q-and-A-with-Miss-Manners.html

Inherit the Wind

Clarence Darrow's "Loeb and Leopold Closing Argument"

http://law2.umkc.edu/faculty/projects/ftrials/leoploeb/darrowclosing.html

Loeb and Leopold Trial PBS

www.pbs.org/wgbh/amex/monkeytrial/peopleevents/e_leopoldloeb.html

September 11th

Margaret Atwood's "Letter to America"

www.commondreams.org/views03/0404-07.htm

Brian Doyle "Leap"

www.pbs.org/wgbh/pages/frontline/shows/faith/questions/leap.html

Michael R. Gordon's "A Day on Terror: An Assessment; When an Open Society is Wielded as a Weapon Against Itself"

www.nytimes.com/2001/09/12/us/day-terror-assessment-when-open-society-wielded-weapon-against-itself.html

Natalie Angier's "Of Altruism, Heroism and Evolution's Gifts"

www.nytimes.com/2001/09/18/science/of-altruism-heroism-and-evolution-s-gifts.html

John Winthrop's "A Model of Christian Charity"

http://religiousfreedom.lib.virginia.edu/sacred/charity.html

Thomas Jefferson's "The Declaration of Independence"

www.archives.gov/exhibits/charters/declaration_transcript.html

Franklin Delano Roosevelt's "Four Freedoms Speech"

www.archives.gov/exhibits/powers_of_persuasion/four_freedoms/four_freedoms.html

Elie Wiesel's "Hope, Despair, and Memory Speech"

www.nobelprize.org/nobel_prizes/peace/laureates/1986/wiesel-lecture.html

Romeo and Juliet

Anthony Bruno's "Punk Rock Romeo and Juliet: Sid Vicious and Nancy Spungen"

www.trutv.com/library/crime/notorious_murders/celebrity/sid_vicious/index.html

Bibliography

Bernays, Anne, and Pamela Painter. *What If?: Writing Exercises for Fiction Writers*. New York: HarperCollins, 1990. Print.

National Governors Association Center for Best Practices, Council of Chief State School Officers. *Common Core State Standards for English Language Arts*. Washington DC: National Governors Association Center for Best Practices, Council of Chief State School Officers, 2010. Web.

Noden, Harry R. *Image Grammar: Using Grammatical Structures to Teach Writing*. Portsmouth, NH: Heinemann, 1999. Print.

Olson, Carol Booth. *The Reading/Writing Connection: Strategies for Teaching and Learning in the Secondary Classroom*. Boston: Allyn and Bacon, 2003. Print.

Padgett, Ron. *The Teachers & Writers Handbook of Poetic Forms*. 2nd ed. New York: Teachers & Writers Collaborative, 2000. Print.

Sebranek, Patrick, Verne Meyer, Dave Kemper. *Writers INC: A Student Handbook for Writing & Learning*. Illus. Chris Krenzke. Lexington, MA: Write Source, 2001. Print.

Strong, William. *Write for Insight: Empowering Content Area Learning, Grades 6–12*. Boston: Pearson Allyn and Bacon, 2006. Print.

MAXIMUM
CANADA

MAXIMUM CANADA

TOWARD A COUNTRY OF 100 MILLION

DOUG SAUNDERS

VINTAGE CANADA

To Griff and Maud,
twenty-first century Canadians

Published by Vintage Canada, a division of Penguin Random House Canada
Limited, in 2019. Originally published in hardcover by Knopf Canada, a division
of Penguin Random House Canada Limited, in 2017. Distributed in Canada by
Penguin Random House Canada Limited, Toronto.

Vintage Canada with colophon is a registered trademark.

www.penguinrandomhouse.ca

Library and Archives Canada Cataloguing in Publication
Maximum Canada / Doug Saunders.

ISBN 978-0-7352-7310-8
eBook ISBN 978-0-7352-7311-5

1. Canada—Population—Forecasting. 2. Canada—Social conditions—
21st century. 3. Canada—Economic conditions—21st century. I. Title.

HB3529.S38 2018   304.60971   C2017-901762-4

Cover design: Jennifer Lum
Cover image © Arthimedes/Shutterstock.com
Text design: Andrew Roberts

Printed and bound in Canada

2 4 6 8 9 7 5 3 1

Penguin
Random House
VINTAGE CANADA

CONTENTS

PART ONE
THE MINIMIZING IMPULSE

PART TWO
A PLURAL NATION

PART THREE
OUR COUNTRY'S CAPACITY

PART ONE
THE MINIMIZING IMPULSE

CHAPTER 1

The War against the Outside

Around midnight on an early winter evening one hundred and eighty years ago, my grandmother's great-grandmother stood in fury as a crowd of armed rebels forced their way inside her Brantford house, demanding the rifles and pistols that she and her Welsh-born barrister husband, William, had spent the day hiding. The couple had armed themselves that autumn, and William had worked to organize a local militia, in the certain belief that they would soon be joining an all-out civil war over the size, composition and purpose of Canada.

"Twelve of them came down to us in the middle of the night demanding arms—they had each suspended to their sides swords and rifles. They searched the house but William, being a strong Tory, had the precaution to hide his guns and pistols and etc.," Catherine Lloyd-Jones, then thirty-six and a mother of three, wrote her mother in England. "They left disappointed but told us to beware of the rabble." As the men departed in frustration,

William yelled after them that he would be joining the fight, but not on their side. The couple knew these rebels: Canadian men from the nearby village of Scotland, men who had resided in Canada far longer than they had. But Catherine denounced them and their fellow rebels as "Americans," for she and other Tories saw their expansive and democratic ideas, their support of public education and open borders and elected governments, as treasonous and foreign.

"I then felt alarmed and rather dreaded the consequences of refusing them arms," Catherine wrote. "Fancy me close to William's elbow, pale as death in my night dress covered with a cloak—I think I could almost have fired at them myself." They spent the next several weeks sleeping fully dressed with weapons at their side, prepared to flee the house, pistols in hand, and join the coming fight.

"What a country this is, my dear Mother," Catherine lamented to her overseas family. "This is to come to nothing but war—and civil war the worst of all—being in danger of being shot by our neighbours. People are in danger of their lives unless armed with their pistols even to go a mile from their own home. . . . Little did we anticipate a bloody war which will eventually take place."

Catherine's fears were only partially realized. Civil violence, rifle battles and a serious national crisis did ensue, but the "war" that took place in the days after Catherine's letter, today known as the 1837 rebellions, would not prove as bloody or as lengthy as my ancestors feared. The pro-democracy uprisings in Upper and Lower Canada, including the events Catherine and William experienced in Brantford (an abortive effort by settlers around Brantford and Hamilton, led by prominent Reform politician Charles Duncombe, to lend their support to the Toronto rebellion), would be crushed by colonial troops in a few weeks. The Reformers who launched and fought in the rebellion were tried and transported to Australia, forced to flee to the United States or executed. The Lloyd-Joneses, one of the few regime-supporting Tory families in their region, would keep their handsome house outside Brantford. Their son Thomas would turn his father's volunteer militia, the Burford Troop of Volunteer Cavalry, into a standing regimental division designed to protect Upper Canada's closed colonial regime for the rest of the century.

What Catherine had in mind was the far larger but less violent civil war that had been underway as long as she'd lived in Upper Canada, one that had been launched by Canada's British occupiers almost the moment the War of 1812 had ended a quarter-century earlier. It was a war to limit British North America's ambitions, its size and its purpose. While the enemies were often described as "Americans," all of them were in fact long-standing residents and subjects of the Canadian colonies. The border with the United States had been slammed shut to migration after 1815, so that the U.S.-born families of Canada (who until the 1830s were the majority of Upper Canada's population) had lived there much longer than most British-born settlers and had a greater claim to being "real" Canadians.

The colonial rulers did not hesitate to call this clash of loyalties and visions a war and to specify what they were fighting. Sir Francis Bond Head, the Tory lieutenant-governor of Upper Canada, had urged British Anglicans (among them Catherine and William) to emigrate to the colony after 1815 by telling them they'd be soldiers in a "moral war . . . between those who were for British institutions, against those who were for soiling the empire by the introduction of democracy."

The conflict involved much more than democracy versus British institutions, though. It was an all-out struggle to ensure that the emerging Canada would be a closed, ethnically homogeneous colony whose political and economic function would be limited to the provision of raw materials to the imperial capital, and whose population would be restricted mainly to small-hold farming. This was a vastly different place from the pre-1812 Canada. Though tiny and sparse, that earlier Canada had been defined by an ambiguous and open border, diverse immigration and a free-flowing trade in goods, people and ideas with the new-born United States—all of which were now forbidden. This was a war against expansion and openness.

Catherine and William saw their ideas triumph (though William would die eight years later when he fell from a wagon). Canada's border would remain closed and tariff-walled for decades. Its immigration policies would allow only a certain sort of British person; its economy would remain colonial, rural and resource-based. This victory would exact a heavy and lasting cost on Canada. For the rest of the nineteenth century, and much of the twentieth, the new country would fail to attract people, despite constant efforts to do so. Underpopulation would become a constant and lasting problem.

For most of the rest of the century, the colonies and later the provinces of Canada became places where initiative, entrepreneurship, diversity and the immigration of anyone other than British Protestants were discouraged and sometimes punished. Trade with any place but Britain was restricted by heavy tariffs. The economy became closed and restricted to the extraction of fur, fish, timber and other raw materials. Relations with the indigenous nations turned from mutual cooperation into subjugation.

And, as both a consequence and a cause, embryonic Canada would be severely hampered in its efforts to develop an autonomous economy and civic life.

This spiral of self-defeating factors was readily visible in Catherine and William's time. The Scottish writer John Howison, in his 1822 travelogue *Sketches of Upper Canada*, described the colony's choked-off economy: "The farmer is discouraged from raising grain or making agricultural improvements; mechanics and artizans cannot prosecute their labours with advantage; and the merchants are obliged to impoverish and oppress the people by exorbitant charges."

Not only were the colonists' economic opportunities restricted, they often relied on expensive and awkward barter schemes for income because there were hardly any coins or banknotes to be found. The colonies lacked a manufacturing economy or a substantial commercial farming sector, so almost everything in Canada had to be purchased from the United States (at inflated prices, due to heavy tariffs) but almost nothing could be exported to the United States. As a result, most specie currency was rapidly shipped out of the country in a strikingly physical manifestation of a balance-of-payments crisis. "Formerly," Howison wrote (meaning before 1812), "the farmers received cash for their wheat, because Montreal and Quebec then afforded a ready market; but things are now altered, and the agriculturalist rarely gets money for any kind of home-produce, in consequence of its being unsaleable abroad." Equipment could only be bought at a high price, and produce couldn't be sold at any price. It was an exaggerated version of a situation that would afflict Canada throughout the next 150 years.

Howison described a country, two decades into the nineteenth century, that was determined to remain provincial. Gazing across the U.S. border, he saw communities that thirty years earlier had been nearly identical but had followed dramatically different paths: "The villages on the American frontier, indeed, form a striking contrast with those on the Canadian side. There, bustle, improvement, and animation, fill every street; here, dulness, decay, and apathy, discourage enterprise and repress exertion."

Canada was making a concerted effort to be small in size and limited in function. This would be a recurring trend through the next two centuries—but it would constantly be in conflict with another, larger idea.

The starting point for this book is an often overlooked fact about Canada: it is a country that has long had trouble keeping people. During most decades of the nineteenth century, and for many decades in the twentieth, Canada sent more people to other countries than it received as immigrants. When the largest emigration boom in history was sending more than 40 million people from Europe to the New World in the second half of the nineteenth century, Canada suffered a net migratory loss—mostly to the United States. Only as it approached its centennial did Canada begin to grow and develop in a way that other Western countries had begun a century earlier. As a consequence, Canada still faces the structural problems of underpopulation—with so few people inhabiting so much geography, it is difficult to build durable institutions and economies.

This was not an inevitable fate. In fact, much of Canada's early colonial history pointed toward another trajectory, one of expansive economic and human development. It took a surprising confluence of circumstances and individuals, in Britain and in the colonies, to launch Canada into a spiral it would not escape for a century and a half.

My colonial ancestors and their allies played a specific and formative role in this development, one that affects Canada's structure, economy and role in the world today. They were defenders—sometimes with arms and always with influence—of a set of ideas about Canada, how Canada should relate to the world, and who should call themselves Canadians. I call this set of ideas, and the vision that unites them, the "minimizing impulse."

The minimizing impulse has existed throughout Canadian history, both pre- and post-Confederation; for most of that history, it has been the dominant governing idea. And it continues to have a strong body of advocates today.

These are its elements:

Restrictive immigration. Sometimes the impulse began with a desire to prevent newcomers from settling in Canada, or with a policy aimed at having only certain sorts of people settle. During much of the nineteenth century, there was a push for British (as opposed to American or wider European) immigration; in much of the twentieth century (from 1911 until the 1960s), immigration numbers were severely limited, as they were restricted to a narrow pool of white Western Europeans.

Ethnic homogeneity. Immigration restrictions were often rooted in an official desire for the country's population and character to be ethnically British and Anglican, or, more rarely, to remain "two races" or "two nations." Theories of ethnic nationalism—the idea that a nation-state is associated with a single ethnic or racial group—emerged in Europe in the late nineteenth century and developed an incongruous following in Canada, where multiple ethnic groups and languages had always been components of the country.

Extractive economic policy. Often, restrictive immigration and population policies have been the result of a view of Canada as a source of staple exports drawn from farms, forests and fisheries, and then from mines and oil wells, to provide low-cost materials to the imperial centre in Britain (and later to other economic centres), and not as a country with its own industrial and entrepreneurial economy. This view was often a driver of ethnic-homogeneity policies, too. British and other Protestant immigrants were seen as natural employees suited to hierarchical work in a resource economy.

A view of indigenous communities as problems, not partners. The minimizing impulse historically led to relations with indigenous nations based on control, restriction and subjugation. An economic model that relies on sovereign control of land and resources rather than on the creative potential of communities is going to view the original peoples of Canada as obstacles to control rather than as partners in Confederation. An economic policy that called for a small population exercising control over a large land gave rise in the mid-nineteenth century to Canada's adversarial, paternalistic approach to "Indian affairs."

Restricted relations with the United States. The minimizing impulse is usually built on a rejection of North American economic integration in favour of colonial trade relations with Britain or attempts at economic self-sufficiency. This insular approach tends to be self-defeating. Anti-U.S. policies have almost always led to constricted population growth. More ambitious immigrants have avoided Canada during such periods, further hindering our population and economic growth.

A shortage of people. The combination of these views has meant that Canada's population has grown slowly, and sometimes not at all, during periods when the minimizing impulse was the governing ideology. The minimizing impulse causes, and is a result of, Canada's having insufficient population density, market size and taxpayer base to service its geographic, human and economic needs.

Canadian governments have rarely sought minimal population as a desired goal. During many periods before and after Confederation, they recognized underpopulation as a problem and employed immigration drives to solve it. But these drives were foiled by other minimizing trends, such as extractive or colonial economic policies or closed relations with the United States. Without an expansive economic and development policy, a growing population and a thriving civic life are impossible.

The elements of the minimizing impulse might sound disparate and unrelated. But throughout Canadian history, they have tended to move together. A strong push for one minimizing factor (such as a closed U.S. border or strong restrictions on immigration) tends to trigger the others.

Sometimes Canada's governing authorities have supported only one or two of these elements and tried to keep the others in check; they have almost always been disappointed. For example, the lavish immigration campaigns of the Confederation era proved unsuccessful because of the collapse of free trade with the United States and Ottawa's insistence on an agrarian resource-extraction economy. It's a lesson that has been illustrated over and over through Canadian history. To have an expansive, inclusive and successful country, you need people; to attract and keep people, you need to give them a reason to come, a sense of a better future, a source of hope.

Ever since Samuel de Champlain first established a settlement in 1608, the organization of Canada has been a series of answers to one fundamental question: Should this place remain a colony whose sole role is the provision of raw materials for an overseas master, or should it become its own place, one whose economy and governance serve the mutual needs and interests of the original inhabitants and the settler populations?

Champlain himself had a surprising answer to that question, one that his royal benefactors would not have agreed with. He largely ignored the orders from the King's authorities in Paris to "populate the country with native-born French Catholics" and actively encouraged his settlers to mate with Scottish fishermen, settlers from the English colonies to the south and, most significantly, members of the indigenous tribes. This somewhat pluralistic view was born of necessity. During the entire century before 1700, only six thousand Europeans were persuaded to come and stay in Canada (compared to tens of thousands who went to other colonies), and most were male.

Champlain famously declared to the Huron and Montagnais chiefs in 1633 that "our young men will marry your daughters, and we shall be one people," a message that seemed to have been welcomed among all three communities. At first, it didn't work. Although there had been a significant number of marriages between French fur trappers and indigenous women in the decades before Champlain uttered those words, historians Denys Delâge and Mathieu d'Avignon could find records of only five such ceremonies between farming seigneurs and indigenous brides during the three decades that followed. It was only after 1663, following the arrival of French soldiers in New France, that the independent traders who would later be known as coureurs de bois pushed westward toward the Red River and began marrying indigenous women. This largely cooperative and respectful meeting of two more or less nomadic peoples (albeit one conducted with a heavy-handed Christianizing mission) gave rise to the Metis people. Elsewhere, in Nova Scotia and Acadia and among the trappers of the Hudson's Bay Company, a similar meeting and interbreeding of peoples was taking place. (As John Ralston Saul notes, "anyone whose family arrived before the 1760s is probably part Aboriginal.") The result was a hybridized culture that Delâge and d'Avignon call "a religiously monolithic but ethnically and culturally pluralistic project of alliance and interbreeding rather than apartheid."

There were some efforts, during the 150 years of settlement in New France, to move away from basic resource extraction and create the kind of autonomous, diversified entrepreneurial economy that was emerging in the English colonies to the south. Jean Talon, the colony's first intendant appointed by Louis XIV, used a system of grants and incentives to encourage settlers to become less dependent on trapping and subsistence farming and to set up enterprises in shipbuilding, mining, brewing, and production and processing of commercial crops such as hops, flax and hemp for trade with other colonies.

Realizing, as Canadian leaders would in later centuries, that none of these industries could thrive without a reasonable population density, Talon launched several programs to raise the population through immigration, most famously his import of the eight hundred French orphan women known as the filles du roi. (It is estimated that two-thirds of Quebec's current ethnic French population are descended from these women.) But this was not enough. The industries generally died out, and the fur trade continued to account for at least 80 percent of New France's economy throughout its existence. An economy built on the gathering of unprocessed raw materials is not conducive to growth or sustainable population density. In all, only about nine thousand people ever immigrated permanently to New France throughout its entire 150-year history; that Canada's population had reached seventy thousand by the time of the British conquest in 1760 is a testament to the extraordinary fertility of its settlers, not their economic success.

After their victory in the Battle of the Plains of Abraham, the British governed vast and sparsely populated territories whose majority population was either ethnically and linguistically French or indigenous. London officials realized that they could not maintain control of this territory without acknowledging these existing nations—and that they could use these populations to check the expansive and increasingly independent-minded instincts of their American settlers.

Their negotiated solution, the Royal Proclamation of 1763, was the first recognizable constitutional document in Canada. It was intended to add the new colony of Quebec (along with the Florida colonies and Grenada) to the existing thirteen without triggering a war with the continent's indigenous nations or conflicts between French and English settlers. As such, it established a legal precedent for recognition of First Nations as more or less equal and autonomous communities with control over their territories and alliances. (With the Quebec Act of 1774, these territories were extended southwest to the Ohio River Valley and northwest through the Prairies and Hudson Bay.)

The proclamation was also intended to fix the increasingly evident demographic shortcomings of the Canadian colonies, by encouraging the emigration of English-speaking settlers in the Thirteen Colonies north to Quebec and Nova Scotia, promising land and eventual responsible government to those Americans willing to move. This attempt at attracting American emigrants initially had little effect: immigrants didn't want to come to a place with a restricted and limited economy and an indifferent colonial government. And those immigrants who did come weren't interested in quietly fitting into the colonial resource-extraction economy.

The only English-speaking settlers who came to Quebec in decent numbers were American merchants seeking to do business there, and their entrepreneurial sensibility horrified the colony's British rulers. "Although relatively small in numbers," Valerie Knowles writes in her history of immigration, "this rising Anglo-American business class would spar frequently with British administrators, military men, and governors, who came to regard them as grasping, self-seeking demagogues, bent on controlling the province's political institutions to serve the promotion of commerce." This fear of commerce would become a driving force behind the minimizing impulse during the next century.

First, though, the proclamation's North American settlement project would experience a surprise four-decade reprise, during which a different sort of Canadian future almost became visible. Its cause was the American Revolution.

It is misleading to think that Canada was settled by British and French colonists. Very few made the crossing during the first two centuries, and most of them didn't stay. In fact, during Canada's crucial formative period the land was overwhelmingly settled by emigrants from the United States.

Americans were the first major population group to settle permanently in Canada in more than token numbers, and they dominated Canada's population for six decades. From the 1770s until the 1830s, the majority of English-speaking Canadians were U.S.-born. And they brought with them a set of ideas that directly challenged the minimizing narrative of the colonial rulers.

It is popular nowadays to think of those American emigrants as loyal British subjects who fled to Canada out of opposition to the Patriots' victory in the revolution. But the United Empire Loyalists, as they later called themselves, were never more than a small portion of the influx of Americans, most of whom had no interest in the colony's system of rule and many of whom opposed it. To be sure, between 1775 and 1784 the revolution violently divided Americans, and those who fled the conflict or were forced into exile during those years were indeed motivated by political affinity, but their legend outshines their proportion.

No more than about 43,000 loyalists settled in Canada during the Revolutionary War. They were Canada's first wave of refugees, and they were deployed strategically. Most (about 35,000) settled in the Maritimes and about 2,000 in Quebec; the remaining 6,000 or so were ordered or enticed in 1784 to settle, in an attempt to build a counter-revolutionary regime adjoining the newly independent United States, in the hard-to-reach lands west of Montreal along the St. Lawrence and Great Lakes. Those lands—today's Ontario—were at that point inhabited by prosperous indigenous tribes and a few scattered trappers. It is often forgotten that many of those loyalist settlers were indigenous— the initial U.S. settlers of Upper Canada included two thousand native Americans who had fought for the British—and also black, including some three thousand free black Americans who fled mainly to the Maritimes.

But the really substantial northward migration of Americans got underway after the war was over and U.S. independence had been negotiated, and it had nothing to do with loyalties or empires. These immigrants were attracted not by ideology but by the promise of free land and lower taxes. (The United States, in order to pay off debts incurred during its War of Independence, taxed its citizens harder than the British colonies taxed their subjects. It also sold large tranches of public land to speculators who drove up the price of private property.) The American influx helped drive the Canadian population up from 90,000 in 1775 to more than 430,000 in 1814.

Of course, British officials hoped that the Americans would be, in the words of Home Secretary Lord Sydney, not entrepreneurial and self-starting North American opportunists but simple farmers who were "sufferers under the ruinous and arbitrary Laws and Constitution of the United States."

But by 1783, any Americans who held monarchist sentiments had already fled to Canada or returned to Britain. Historian John Little characterizes the Americans who settled in Lower Canada's townships after 1783 as "neither British Tories nor American republicans[;] most were political pragmatists who valued property ownership, economic development, and liberal political institutions." The first of these they had; the absence of the second two would soon cause problems.

While free land and lower taxes attracted Americans, they would not stay if the Canadian economy and government proved inhospitable. Remember, there had also been a substantial emigration of Canadian settlers southward during and after the War of Independence, and there was a real risk that these U.S.-bound anti-loyalists would outnumber the northward-moving Americans.

Worried, the British Parliament entered a lengthy and heated debate over the question of what sort of place Canada should be, a question that could shape the future of the British Empire and the world economy. On one side was Lord Shelburne, the Whig prime minister, who had negotiated Britain's post-revolutionary peace treaty with the Americans on fairly generous terms. Shelburne had come to understand (in large part through detailed conversations with economists David Hume and Adam Smith) that prosperity depended on open trade with economically autonomous trading partners—including the United States. In his view, the world economy could return to growth, and therefore the British economy to prosperity, only if both the British and the independent parts of North America were encouraged to develop an autonomous, successful economy that would be a prosperous market for British goods and a provider of products (and not just raw materials) to British consumers.

In 1783 Shelburne proposed granting the newly independent Americans free trade with the British Empire and opening colonial ports to U.S. merchant ships. (This would benefit both U.S. producers and the export economies of the British West Indies, as well as Canada.) For Canada to thrive and avoid the revolutionary fate of the Thirteen Colonies, it would have to become attractive to newcomers and free from the deprivations and resentments that had prodded the Americans into rebellion. To make this possible, he proposed replacing Canada's paternalistic colonial rule with a more liberal government and more open trade. In essence, he would stave off revolution by giving the Canadians the open economy, free trade and self-government many of them craved, while keeping the imperial hierarchy in place. Had Shelburne succeeded, Canada's history would have followed a very different path, its nineteenth century dominated by maximizing rather than minimizing impulses.

Shelburne's proposal ran headlong into the wrath of Britain's Tories (and some Whigs), who were already incensed by the non-punitive nature of his American peace treaty. In their view, the American Revolution had been provoked not by restrictive colonial measures, but by indulging the Thirteen Colonies' desire to develop their own autonomous economy and political system. This, in their view, had spiralled toward revolution, and must never be permitted to take place in the remaining northern colonies. Any gain in American trade, the Tory view held, would be a loss for the Royal Navy, which secured the British monopoly on sea trade. Given the rapid growth of the U.S. economy, a free-trade regime could lead the United States to displace Britain as the leading sea power.

The Tories' proposed solution was to lock down the Americans, restrict their trade and empower Canada's loyalists as the sole providers of resources, lumber, fish and grain to Britain and its colonies. As Guy Carleton, the arch-Tory governor general of the Canadian colonies, told the British Privy Council, "the only firm hold that Great Britain has upon the remains of the American Dominions is certainly by means of the Loyalists." That Tory view, of a closed and restricted Canada serving as an imperial backstop and storehouse, prevailed. Shelburne was driven out of office later in 1783, in large part through opposition to his belief in a more autonomous and expansionist British North America.

Shelburne's loss would have lasting consequences. First, it forced Canada's economy into dependency on the imperial core. And second, the attempt to isolate the United States by limiting its seagoing powers and enforcing the British right to board any U.S. ships and impress their British-born sailors into military duty provoked two outcomes: a decade-long economic depression in the United States during the 1780s, then a furious response to British control of the oceans and seaports that became the principal cause of the War of 1812.

A former redcoat officer who made his reputation burning Patriot villages in the War of Independence, John Graves Simcoe was appointed the first governor of Upper Canada in 1791 and immediately understood that the British notion of a closed and limited Canada contradicted the empire's goals of keeping the United

States in check. It also contradicted his personal goal of defeating the United States in a future war he desperately hoped would take place. To succeed in these goals, the new colony would need many more people and a lot more trade. Upper Canada would have to be "the grand Mart and Emporium of the Western World," Simcoe's deputy Peter Russell declared, so that the British could "extend their Arms round the United States, and hanging as a two-edged Sword over their Necks Secure at last to this Country (by force of Terror) all those advantages" of imperial rule. Simcoe also realized that the only feasible way to bring about this economic and demographic mastery—since Britons were supremely uninterested in emigrating to the Canadas—was to open the border and populate the place almost entirely with Americans.

Therefore, the Constitutional Act of 1791 both created Upper Canada and tried to make it appealing to land-hungry Americans, by guaranteeing two hundred acres to anyone who took the oath of allegiance to the King. On top of this, Britain heavily subsidized the colonists by underwriting most of the costs of government salaries, military garrisons and payments to indigenous tribes (that is, most of the costs of government), thus ensuring that taxes would be extremely low; in fact, they were one-fifth the rate paid in New York State.

So Americans arrived, in great numbers. By 1812, Upper Canada had 100,000 residents and 90 percent of them were U.S.-born. Less than a fifth of this population were the legendary loyalists: they were outnumbered by the Americans who filled Upper Canada in the decades after the revolution, at a rate of about 2,500 per year.

Simcoe rather optimistically dubbed these settlers "Late Loyalists," but there is no evidence that any of them were motivated by loyalty to the King or that Canada expected such loyalty. These New World Canadians barely even acknowledged the Canada-U.S. border. Families, merchants, preachers and farmers moved back and forth across it, many families straddled it, and trade and commerce began to develop between New York State and Upper Canada. Commercial farming of the sort that was flourishing in the United States did not generally take hold among Upper Canadians, since shipping export produce up the rapids to Montreal was difficult and expensive (and impossible in the winter months). So the United States was the only market, returns were poor and most farming was subsistence-level.

The newly constructed Anglican churches of Upper Canada found their pews bypassed by the colony's swelling Baptist and Methodist congregations, often served by itinerant border-crossing U.S. preachers. Their individualistic message of self-salvation and personal witness of God was sharply at odds with the acquiescent and hierarchical messages of the Church of England and the Roman Catholic Church. Canada, desperate for population, settled large communities of pacifist Mennonites, Quakers and Germanic members of the Church of the Brethren ("Dunkers"), granting them entire townships and allowing them to self-segregate and self-govern in order to avoid integrating. "Scattered through an immense forest, Upper Canada's distinctive communities had little cause or desire to cooperate, much less to meld," writes historian Alan Taylor. "Upper Canada was an ethnic and religious mosaic rather than a melting pot."

Officials in Simcoe's circle warned him that the new Canadians from the south were a threat to British values—and rule. "I could wish we had not so many emigrants from the States as I much fear the turbulent seeds of fanaticism and rebellion are not sufficiently eradicated from their breasts," Simcoe's friend and deputy Captain Charles Stevenson warned him in 1793. But Simcoe insisted that they would be won over to the British side. His rapid-population scheme was tolerated by his overseas masters, but not his lust for war with the United States. That, at a moment when Britain was expensively at war with France, was a step too far. He was reassigned back to Britain (at higher military rank) and died in 1806, six years before his long-anticipated war actually took place.

The War of 1812 would test the ideas of domination-by-population that Simcoe had introduced. What unfolded over two chaotic years was at once a war between the republic to the south and the colony to the north, a confrontation between the defensive British Empire and the expanding American economy, and a conflict within both nations between competing sets of ideas about how North America should be run. In Canada, the War of 1812 began as a test of loyalties for the colony's British, French, American and indigenous residents, with ambiguous responses.

The war's first sobering lesson for the British was that North Americans did not especially want to fight each other. The call for military volunteers received extremely limited response from Canada's men, who weren't interested in abandoning their crops to wage battle against their relatives and former neighbours in the name of their new country's king. Those who were conscripted or press-ganged into battle deserted in large numbers. (The Americans also suffered large-scale desertion, for similar reasons but also because the pay was poor.) Britain then enlisted Irishmen in substantial numbers, hoping they would see military service as a way out of poverty, but a majority of them promptly deserted upon arrival in Canada and moved to the United States in what became known as "emigration enlistment"—use of the army as free passage across the Atlantic. At times, it seemed as if Britain was devoting more resources to tracking down Canadian and Irish deserters than it was to fighting the war.

Britain would turn for the defence of Upper and Lower Canada to a group who still represented a majority population of Canada, the British-allied indigenous tribes. The guerrilla warfare acumen of the Iroquois Confederacy proved decisive in many of the war's key battles. They were fighting to maintain contiguous control of their Ohio River territory from the U.S. settlers, whose hostile and racially intolerant approach to indigenous groups was a stark contrast to the autonomy that indigenous nations had been granted in Canada. The tribes were also granted promises of land in exchange for joining the fight in 1812, and they were infuriated in 1814 when the war-ending Treaty of Ghent failed to give them anything they'd been promised. (They would be further betrayed when, within a decade of the war's end, the minimalist-minded postwar Canadian leaders would neglect the treaties and begin seizing their land.)

In the end, the War of 1812 was a shambolic affair in which both sides lost sight of any goals or principles they had held at the outset. The Americans, woefully underarmed and abominably led, soon lost track of any purpose for their scattered attacks. In 1812 their Republican Party politicians had talked of defeating the British occupier by crossing the border with messages of solidarity and warming the Canadian settlers' hearts; by 1814 they were making raids across the border to burn the Canadian settlers' homes.

Many U.S. Republicans had seen the war as an opportunity to extend popular sovereignty and democratic rights to the remaining British-occupied corners of the continent; they imagined the final phase of a North American democratic revolution. Some speculated (probably correctly) that a majority of Canadians had little use for the King or the authoritarian elites who ruled them. But the Americans were divided over this goal (many southern Congressman feared that a conquest of Canada would make northern anti-slavery states a majority, and northern Federalists considered it a waste of money), and their Congress declined to fund enough military resources to make 1812 anything other than an attempted revenge strike against Britain for its shipping policy. It's interesting to speculate what the larger regime-change campaign, if successful, might have done to improve the future development of both territories. Regardless, what actually occurred was two years of pointless and inhumane war that soiled the image of Americans and turned even many anti-loyalist Canadians against them. It also showed the British to be lacking popular support and unable to hold their border without expensively purchased indigenous assistance.

When the war finally ground to a halt, the border should have opened once again and the two North American entities should have resumed their awkward but mutually beneficial relationship. As it happened, Americans soon forgot about the war. Canada's British rulers, on the other hand, decided to make it permanent.

The minimizing vision of Canada was born in 1815. What the British colonel Sir John Le Couteur described as "a hot and unnatural war between kindred people" was followed by a dramatic and total severance of that kinship. That was not an inevitable outcome of the war, but rather the result of postwar policies designed to prevent Canada from becoming anything like the United States. As soon as the war was over, the Canadian ruling elite erected a set of barriers between their subjects and the fast-expanding North American culture and economy.

The war taught the ruling officials of Upper and Lower Canada that Canadians were not to be trusted. Those ruling officials—in Upper Canada, a closed circle of British Tories who became known as the Family Compact, and in Lower Canada a similar circle of Tories with a handful of wealthy French-Canadian traders who became known as the Château Clique—had long remained aloof from the population they governed; now they feared and resented that population. "The events of the war demonstrated that a significant portion of the province's approximately one hundred thousand inhabitants were either indifferent or hostile to the British cause," historian Colin Read writes of the quandary facing Upper Canada's leaders. "How to purge the province of this lamentable pro-American element was clearly a major question."

The Family Compact turned angrily against Simcoe's erstwhile immigration policy and the American-born majority with its entrepreneurial, expansionist, non-agrarian thinking. Bishop John Strachan, an Anglican firebrand who did much to shape post-1812 Canada, declared that the war's outcome had allowed the Family Compact to distinguish "our friends from our foes, and rid us of all those traitors and false friends whom a short-sighted and mistaken policy had introduced among us."

The English-speaking population of Lower Canada was, if anything, distrusted even more. British authorities there, who already feared a French-Canadian insurrection, found themselves very much on the defensive. Historian John Little quotes one British officer in the Eastern Townships, Lieutenant Colonel Paul Holland Knowlton of Lac-Brome, describing the population of his Quebec region as "a few Loyal from principal, many who have come to the country for some years passed who are in nature and education perfectly hostile to British Institutions. . . . None of these have any gratitude for the protection they have enjoyed under this Government, and are notwithstanding abundant Loyal professions, daily plotting with sympathizers and Rebels." (Knowlton himself would later be relieved of his command for signing a petition calling for Lower Canada's annexation to the United States.)

These elites answered first with a ban on Americans immigrating to Canada and on U.S.-born residents of Upper Canada taking the oath of citizenship. These Canadians of American descent, most of whom had been settled in Canada for decades, were forbidden from holding land or participating in assemblies or government bodies. (Only in 1828, after years of debate on "the alien question," were American-born Canadians allowed to take the oath of loyalty to the King.) The border was closed to most forms of export commerce.

Second, they began a concerted campaign to prevent expansionist ideas from spreading. Newspapers and postal services were censored and restricted. The ruling authorities of Toronto and Quebec City distrusted public education as seditious, and they supported schools only for the wealthy. The Canadian colonies fought the introduction of mass public education, even at the primary school level, lest it spread American ideas; advocates of public schooling, such as Toronto's Egerton Ryerson, were denounced as unpatriotic "Americans." Free and compulsory public schooling would come to Ontario only in 1871, three decades after its introduction in the United States. It would arrive even later in Quebec, where public schools were seen as a threat to both the British regime and the Roman Catholic Church, which would be given control of the education system there in 1875.

Third was the imposition of a very limited ethnic and religious identity on the colonies. One-seventh of all the unsurveyed land in Upper Canada was given to the Church of England; an even larger share of Lower Canada's land was controlled by the Roman Catholic Church. Baptist and Methodist preachers were barred from entering Canada, and dissenting faiths were discouraged.

Fourth was a concerted effort to change the demographic makeup of the colonies. Alexander Macdonell, the Catholic bishop for Upper Canada, warned after the war that Canada needed to subsidize a great wave of Scottish immigration if it was to guard against the "contagion of democracy."

The solution, Britain and its colonial leaders decided, was to import people who were loyal—but not necessarily inventive or talented or ambitious. The colonial administration was soon paying cashiered soldiers from the Napoleonic Wars and bankrupt but loyal British farmers to make the crossing. Reform politicians in Upper Canada complained that the colonial elite had issued a large number of land patents, often for sizeable estates, to loyal Tories in Britain without regard for any other qualities (this is likely how the Lloyd-Joneses ended up in Canada).

The strategy worked. The U.S.-born, who were a majority in 1815, had fallen to only 7 percent of Upper Canada's population, which had more than tripled to 487,000, by 1842. But it also had the effect of choking the economic and civic life out of the nascent Canada, at a moment when the Industrial Revolution was beginning to transform the rest of the Western world. Alan Taylor describes the self-perpetuating spiral of factors that hampered the development of an autonomous economy or society in the first half of the nineteenth century:

> Upper Canada offered cheap land and paltry taxes, but the settler had to accept a lower standard of living than in the United States. That prospect screened out ambitious men. . . . The scarcity and high wages of labourers also discouraged prosperous farmers from settling in Upper Canada. Few men remained labourers for wages because they could so easily obtain farms in the land-rich colony. Because so few men of means immigrated to Upper Canada, the colony had relatively few millers, innkeepers, or commercial farmers, the sort of entrepreneurs who led rural society in the United States. In sum, the colony had a weak "civil society": a network of private associations and institutions beyond government's control. Distrusting such a civil society, the government officials felt strengthened by its weakness in Upper Canada.

This constricted economy drove people away from Canada. Not only did Europeans favour the United States by a huge proportion, but the majority of those British immigrants who were enticed to come to Canada also moved to the United States—a pattern that wouldn't end with the 1830s. "Between 1815 and 1839," Ninette Kelley and Michael Trebilcock write in their migration history, "between half and three-quarters of the number of immigrants to arrive in British North America emigrated from British North America to the United States. This was the beginning of a recurring trend throughout the nineteenth century." While Canada would change dramatically over the next seven decades and become a sovereign state, its difficulty retaining immigrants would get worse.

CHAPTER 2

Stillborn: The Great Loss of 1867

We tend to think of the dark and constricted era between the end of the War of 1812 and the 1837 rebellions as a Canadian anomaly. In the popular version of nineteenth-century history, the next six decades saw a series of major political changes and economic transformations that created the modern Canada. Britain's dissolution of Upper and Lower Canada and creation of a united Province of Canada, joint English-French rule, responsible government, Confederation, the building of the Canadian Pacific Railway, the opening of the West—these, we imagine, brought about the rise of independence and prosperity in a growing nation.

Viewed through the lens of population, however, these six decades look rather different. The majority of the nineteenth century was marked by a nearly continuous hemorrhage of people. During these decades, underpopulation became a permanent and lasting feature of Canadian economic, political and cultural life.

In response to the political crises of the late 1830s, Britain decided that its Canadian colonies needed a major immigration push in order to displace Lower Canada's francophones and Upper Canada's U.S.-born, democracy-tolerant population. It should have been an ideal time to do it. The middle decades of the nineteenth century saw tens of millions of Europeans emigrate overseas, pushed out by the constricted and sometimes deadly conditions at home, pulled by the prospect of farmland and employment abroad. Canada missed out on most of this unprecedented wave, by insisting on receiving only immigrants from its colonial motherland. Sizeable numbers did come, though: between the 1837 rebellions and Confederation, a million British and Irish immigrants would come to British North America, to the point that by 1867 two-thirds of the population of Canada was British in origin.

But Canada would nevertheless lose more in emigration than it gained in immigration during those decades—in fact, the loss was worse than it had been before 1837. In the words of immigration historian Valerie Knowles, "It appears that once immigrants arrived in the Province most of them kept right on going until they reached Canada's southern neighbour. This diversion or loss of immigration to the United States would be a recurring theme in nineteenth-century Canadian history."

During every decade of the nineteenth century during which immigration records were kept but one, more people chose to leave Canada than arrived as immigrants. Significantly, the one decade when Canada experienced a (slight) net migratory gain was the 1850s—also the one decade during which Canada enjoyed something resembling free trade with the United States, and thus economic conditions (or at least some hope of future economic conditions) that might make it worthwhile to stay.

After the 1850s, and in the three decades following Confederation, the population leakage became a flood. From 1851 to 1901, Canada attracted 734,900 immigrants from England, Wales and Scotland and lost at least 1.2 million emigrants, mainly to the United States—a net migratory loss of Canadian population of 433,000 people.

Canada's population growth until the twentieth century was entirely due to fertility. Large families permitted the population to rise to 5.3 million, despite the near-constant exodus away from the country's flailing economy. That population would have been millions more if not for the migratory loss.

By comparison, during the five decades when aggressive immigration campaigns by Canadian agents attracted only 734,900 British and Irish people to Canada, the United States received 3,116,600 immigrants directly from Britain (on top of the 1.2 million, many British in origin, who moved from Canada to the United States), as well as tens of millions of people from European countries whose émigrés Canada wasn't even considering for admission. The United States had by 1900 achieved a population of 76 million, enough to provide it with a substantial domestic market, a fiscal base of sufficient size to build important and lasting institutions, and a sufficiently autonomous economy to make Canada an insignificant part of its economic orbit.

"Over the course of four decades [1860 to 1900]—decades which were otherwise politically formative for the Dominion," economic analyst David Verbeeten writes in a study of migration statistics, "the population of Canada actually expanded at a rate below that of natural increase. Immigration only began to contribute significantly to population growth after 1901. . . . Canada largely missed out on the migrations of the nineteenth

century—human movements which were otherwise unprecedented in size and scope. . . . For much, if not most, of its formative history, Canada was not a country of immigrants, but rather
a country of emigrants or transients."

This was not mainly or even predominantly an Anglo-
Canadian phenomenon. In fact, Quebec lost an even higher
proportion of its francophone population to the United States.
Between 1840 and the end of the 1920s, an estimated 900,000
French Canadians left Canada, almost all of them for New
England; about 70 percent of this migration occurred before
1900, when Quebec had a population of only 1.6 million.

As historians Damien-Claude Bélanger and Claude Bélanger
concluded in an analysis of this southward Québécois emigration,
"Around 1900, there would scarcely have been a French-Canadian
or Acadian family that did not have some of its members living in
the United States. . . . In the absence of emigration [to the United
States], there would be 4 to 5 million more francophones living in
Canada today."

The cities of the northeastern United States became peppered
with "petits Canadas"—Québécois arrival cities. New England
cities had their own French parishes and French-language Catholic
schools, newspapers and social clubs. New England had as many
French-language daily newspapers (almost two hundred) as did
the whole province of Quebec. By 1900, Fall River, Massachusetts,
with a Franco-American population of 33,000, had become the
third-largest French-Canadian city, after Montreal and Quebec
City; the fourth largest was Lowell, Massachusetts, with 24,800
Québécois. New England contained ten cities with more than ten
thousand French Canadians; Quebec itself contained only five
cities of more than ten thousand.

And no, it wasn't the weather. The chief destination for the hundreds of thousands of Quebecers who fled during the nineteenth century was climatically identical New England; for the immigrants to the Canadian Prairies who abandoned their homesteads in droves, it was the Dakotas. While Toronto, Montreal and Hamilton did see their populations grow, immigrants chose to settle in vastly greater numbers—and stay—in Chicago, New York City and Boston, all of which have very similar climates. It was not snow and ice repelling newcomers, but Canada's economic circumstances and the political conditions that created them.

In the early twentieth century, Canadians came to recognize the scale of their population loss. Political economist (and future cabinet minister) Oscar Skelton chronicled the scale of the phenomenon:

> The Dominion as a whole increased at less than half the rate of the United States, and Sir Richard Cartwright [Laurier's trade minister] had little difficulty in establishing the alarming fact that in recent years one out of every four of the native-born of Canada had been compelled to seek a home in the Republic, and that three out of every four immigrants to Canada had followed the same well-beaten trail. There were in 1890 more than one-third as many people of Canadian birth and descent in the United States as in Canada itself. Never in the world's history, save in the case of crowded, famine-stricken, misgoverned Ireland, had there been such a leakage of the brain and brawn of any country.

In no other present or former colony was the number of settlers who arrived in the nineteenth century outnumbered by those who decided to leave. In the midst of the world's largest immigration boom, underway even as Canada achieved nationhood through Confederation, the country not only failed to attract people but provoked millions of its own residents to depart—an enormous missed opportunity from which Canada has not yet recovered.

In the wake of the 1837 rebellions, Britain's Whig government dispatched John Lambton, the Earl of Durham, to investigate what exactly had gone so terribly wrong in the North American colonies. They appointed him governor general and high commissioner of British North America in order to determine the rebellion's root causes.

The Durham Report, released in 1839, begins with a bold assessment of colonial economic conditions that provides a surprisingly precise denunciation of the minimizing impulse:

> While the present state of things is allowed to last, the actual inhabitants of these Provinces have no security for person or property, no enjoyment of what they possess, no stimulus to industry. The development of the vast resources of these extensive territories is arrested; and the population, which should be attracted to fill and fertilize them, is directed into foreign states. . . . The principal evils to which settlers in a new township are subject result from the scantiness of population. . . . These blocks of wild land place the actual settler in an almost hopeless condition; he can hardly expect, during

his lifetime, to see his neighbourhood contain a population sufficiently dense to support mills, schools, post-offices, places of worship, markets or shops; and without these, civilization retrogrades.

That, at least, is what Durham wrote after examining the conditions of Upper Canada, where he broadly agreed with the Reformers who had led the Upper Canada Rebellion. But Lower Canada, despite having endured similar restrictions at the hands of its Tory elite, provoked another infamous response that dominated Durham's report. He concluded that the root problems there, and therefore of Canada in general, were not political or economic but racial. After having spoken to none of them, he concluded that the French Canadians were an inferior race doomed to drag down the colonies as long as they remained a majority anywhere, and that the colonies therefore needed to be flash-anglicized through forced assimilation and mass immigration of subservient Orangemen from Britain. "The language, the laws, the character of the North American Continent are English; and every race but the English appears there in a condition of inferiority," he wrote. "The French Canadian is cast still further into the shade, by a language and habits foreign to those of the Imperial Government. . . . They are a people with no history, and no literature." And therefore, "tranquility can only be restored by subjecting the province to the vigorous rule of an English majority."

At a moment when the Industrial Revolution was becoming a central fact throughout the Western world, when the old closed and protected colonial trade patterns were being replaced with open international competition, when subsistence agriculture was giving way to urban economies and capital intensive commercial farming, the British government concluded that Canada's most pressing problem was that it had the wrong sort of people.

This estimation had ominous effects on Canada's development. Canada became embroiled in a thirty-year period of chaotic struggle, including violent and sometimes deadly battles between Orange Order terrorist gangs and reformist crowds over ethnopolitical identity and colonial fealty. Decades of instability and ambiguity deterred countless more knowledgeable and entrepreneurial settlers from landing there, leaving Canada constricted and agrarian at the very moment when the United States was taking in huge numbers of people to populate its cities and build its industries.

And it marked the beginning of a century-long racialization of Canadian politics. By the final decades of the nineteenth century, the dominant voice in Canada had concluded that indigenous Canadians, French Canadians and other minorities should be seen not as partners but as obstacles to English supremacy and territorial expansion. Rather than trying to build successful economies and communities—a process that implies cooperation and compromise—Canada during much of this period would simply attempt to fill territory through mass importation of anglophones. Combined with a crude mercantilist vision of agriculture and resource extraction, this meant that Canada would view its indigenous peoples, during a crucial period of growth, as hindrances rather than as collaborators in its development—again, with ominous effects.

While the Durham Report did cause Upper and Lower Canada to be combined into the single Province of Canada for a quarter-century and spurred the eventual rise of responsible government, neither Durham's liberal economic suggestions nor his ethnic-nationalist assimilationist proposals would become realities. The latter is to the enormous historical credit of the Province of Canada's Reform politicians, especially Louis-Hippolyte Lafontaine and Robert Baldwin. Their joint English-French rule, against Britain's wishes, preserved the polyglot traditions that had given Canada its most hopeful moments and prevented Quebec from becoming the outpost of English chauvinism that London had envisioned. The Lafontaine-Baldwin shared-society approach was also built on the importance of liberal institutions: local government, universal public education and open trade. By introducing them, Lafontaine and Baldwin would plant the seeds of a different, maximal sort of Canada, one that would be cultivated in the next century.

Up to this point, the chief causes of Canada's constricted development and limited ambitions had mainly been located in London. In the eyes of the British Empire, its North American colonies served chiefly as storehouses of raw materials for Britain's commercial and industrial growth. In the mercantilist view that had dominated imperial economic policy, trade was a closed loop in which fish, fur, lumber and later grain departed Canada for Britain and its other colonies on ships whose trade monopoly was protected by the Royal Navy, and in return British manufactured goods (and sometimes immigrants) were sent back on those same ships. Since 1825, exports from the Canadas had entered Britain and its other colonies at a 2.5 percent duty, while exports from the United States and other non-imperial sources had paid duties as high as 30 percent. (Key colonial exports such as salted fish, furthermore, were prohibited from import to Britain outside the imperial loop.)

These imperial preferences had given the Canadian colonies a guaranteed and usually lucrative market for their unprocessed exports. They also discouraged any expansion into more productive economic activity, and kept imports—including farm equipment—much more expensive than they were in the United States. Thus, they discouraged immigrants from settling. Imperial preferences and mercantilism were the root of the minimal-Canada model, since maintaining this closed-loop imperial extraction-and-trade model benefited the colonial elites within Upper and Lower Canada as much as it did the landowning classes in Britain. This was all about to change.

It had long been apparent to knowledgeable officials in Britain and the colonies that the mercantilist model wasn't working. Imperial preferences benefited thousands of producers, farmers and resource exporters by providing secure rewards, with little need for innovation or employment. But they were deeply detrimental to millions of consumers and putative entrepreneurs, driving up both goods and equipment costs in the colonies and, crucially, food costs in Britain and Ireland. And they were punishingly expensive to maintain.

The British Empire operated at a net loss, its colonies costing more to administer and secure than they delivered in savings on raw materials. And those weren't really "savings," as economists had known since Adam Smith first pointed out in 1776 that Britain would be more prosperous if it simply bought what it needed from the cheapest supplier, colony or otherwise. Empire may have made Britain powerful, but it didn't make British people prosperous—and by the middle of the 1840s, it was starving them to death.

The reorganized Province of Canada started the 1840s well. After the post-1837 economic depression died down, a building boom sent record shiploads of timber, harvested in New Brunswick and Upper Canada by firms owned by monopoly-holding lumber barons and floated down rivers and newly built canals in great rafts, to Britain at preferential imperial tariff rates. The ships returned with their hulls crudely converted to hold immigrants, sometimes known as "paying ballast," who were dropped off at Quebec City. By the middle of the 1840s, wheat and flour had also become important Canadian exports.

Still, there were early signs that the immigration half of the equation wasn't quite working. In 1842 Britain, anticipating a canal-building boom in Canada, recruited more than 44,000 labourers to emigrate to Canada. But they failed to find employment, and the closed economy offered few other opportunities, so most of them departed for the United States, and reportedly 9,500 of them subsequently returned from New York back to Britain. During the next couple of years, immigration rates declined. Then a new force began to send people fleeing to Canada in unprecedented numbers: mass starvation and famine.

The near-simultaneous combination of potato blight in Ireland and the failure of the British and northern European wheat and rye crops in 1846 was a humanitarian and political catastrophe on a level Europe had not seen for centuries—and worse, the famine's deadliness was largely the fault of protectionist imperial trade policies whose dangers had long been known. As reports flooded in of the million starvation deaths in Ireland and the widespread famine and ruin elsewhere, even the most staunch defenders of Britain's Corn Laws, which banned import of wheat and flour from outside the British Empire, could no longer stand up for a protectionist policy that was cutting off Britain's food supply in order to benefit wealthy landholders. When Sir Robert Peel's Tory government repealed the Corn Laws in the summer of 1846, it more or less instantly ended Canada's imperial preferences; the preferential lumber tariff was also cancelled that year, ending Canada's decisive lumber-price advantage over Scandinavia. By 1849 the last imperial preferences had ended and Britain was trading more or less freely with the world, which meant that the United States almost instantly became its biggest trade partner. Canada was suddenly no longer vital, nor really necessary, for British well-being.

The minimizing impulse had never been a sustainable way to govern or develop Canada autonomously. It represented the politics of an artificial economy built on subsidies to Canada in the form of imperial tariffs and militarily enforced trade prohibitions against competitors. When those subsidies abruptly ended in 1846, the entire illusory economy vanished, the colony's export goods suddenly lost their competitive value, and Canada's elite were left without an alternative plan. Michael Hart, in his economic history of Canada, describes the scope of their sudden reversal of fortune:

First fish, then furs, and later lumber and grain, had dominated Canadian production and geared Canada's productive capacity and infrastructure toward the export of staples at relatively low levels of processing. . . . The commercial policies of the metropolitan country [Britain] ensured that the colonies could continue to concentrate on producing staples for export to the home country and to import their other requirements from it. Tariff and other policies discouraged the development of native industries to upgrade the staple before export or other more sophisticated economic activities. . . . Once that preference was removed, all the disadvantages of a small economy with a slender population base strung out along several thousand miles of inland waterways and hinterland stood out in sharp relief. . . . Britain had abandoned the colonists.

For Canadians, the immediate effect of Britain's embrace of free trade was a two-year economic depression triggered by the collapse of Canadian staples prices. To make matters worse, the first major system of canals to the St. Lawrence River, completed in 1848 with high-volume imperial trade in mind, suddenly lost much of its financial rationale. The Province of Canada was on the hook for the substantial debts it had accrued for the waterway's construction, but the revenues weren't coming. The government's largest income source had been its own colonial tariffs, which, unlike the British imperial tariffs, were designed more to generate revenues than to block imports. That era was ending elsewhere: the United States and Britain were shifting from tariffs to domestic taxes as their main sources of state revenue. Canada lacked the population base or political will to follow this shift, so it was forced to keep its imports expensive even as export earnings collapsed. As a consequence, both the private and public economies crashed.

And, inconveniently, this was exactly when people started coming. In 1847, a record-breaking 105,000 people, or more than 7 percent of Canada's population, arrived in British North

America—almost all of them starving Irish peasants, many infected with cholera, a disease that killed more than 30,000 of them that year alone. They were so destitute and ill that the Canadian government had no choice but to establish a costly financial aid program to keep them alive and off the streets. The Irish (a large proportion of whom were Protestant and settled in rural areas, contrary to the popular image) would dominate immigration through the next seven years, during which some 300,000 more would arrive. This wave marked the last time in the nineteenth century that Canada would settle more newcomers than it sent away.

In the 1850s, Canadians were forced to confront a basic truth that had previously been half-concealed by the artificial economies of empire but was evident to anyone living in its cities: that Canada is part of a North American economy and culture, not a European one. Britain was increasingly uninterested in maintaining and paying for a North American territorial outpost, but Canada's borders and political relations with the United States remained largely closed. The next several years embroiled Canada in a debate over how to open them and how to turn away from the minimizing vision.

One popular answer was for Canada to become part of the United States, which was far more prosperous and developed, enjoyed a much higher standard of living and was at this point home to at least one relative of almost every Canadian. The movement to join Washington had a substantial following in the 1850s, centred in Montreal (and this movement would reappear more than once both before and shortly after Confederation). It faced considerable resistance, though—in part because the United States was having one of its periodic convulsions of nativist politics and a furious debate over the slave trade. In fact, the U.S.-annexation movement would receive its final rebuff not from colonial-minded Canadians but from the Confederate states, who feared that the addition of the British North American colonies to the 31 states would tip the political balance of power away from slavery.

A more viable approach to building a less minimal Canada was free trade with the United States—known then as reciprocity, because it didn't propose to banish all duties and tariffs (which were still needed for revenue) but rather to eliminate them on certain key goods and harmonize them on others. There had long been a Canadian movement for reciprocity; suddenly it became the only way to fill the loss of Britain's largesse. Franklin Pierce, the expansionist U.S. president, saw reciprocity as an opening to full annexation of Canada, which he ardently if vaguely desired. The only major barrier was Canada's insignificance. While Canada desperately needed a North American market, the Americans were already making strong inroads into the British market. They saw Canada, with its small and mainly non-consumer population, chiefly as a set of transportation and fishing opportunities. Their exporters wanted to use the Great Lakes and the Canadian canals, and their fishermen wanted access to Maritime waters. They believed in free trade, but it was such a low priority that negotiating a deal took five years, becoming law only in 1854.

This was a fulcrum point in Canada's economic history. For the first time, Canada's resource-based economy and its population were both growing at rates comparable to the fast-expanding U.S. industrial economy, creating a historic opportunity to develop the sort of self-sufficient, export-oriented manufacturing economy that the Americans were. But Canada's manufacturers—dominated by populations of loyal but unambitious Orangemen who had immigrated in the 1820s through 1840s—had little vision of markets beyond their closed colonial confines. They impressed their protectionist views on a colonial government whose main clients were the colony's lumber, grain and fishing interests. As a result, when Governor General Lord Elgin launched reciprocity negotiations on behalf of Canada and the Atlantic colonies, he made it clear from the beginning that the colonies wanted free trade only in raw materials, not in any form of manufactured or processed goods.

Lord Elgin finally persuaded a reluctant U.S. Senate that reciprocity was a safer option than annexation of Canada, and the first Canada-U.S. free-trade deal (and the only one successfully concluded until 1988) took effect on January 1, 1855. It provided duty-free trade in "the growth and produce of the aforesaid British colonies or of the United States"—that is, in the unprocessed products of forests, oceans, mines and farms, plus a few lightly processed products such as sawn lumber, ground flour and preserved meats. In exchange, the United States got unlimited rights to the Atlantic colonies' offshore and inland waters for fishing and the Great Lakes and the St. Lawrence River system for navigation rights, plus a tacit understanding that Canada would not raise tariffs on U.S. manufacturing exports. (Canada would break this promise, raising them in 1858 and 1859.)

Despite being a very limited deal, reciprocity coincided with Canada's most successful decade of nineteenth-century population growth, export growth and economic growth. (It is estimated that the deal itself added 2 to 3 percent to Canada's gross domestic product.) As some economists have pointed out, the growth in exports began a couple of years before reciprocity; this suggests that the larger maximizing impulse in politics and commerce, of which more open borders were only a part, created an environment that encouraged immigrants to stay, boosted exports and built Canada's cities. It didn't last long enough, or provide the necessary tools, for Canada to transform itself into something other than a resource economy. Immigration declined in the late 1850s because of improved conditions at the sending end, and trade stagnated during the American Civil War (1861 to 1865). But the reciprocity decade taught Canadians that population, trade, immigration and diversification are linked and are rooted in an intensified economy, not in territorial growth. And it provided Canadians with an example of a better sort of North American economy, one that they would attempt to revisit many times over the next century and a half.

When reciprocity ended in 1866, it wasn't because Canada had become protectionist but because Canada was British. Washington's fury at Britain for having effectively sided with the Confederacy during the Civil War led Congress to cancel the deal and raise tariff walls amid a worldwide rise in protectionist sentiments. As the United States struggled with Reconstruction and contemplated its new role as a heavily armed military superpower, Britain began to see its string of colonies along the U.S. border as expensive and risky liabilities. For two decades, Britain had sought free trade in manufactured goods with the United States, and by the 1860s many parliamentarians believed that Britain's Canadian colonies, and the resultant British military presence in North America, had become the chief barrier to better political and economic relations between Britain and the United States. Many of them were willing to abandon Canada to win this.

The case for turning Canada into a sovereign nation was pressed aggressively during the Civil War by William Gladstone, chancellor of the exchequer for Britain's newly created Liberal Party (he would soon serve as prime minister). "We cannot place wholly out of view the danger, first, that we might have a war with the United States following after the termination of their present struggle; and, secondly, that the war might involve the invasion of the British North American Provinces," he wrote in an 1864 memorandum. It went on:

> To meet that change, it is above and before all things necessary that the people of those Colonies should cease to have the sentiment and habits of mere dependencies: that we should encourage and aid them to acquire as among themselves more of a corporate and common feeling . . . that they should be themselves, through their Representative and Constitutional Government, the first and chief judges of what may be the proper system and the proper measures of defence for the country . . . [we] should, in a word, shift the centre of responsibility from this metropolis to the capital of Canada. . . . The more Canada and the British Colonies are detached, as to their defensive not less than their administrative responsibilities, from England, the more likely the Union will be to study friendly relations with them.

Privately, he went further. "Canada is England's weakness," Gladstone told a junior minister in 1865. "Till the last British soldier is brought away & Canada is left on her own, we cannot hold our own with the United States." Many British officials (on both the Liberal and Tory benches) agreed that the United States was resistant to opening trade with the United Kingdom because Britain's colonial presence in North America seemed a threat. Some, like Gladstone, imagined a fully independent Canada helping to forge an integrated North American economy whose stability and trade relations would be beneficial to Britain. Some, including Governor General Charles Monck, even suggested that Canada's Confederation should be a first step toward union with the United States. Others simply saw the colonies as an unnecessary expense.

Canadians weren't ready to go as far toward independence as their imperial masters wished. John A. Macdonald expended considerable energy persuading Anglo-Canadian voters that he was not actually seeking independent nationhood, that they would remain British subjects and that Canada would still be a colony. To suggest otherwise was political suicide. And to suggest that Canada might use Confederation to become part of a thriving North American economy, one with a considerably higher standard of living, was also a risky move. While many, including Reform leader George Brown, argued that Confederation could free Canada from its limited mercantilist wood, fish and grain economy and permit a modern economy to grow, this was by no means a popular idea. By 1867 anti-Americanism had become a potent Canadian ideology.

This view was partly a product of demographics. Over the preceding decades, most ambitious and inventive immigrants to Canada had quickly departed for the United States. The colonies were left with a self-selected group who didn't want much from life: an agrarian, very religious, austere population of peasants and labourers who tended to see change and growth as a threat rather than an opportunity and a consumer economy as generally sinful excess. In 1867, about 80 percent of Canada's 3.3 million people were farmers; the majority of them were subsistence farmers, growing only for their own consumption. Among the 25 percent of Canadians who were paid for work, four in ten were employed on farms, a quarter were lumbermen and 10 percent were fishermen. Industrial labour accounted for a small share of the rest, and it was mostly in support of extractive industries: the shipbuilding industry in the Maritimes and the thriving Massey agricultural equipment works in Toronto (its rise a product of trade protectionism). Even the biggest cities, Montreal and Toronto, were mainly agriculture-processing centres; it was not unusual to see herds of cattle driven down Toronto's Yonge Street. The enormous changes that had transformed the Western world in the middle of the nineteenth century—the Industrial Revolution, the rise of great cities and new technologies, and the use of government to ameliorate social ills—had almost entirely bypassed Canada.

So when John A. Macdonald and George-Étienne Cartier began promoting the idea of Confederation, they didn't talk about building an economy and a population capable of thriving in North America. Rather, they spoke of building an alternative east-west economy that would supposedly be a patriotic substitute for the loss of U.S. trade in 1866 and the loss of protected British trade monopolies in 1846, but would maintain Canada's largely resource-based culture. The Canadian provinces, Macdonald's argument went, would thrive and grow by trading with the Canadian provinces.

That idea never really added up. While George Brown boasted that Confederation would bring to the Province of Canada "the addition of nearly a million people to our home consumers," and Macdonald said that it would "give us the control of a market of four millions of people," they knew this wasn't really the case. Because the colonies all produced and exported more or less the same things (timber, grain, fish), there was little to be gained by building internal trade links. And those links didn't really require Confederation anyway. "Let us not," wrote liberal journalist and politician Jean-Baptiste-Éric Dorion, "be lulled with fancies of the great commercial advantages we shall derive from a Confederation of these provinces."

It came back to the root problem of Canada: it did not have the population base to provide sufficient markets to get a robust manufacturing economy going or a tax base to support the kind of institutions and infrastructure a modern country needed. And as long as manufactured goods and equipment could be bought only at a steep duty markup, people weren't going to stick around to set up businesses. As historian Ged Martin concludes, "As consumers, the half-million people of the Maritimes barely qualified as a substitute for Reciprocity with the 31 million people of the United States."

Macdonald was, in principle, in favour of reciprocity in the 1860s, and he would pursue it sporadically but fruitlessly during the first decade of Confederation. But all the while he campaigned against the sort of Canada that would benefit from free trade. In 1876, he would abandon economic change entirely by introducing the National Policy, his signature package of high tariffs on manufactured imports. This policy, which would remain in place in one form or another until after the Second World War, created an economy of protected Canadian copycat manufacturing firms in the major cities and U.S.-owned branch-plant firms in most towns and cities, and it meant that the industrial-age surge in invention and innovation would bypass Canada. It also guaranteed that commercial goods, many foodstuffs, farm equipment and domestic supplies would be considerably more expensive in Canada—a set of factors that deterred immigrants and drove Canadians to emigrate.

A protectionist policy would have made some sense in a country that already had a robust population and fully developed cities and consumer markets. Other countries, including the United States, used protective tariffs in their formative years to build successful industries within large and prosperous domestic markets that could later trade internationally. But Canada, with a tiny and widely dispersed population consisting mainly of poor farmers, did not yet have the population or consumer economy to make such a policy work. As a resource-extraction economy, Canada was dependent on the export of raw materials (the majority of which, by 1867, were going to the United States) and, as a result of the National Policy, on the import of foreign investment. The United States found itself in the opposite position. Its industrial success meant that it imported materials and exported investment capital. Under Canada's National Policy, this contrapuntal relationship would turn into a century-long spiral.

Macdonald's ambitions were nominally expansionist—but he saw expansion primarily as a set of geographic goals; demographic and commercial growth were only means to that end. He recognized the need for a larger population, although only insofar as it would be useful for populating the Prairies and the West. This itself was a form of Canadian exceptionalism: while the Americans had populated their western regions two decades earlier as a response to economic demand and immigration, the Canadians were trying to spur immigration and commercial activity as a way to populate the West. Macdonald saw Western expansion almost exclusively as a strategic and security necessity, as a way to keep the Americans at bay. His major technological goal, a transcontinental railway, was sold to investors and to the British government as a way to defend the frontier and deliver waves of British soldiers should the Yanks attack. (This idea eluded the understanding of military officials, who correctly saw a railway line as a target rather than an asset.) The only time the railway would be used for explicitly military ends would be in 1885, when it was employed to attack fellow Canadians during the North-West Rebellion.

Macdonald cheerfully admitted that the railway was not going to do anything for Canadian economic growth. "It cannot be denied that the Railway, as a commercial enterprise, would be of comparatively little commercial advantage to the people of Canada," he told a Halifax audience in 1864 while selling them on Confederation. "Whilst we have the St. Lawrence in summer, and the American ports in time of peace, we have all that is requisite for progress." Which wasn't quite true: Canada had the right ports and the right canals and riverways for progress; what it lacked was people.

Even the most conservative politicians knew that the long-term success of Confederation would require more people. Its first thirty years involved a near-constant campaign to persuade people, mainly British people, to settle in Canada. The complete failure of this campaign was not from lack of trying—Canada developed its first immigration bureaucracy during these decades. The new country initially placed very few legal restrictions on who could immigrate—but in practice, there were heavy restrictions on what sort of people were sought. Ottawa made it very clear, from the outset, that Canada did not want those who would immigrate to the United States: educated people, merchants, entrepreneurs, urbanites. Canada wanted farmers, and not much else. As Valerie Knowles recounts,

> No sooner had the fledgling dominion come into being than measures were taken to establish a network of emigration agents to advertise this country's attractions to prospective immigrants. Until the advent of the First World War, these immigration salesmen would target farmers with capital, agricultural labourers, and female domestics, preferably from Great Britain, the United States, and northern Europe, in that order. In the picturesque words of one assistant superintendent of immigration, those sought were "men of good muscle who are willing to hustle." Not so welcome were individuals with professions, clerks, or other prospective immigrants of sedentary occupation. They were actually discouraged from emigrating to Canada, while artisans, mechanics, and tradesmen, if not discouraged from doing so, were certainly not courted.

This lack of ambition led, from the outset, to a lack of results. Immigrants weren't staying in Canada, and a good number of established Canadians were departing with them. "Although thousands of foreigners passed through Canada every year, only a small proportion settled here," Kelley and Trebilcock write. "Most of these arrivals were actually in transit to the United States. In passing through Canada, they were joined by hundreds of other immigrants and Canadian residents who, disillusioned with their prospects in Canada, were attracted by the relative prosperity experienced by the nation to the south."

Even those creative and entrepreneurial people who did emerge from Canada's population—and many did—soon found that in order to profit from their talents, they needed to leave Canada, which lacked the resources, markets and institutions they needed to make their ideas work. Alexander Graham Bell came from Scotland to Brantford, Ontario, in 1870, loved the place, and used it as his base for experimentation and repose. But he had to leave for Massachusetts, resettle in the United States and take citizenship there in order to find the investors, laboratories and circles of creative talent he needed to invent, patent and profit from the telephone. It was an American invention produced by a sometime Canadian who couldn't make it work at home.

This problem would continue. Dairy farmer and inventor James L. Kraft of Fort Erie, Ontario, found Canada's markets too limiting and its equipment too expensive. In the 1890s he moved to Illinois to find a sizeable enough market for his high-technology cheese-making ideas. Kraft ended up patenting an orange product that became known as processed cheese or, most tellingly, "American cheese," turning this Canadian's idea into an icon of American culinary identity. The same went for James Naismith, the McGill University graduate and instructor who found Canada's educational institutions too limited and underfunded and had to move in 1891 to Springfield, Massachusetts. There, a large YMCA youth-instruction academy of a sort Canada was incapable of building gave him the freedom and resources he needed to invent and develop the game of basketball. This pattern endured for more than a century: without a big enough domestic market, tax base or institutions, Canadians have had to go abroad to do their greatest work.

Not only was Canada incapable of attracting or keeping its most ambitious people, but many of its leaders were also surprisingly nonchalant about this loss. When George-Étienne Cartier, a Father of Confederation, was told of the huge loss of French Canadians to New England, he is said to have denounced the emigrants: *"Laissez-les partir, c'est la racaille qui s'en va."* (Let them go, it's the riff-raff who are leaving.)

The Canadians fleeing southward weren't riff-raff. While many were poor, they were generally the more ambitious members of struggling communities, the ones who had connections and knowledge and an ability to seek better opportunities. And they were responding sensibly to the Canadian and provincial governments' economic policies, whose logical outcome was a loss of population. The large-scale exodus of French Canadians into New England, Bélanger and Bélanger conclude, was a result of the gross inequality between levels of rural development in Canada and the United States in the nineteenth and twentieth centuries. This wasn't just a matter of Quebec's having a smaller population and more expensive imports; it was the Canadian government's lack of interest in building the markets, financial and government institutions, and trade relations necessary to make the shift from subsistence farming to commercial agriculture and industry. Canada focused its immigration policy almost entirely on farmers but had few financial institutions that could provide financial credit—a crucial agricultural resource—to farmers, especially in Quebec.

"Without proper alternatives, the people of Quebec were condemned to rural life," Bélanger and Bélanger write. "Without credit they could not improve their condition and, consequently, they fell increasingly into poverty. . . . Farmers all over Quebec would have to migrate to big cities in order to find work either to pay off their debts, or after their farms had been foreclosed. Furthermore, lack of credit hampered agricultural modernization which, in turn, engendered un-dynamic, unprofitable farming. Overall, these factors combined to generate poverty even within the most fertile of Quebec's regions."

If those minimizing policies led to a painful loss of French-Canadian population, their consequences in the Prairies were absolutely devastating, and they are still being felt today. Because Macdonald's objective in populating the Prairies was strategic rather than economic, his policy was designed not to build a functioning economy or a sustainable population in the West but rather to fill geographic space. Under the Dominion Lands Act of 1872, willing settlers were given 160 acres for a ten-dollar registration fee, as long as they'd cultivate thirty of those acres and build a house. These settlers found themselves on isolated and relatively unfertile land, located in territories that didn't yet have towns, institutions or distribution networks to connect farmers to markets.

To make matters worse, homesteads could not be established within twenty miles of a train track, because the railways had been granted that prime land by Parliament for future development. Once farmers had covered the extra cost of shipping their produce from their farm to the nearest rail depot, they were charged monopoly railway transportation fees, much higher than those south of the border.

There had been a population living on the Prairies who knew how to make a good living off the land. For the previous two hundred years, those lands had been recognized by Canada as the sovereign territory of the Cree, the Assiniboine and the other indigenous nations of the plains, who had used international trade ties to French and British fur markets and strategic relationships to maintain successful societies there. But the post-Confederation economic mindset, with its basis in territory rather than economies, saw the First Nations and their knowledge as obstacles—a historic shift in Canadian thinking. In 1871, Canada concluded the first of a set of numbered treaties intended to shift these nomadic peoples onto reserves in exchange for promises of cash grants, farming equipment, continuing economic support and medical care.

The entire program of settling the Prairies was a failure. Farmers were spread out over such huge distances without urban development that they wouldn't have crucial markets and networks of mutual support to sustain their agricultural businesses. Those markets and networks quite visibly existed just across the border. As a result, the Canadian West barely grew. In 1881, four years before the Canadian Pacific Railway launched its campaign to populate the Prairies, 180,000 people lived there; after a decade of intensive promotion, that population had risen to only 250,000. During the same period, the U.S. Dakota Territory alone (which became the states of North and South Dakota) grew from 135,000 to 510,000. A good number of those settlers on the American Prairies had passed through Canada first, only to find too many deterrents to stay.

Canadian officials, noticing this loss, at first blamed the weak domestic economy, then the lack of transportation links, then the worldwide economic depression that began in 1873. But economies improved and, in 1885, the transcontinental railway was completed. People kept giving up their homesteads and flooding out of Canada, right up until the final years of the 1890s.

The failure to populate the Prairies, Skelton concludes, was a direct result of economic and trade policies intended to restrict Canada's economy to strictly national confines:

> Manitoba chafed under a 35 per cent tariff on farm implements.... The Canadian Pacific Railway had given the much desired connection with the East and had brought tens of thousands of settlers to the province, but it had not brought abiding prosperity or content. The through rate on wheat from Winnipeg to Montreal was ten cents a bushel more than from St. Paul to New York, an equal distance; and, from the farm to Liverpool, the Minnesota farm had fifteen cents a bushel the advantage of his Manitoba neighbour.... Coal and lumber and general merchandise cost from two to four times as much to ship as for equal distances in the eastern provinces. ... A more effective means of stirring up ill-feeling between East and West and of discouraging immigration to the prairies could hardly have been devised.

In its haste to plant the flag on the plains, the Canadian government failed to provide any of the economic, infrastructural or municipal resources the settlers needed to make a sustainable living. And in its haste to get the original, economically successful inhabitants of the plains off that land, Canada failed to provide most of the resources promised in its treaties. Instead it pursued a policy that all but eliminated the original peoples.

Health scholar James Daschuk concludes, in *Clearing the Plains*, his study of the sudden and dramatic decline in the health and human development of the plains tribes, that the Prairie-settlement policies had "displaced the indigenous people from their once lucrative position on the periphery of the global economy. It was the alienation of the First Nations from a viable economic base in the world system and the imposed environmental constraints of the reserve system that played a key role in the decline of their health in the late nineteenth century." To persuade Cree to give up their land and move onto appointed reserves, government officials withheld food, "forcing them to trade freedom for rations" and permanently excluding them from participation in the emerging agrarian economy. Once they were on their reserves, the medical aid and famine relief failed to materialize and "food placed in ration houses was withheld for so long that much of it rotted." Food aid was withheld throughout the famine of 1878–1880, creating the ecological preconditions for a massive tuberculosis outbreak. The formerly thriving First Nations, deprived of economic relations and open trading, "fell into a decades-long cycle of malnutrition, suppressed immunity and sickness from tuberculosis and other diseases."

The cooperative, equal-nations approach to indigenous relations that had defined Canada in its early centuries withered during the constricted years of the nineteenth century and came to a complete and violent end in the 1880s and 1890s. By pursuing a policy of closed borders, resource-extraction economics, ethnic homogeneity and purely agrarian geographic expansion, Canada was directly responsible for the depressed social and economic conditions that provoked the Metis and Cree uprisings of 1885 in the North-West Rebellion and made violent military attack the only response Ottawa could contemplate. And the view of First Nations as obstacles led to the conclusion that they could be neutralized, or forcefully assimilated, by seizing their children and raising them, away from their families, in residential schools, where they experienced, at best, demeaning treatment and isolation from family and community, and in many cases serious and sometimes lethal physical, emotional and sexual abuse. Those seizures became mandatory under the Indian Act of 1894 and would grow in number for at least half a century.

By 1896, it was readily apparent to most Canadians that Confederation had failed to create the prosperous and self-sufficient country Macdonald had envisaged. Canada's economy, its cities, its standard of living and its population were all too thin and sparse to support its physical expansion across an entire continent. In the well-turned phrase of Macdonald's biographer Richard Gwyn, "Canada's very existence constituted a denial of geography, demography and commerce." By century's end, a majority of Canadians were ready to end the denial.

CHAPTER 3

The Fifteen-Year Canadian Century

By the end of the nineteenth century, it was clear to many Canadians that the minimizing impulse had become a self-reinforcing spiral. Low population density starved the government of revenues and crushed economic productivity, making Canada reliant on tariff walls and unable to build trading relationships beyond raw materials. This drove prices up and choked off business development within Canada, discouraging immigrants from settling and Canadians from staying. The loss of population growth increased ethnic homogeneity and therefore political pressure to remain a colonial resource economy. In an 1891 letter to constituents that was widely quoted and circulated over the next several years, former federal Liberal leader Edward Blake described the effects of this vicious circle:

It has left us with a small population, a scanty immigration, and a North-West empty still; with enormous additions to our public debt and yearly charge, an extravagant system of expenditure and an unjust and expensive tariff, with restricted markets for our needs, whether to buy or to sell, and all the host of evils thence arising; with unfriendly relations and frowning tariff walls, even more and more estranging us from the mighty English-speaking nation to the south. . . . Worse, far worse. It has left us with lowered standards of public virtue and death-like apathy in public opinion; with racial, religious and provincial animosities. . . . It has left us with our hands tied, our future compromised.

How to break this cycle became the great political debate of the 1890s. By 1893 Blake's successor, Wilfrid Laurier, had come up with a formula. It would not be enough to tinker with the details of national policy. Canada would need a shock program in which it would change its approach to immigration and population, its trade relationships and its economic basis.

As a bilingual French Canadian who had experienced the late nineteenth century's effects on his community, Laurier understood the mutually reinforcing relationship between free trade, shared societies, economic diversification and population growth. As an inveterate politician, however, he realized that this package would be a tough sell. In the 1890s, many Anglo-Canadians had become infected with the triple pathogen of anti-Americanism, colonial nostalgia and the new European invention known as ethnic nationalism. And the Montreal and Ontario business communities were enjoying their near-monopoly status under the steep anti-U.S. tariffs of the National Policy and lobbying hard to keep it.

So Laurier, who always put electoral pragmatism ahead of

ideological purity, campaigned in 1896 on a promise to break with his career-long commitment to full reciprocity and maintain Macdonald's tariffs against the United States. He also promised to build closer colonial-style economic relations with the United Kingdom, to strike a compromise on contentious French-English intercommunal issues such as public funding of Catholic schools, and to populate the Prairies more effectively. He persuaded even his most skeptical opponents that he believed in these ideas, leading his Liberals to a strong parliamentary majority—one his party would hold for fifteen years and through four elections.

That decade and a half, viewed from the distance of a century, is the most productive and expansive time Canada has ever experienced—a decisive break with the minimizing impulse and the advent of an entirely new approach to building the country. Never before in its history—and never since—has Canada grown so rapidly and so successfully in population, in economic activity, in urbanization, in ethnic diversity, in scope of government and in standard of living. The vicious circle became a virtuous circle in which demography, economics, trade and urbanization drove one another to new heights. This was a huge and lasting change. A very large proportion of present-day Canadians are descended from the three million immigrants who arrived as part of the Laurier wave; a large part of Canada's current economy is descended from the enterprises and institutions that were born during those years, including the classic big companies of the steel, aluminum, chemical, communication, automobile, food-processing and finance sectors; and the rail, canal and hydroelectric power networks that shaped industrial Canada.

The change in Canada's population and prosperity was unprecedented. Through the first decade of the twentieth century, Canada experienced annual economic growth rates approaching a staggering 10 percent, and similar increases in almost every other measure of well-being. This was in good part because the population of Canadians increased even more dramatically: Laurier and his cabinet had finally found the formula for attracting, and keeping, unprecedented numbers of people. In 1897, only 21,716 immigrants entered Canada, and most were from Britain. By 1901, that number had doubled to more than 50,000 annually; by 1906, it had quadrupled again to 200,000 (and British immigrants had fallen to less than a third). In Laurier's final year in office it hit 300,000 and in 1913, before the Borden government found a way to shut down the Laurier immigration drive, it would reach an all-time peak of 400,000, or 5 percent of the population. For similar growth rates to occur today, Canada would need to receive 1.75 million immigrants per year.

Yet from Laurier's perspective, the fifteen years were something of a disappointment. He came nowhere close to achieving what he had wanted in population, trade and development. He raised Canada's population by 43 percent, to almost eight million, but that was far short of the forty million he estimated that Canada would need by the 1920s in order to function fully. Likewise, he had created a far more integrated North American economy, but free trade eluded and, in the end, defeated him. He was right to be disappointed by the long-term results: it proved not to be Canada's century, as his famous slogan suggested, but rather Canada's fifteen years. He used those years to write the instruction manual for turning Canada into a full and sustainable country, but it would be three generations before anyone seriously picked it up again.

"We are just at the beginning of the twentieth century," Laurier told an audience at Toronto's Massey Hall in 1904. "We are a nation of six million people already; we expect soon to be twenty-five, yes, forty millions. There are men, living, in this audience, [young] men over there, the hope of the country, who before they die, if they live to old age, will see this country with at least sixty millions of people."

This was political hoopla, and it earned eager and sustained applause. But those were not arbitrary numbers. Laurier knew Canada's extensive geography well and had seen the effects of sparse population on economic development and human well-being in Quebec's farms, Ontario's cities and the abandoned Prairies—and on Ottawa's balance sheets. By the time he gave that speech, the United States had attained a population of 84 million—more than twice that of Britain—and was using that huge and flourishing consumer market (and tax base) to dominate the world's economy. The U.S. used that demographic and economic heft to woo Canadian immigrants and citizens and to play a dominant role in the Canadian economy by serving as the main source of investment and often ownership. As Michael Hart notes, during the Laurier years and the decades that followed, Canada's manufacturing economy was "dependent on imported capital, technology and management" from south of the border. Laurier had made the calculations that so many future Canadians would make, and he understood the numbers needed to make the country, and its industry, infrastructure and government, work—and the reasons why those numbers had not previously grown.

This was all changing fast. The world had become a different place by the time of Laurier's 1896 election, in ways that made Canada much more attractive to prospective newcomers. The new technologies of the 1890s had made Canada a more viable prospect for settlers. Most important was the Canadian development of hybrid high-yield, cold-climate grains, especially the hardy Marquis wheat, better suited to shorter growing seasons. Combined with the now widespread availability of the steel plough and the development of dry farming techniques (notably the use of fallow crops), this meant that western Canadian farms were suddenly capable of earning a significant return, even with higher equipment and transportation costs than their U.S. neighbours. It also meant that Canada would from now on be a net exporter of food, often on a very large scale.

This agricultural revolution was centred on Manitoba, which had been settled earlier in the nineteenth century. Not until after 1907 would Saskatchewan and Alberta become major grain producers. But the innovations meant that these provinces would attract a lot of people, including Americans, hoping to take advantage of free land and become part of the Wheat Boom during the first decade of the twentieth century.

Canada was also developing a real urban economy, even on the plains. Western settlement had failed before 1896 in good part because the Prairies had not yet developed the urban infrastructure and networks—transportation, banking, marketing, wholesale and retail—necessary to make commercial farming work. The beginnings of the Second Industrial Revolution (involving steel, electricity, petroleum engines and chemicals) finally allowed the growth of central Canadian cities, which only in the late 1890s possessed the size and development to make industrial economies succeed.

On top of this, at the turn of the century the world had a seemingly limitless supply of people wanting to move. Huge populations in eastern and southern Europe and in Asia were being driven out by wars, famines, pogroms, ethnic-nationalist politics, economic change and overpopulation. The revolution in capital-intensive, high-productivity agriculture was driving people out of the western European countryside, while just as many were wishing to leave the continent's urban slums, especially in Britain. And the farmlands of the western United States were believed to be fully populated and faced rising land prices, enticing many rural Americans to look northward for a better deal, much as they had in the late eighteenth century.

To capitalize on this mass desire for a safer and more productive place to live, Laurier and his colleagues needed to unblock the two major barriers that had prevented people from coming to, and staying in, Canada. First, the high cost of doing business and lack of substantial markets caused by a trade-restricted economy, and second, the near-complete lack of interest among the world's people, especially non-British people, in considering Canada as a place to live.

Laurier understood the barrier to immigration created by trade—but he was trapped, throughout his prime ministership, by the Anglo-Canadian antipathy to reciprocity. In 1897 his finance minister, W.S. Fielding, found a compromise: he eliminated the brick-wall protective tariffs of the National Policy, though still granting preferential rates to Britain and maintaining higher tariffs against the United States. But Fielding had provided a loophole. As soon as any protectionist country—that is, the United States—lowered its tariffs to the same level as Canada's, it would also be granted a preferential tariff rate. In fact, a number of other loopholes added to the policy by Fielding and Laurier allowed U.S. trade and investment to cross the border more freely.

That left Laurier and Fielding to the small matter of convincing a U.S. president, or Congress, to reduce tariffs on Canada. By 1899, Laurier was trying to negotiate a wider tariff-cutting deal as part of a complex joint commission on Canada-Britain-U.S. relations. He botched the negotiation, making genuine free trade a non-starter until 1910, when both Canada and the United States would pursue it aggressively and it would become the key issue in the following year's fateful Canadian election.

Even without a grand agreement, Canada-U.S. trade opened considerably during the first decade of the twentieth century. Ottawa and Washington, under several administrations, believed in a more integrated economy and worked to lower individual tariffs and to eliminate other barriers to cross-border commerce and investment. And in spite of the tariff, ordinary Canadians and Americans began linking their local and personal economies through cross-border movement and business transactions.

The results were spectacular. Canada-U.S. trade soared, and Britain ceased to be the major player in the Canadian economy. By the end of the century's first decade, U.S. imports had risen from half to two-thirds of Canadian consumption, while British imports had fallen from one-third to one-fifth—and this was in spite of Britain's preferential tariff.

Much of Canada's economic growth was financed by the United States. Taking advantage of the loopholes in the Canadian tariff—and an Ottawa administration favourably disposed toward North American trade—the thriving U.S. economy poured capital into the upstart Canadian industrial sector.

Laurier's Liberals were, in effect, building Canada on the back of an illusion. Ottawa showed all the signs of moving closer to the British Empire, from its Union Jack emblems to its preferential tariffs. But Canada was enthusiastically integrating itself into the North American economy at a brisk pace and turning its back quickly on the colonial motherland. As historians Robert Craig Brown and Ramsay Cook describe, the shift from a British to a North American economy was as much a matter of cultural factors as economic ties: "British manufacturing representatives in Canada," they write, "were smug, complacent, and poor. American business firms were aggressive and prosperous. British investors shied away from Canadian development schemes because they were so notoriously speculative; American capitalists, urged on by the Canadian business and political community, gobbled them up."

If Canada could no longer rely on British trade and investment to build its economy, even less could it rely on British immigrants to bolster its population. The single-minded focus of nineteenth-century Canadian leaders on stocking the country with loyal British subjects not only hadn't worked—they, too, had left for the United States—but it had also deprived Canada of the tens of millions of highly productive people who had fled the rest of Europe, and a good part of Asia, to settle in North America.

In his effort to launch Canada's population into the tens of millions, Laurier knew he needed to recruit the majority of new Canadians from beyond Britain and western Europe. And he knew that this would require the sort of recruitment, advertising and promotion campaign that no colony had ever undertaken. He appointed Clifford Sifton, a Manitoba politician who acutely understood the problems of underpopulation, as his interior minister with specific responsibility for immigration.

Sifton approached immigration as a marketing problem: "The immigration work," he declared, "has to be carried on in the same manner as the sale of any commodity; just as soon as you stop advertising and missionary work, the movement is going to stop." To make it work, he hired scores of immigration agents and staff to set up offices across Europe, from Dublin to Kiev and from Turin to Helsinki; across the United Kingdom; and across the western United States, where Canada had as many as twenty-four U.S. immigration offices in operation at any time, most in the West.

The scope of this promotion and outreach campaign, which extended across a dozen countries, is described by Kelley and Trebilcock:

> It included the widespread use of marketing surveys; stylized brochures and promotional pamphlets; large advertisements in the British popular press; billboards in prominent locations; and the exhibition of Canadian grains and produce at agricultural fairs, Canadian government offices, and the offices of leading steamship booking agents. The government also publicized the attractions of Canada in schools by distributing wall maps, atlases, and textbooks

on Canada, and by sponsoring essay contests on the subject of Canada. The agents of steamship companies, colonization organizations, and railways were offered bonuses for every agriculturalist, farm worker, and domestic worker they assisted in emigrating to Canada. Their interests in recruitment were myriad and included the sale of transatlantic tickets, increased passage and freight on Canadian rail lines, potential land purchasers, and, in the case of rail companies, possible workers for their burgeoning construction projects.

A significant proportion of the newcomers to Canada in the Laurier years were de facto refugees who had to flee illegally to other countries before they could be enticed to make a passage to Canada. Many European governments had outlawed the emigration of their citizens, so a big part of Canada's immigration campaign during the Sifton years was a clandestine program to circumvent European governments. Carried out through the misleadingly named North Atlantic Trading Company, the program involved a secret network of shipping agents in key port cities who were paid bonuses by Ottawa to redirect settlers and emigrants to Canada. The agents were paid a fee for every European adult (defined as anyone over twelve) they persuaded to take free passage to Canada.

Significantly, the program operated in a wide range of European countries: Russia, Austria, Germany, Romania, Switzerland, northern Italy, Belgium, Holland and France (the latter was probably used to channel central and eastern European migrants into Canada). Many Canadians considered immigrants from some of these places to be "civilizationally incompatible" with Anglo-American society.

Slavs and southern Europeans in particular were considered not just alien in the early twentieth century, they were widely described as members of different and incompatible races who could never assimilate or intermarry with westerners.

But Sifton and Laurier differed from other politicians of the time, including some in their own party, in that they did not see culture as a major factor to consider when selecting new Canadians (though skin colour would prove to be another matter). They both broadly expressed the opinion that most anyone possessed of agricultural or labour skills could become a successful member of Canadian society. "We have not been disposed to exclude foreigners of any nationality who seemed likely to become successful agriculturalists," Sifton told Laurier in a 1901 memo.

This pluralist view also had strong circles of support in the private sector. William Van Horne, the powerful oligarch who ran the Canadian Pacific Railway, expressed the new ethos in a 1905 speech:

> What we want is population. Labour is required from the Arctic Ocean to Patagonia, throughout North and South America, but the governments of other lands are not such idiots as we are in the matter of restricting immigration. Let them all come in. There is work for all. Every two or three men that come into Canada and do a day's work create new work for someone else to do. They are like a new dollar. Hand it out from the Bank and it turns itself in value a dozen or more times a year.

This included an understanding that immigrants from minority language and cultural groups tend to integrate more effectively—and arrive in greater numbers—if they are permitted to cluster together in self-supporting communities, so they can build up networks of mutual support in their effort to establish themselves. This was known at the time as "block settlement" and was applied especially to the huge numbers of Ukrainians who settled during these years. It went even further with some minority communities and religious sects (notably Mennonites, Hutterites and Doukhobors), who were allowed to form self-sufficient settlements, set up their own independent school systems within those settlements, and in some cases even be exempted from military service. Most of these settlements thrived and, within a generation or two, blended into the Canadian fabric while keeping some distinct characteristics. The Doukhobors (a Russian Christian sect whose settlement in Canada took place because Leo Tolstoy persuaded Canadian scholars and politicians that they would be good farmers and needed asylum from Russian oppression) were less inconspicuous: the activities of their more radical branch, including nude marches and arson, caused public outrage and threatened to discredit the entire settlement system.

Despite such controversies—which led to the replacement of Sifton with the more conservative Frank Oliver after 1905—the clustered settling of non-Western immigrants would continue, and it would largely be a success. The use of self-regulated ethnic settlements is arguably the only pure example of multiculturalism Canada has experienced; the 1970s policy of that name was devoted to a far milder form of pluralism that hardly bears any comparison.

Laurier-era pluralism certainly had its limits—particularly with regard to Asian immigrants, black Americans (only a couple of thousand of whom, at most, were allowed into Canada during this decade, at the height of their Great Migration), and Jews (whom Laurier begrudgingly admitted in limited numbers, including to some Prairie settlements, but generally used policies to discourage). Those self-imposed racial and ethnic restrictions, and the rising backlash from opposition Conservatives against communities of Asians and non-Western Europeans in Canada, would become the most significant impediment to Laurier's achieving his population goals.

The irony is that British immigrants settled (and stayed) in unprecedented numbers, largely as a result of the government's aggressive promotion and outreach campaigns in the United Kingdom. In 1900, before the immigration campaigns had begun in earnest, fewer than 1,200 Britons came to Canada; that number had soared to 86,796 by 1906, when for the first time it exceeded British immigration to the United States. It would then reach a peak of 142,622 on the eve of the First World War. Never before, and never since, have so many British people moved to Canada.

But even as their numbers reached a historic high, British-Canadian immigrants became a minority. The United Kingdom, even at its peak, could not provide anywhere close to the number of immigrants Canada needed to fill its basic economic and demographic needs, so the majority of Canada's immigration originated elsewhere. "To the chagrin of Canada's contemporary ethnocentrists," David Verbeeten writes, "as the absolute number of immigrants from Britain went up, so did the relative proportion go down."

By the time British immigration numbers peaked, only 38 percent of immigrants to Canada were British or Irish (that percentage had dipped as low as 22 percent in the first years of the century). Another third of Canada's immigrants, almost as many as those from Britain, were coming from the United States (and they were Americans of many ethnicities, including a great many German Americans, Italian Americans, Hungarian Americans, Icelandic Americans and Scandinavian Americans). For the first time in a century, the number of Americans moving to Canada outnumbered the Canadians leaving for the States (though it is estimated that a million Canadians nevertheless moved southward in the century's first decade).

What really changed the nature of Canada's population and future growth, however, was the 25 to 30 percent of immigrants during each year of the Laurier era who were considered to be of non-Western origins—Slavic, Nordic, southern European and Asian. These new Canadians—whose backgrounds did not represent either of Canada's historic colonial occupiers or its indigenous peoples—were a rising force in Canadian life, culture and politics. By 1911, these "other" Canadians had risen to 9 percent of the population. By 1921, they were 15 percent. Their proportion would continue to grow through the century, even during the decades when immigration numbers all but stopped or reversed. Without really noticing, Canada had become a country whose ethnic identity was no longer connected to its colonial origins.

However, the shift to non-imperial immigration sources was certainly not a result of generosity or pluralist sentiments—not in 1897, and not when it next arose in the 1950s, either. Canadian governments looked beyond Britain because British emigrants were both too few and too uninterested in the types of labour Canada thought it needed.

This was particularly true of British immigrants in the early twentieth century, who showed a distinct lack of interest in becoming farmers. During the Laurier era, only 18 percent of British immigrants ended up starting an agricultural homestead, versus 33 percent of American immigrants and 29 percent of continental Europeans. (Britons weren't respected by Ukrainian and American farmers on the Prairies, either: it was not uncommon for Calgary and Edmonton job advertisements to carry the phrase "No English Need Apply.")

Those homesteading numbers betray another important fact about the Laurier-era population boom. Only a minority of immigrants of any origin ended up going into agriculture. This was rarely mentioned or even noticed at the time because of a second, even more pervasive illusion the Laurier revolution was built upon. It was a myth epitomized by Canada's chief marketing symbol, emblazoned across every immigration-promotion wagon in Europe and every patriotic advertisement from Ottawa: the bundled sheaf of wheat.

It was an article of faith that Canada's success, both in population and in economic growth, was a result of the Wheat Boom. Canada believed itself to be a rural country and ardently believed that its economy was fundamentally agrarian and resource-based—after all, it had been so throughout the nineteenth century. While Canadian officials at the time noticed that the cities and their industries were expanding at an almost unmanageable pace, they believed this to be a side effect of the Wheat Boom. Surely all those factories were simply there to supply the demand for equipment and goods created by the farmers and their railways. And surely the reason the great majority of immigrants were settling in the cities, and in central

Canada, was to bide their time until they had saved enough money to start a homestead. A good number of scholars and politicians continued to believe this wheat-led vision of Canadian growth for generations after the Laurier era.

Laurier and his officials certainly believed it—in fact, they believed it to the extent that they abjectly refused to admit any immigrants who did not have rural backgrounds and avowedly agrarian intentions. They actively discouraged, denied and sometimes turned away immigrants who sought to work or start businesses in technical, industrial or urban service-industry fields.

"Our desire is to promote the immigration of farmers and farm labourers," Sifton told Laurier. "It is admitted that additions to the population of our cities and towns by immigration is undesirable from every standpoint and such additions do not in any way whatsoever contribute to the object which is constantly kept in view by the Government of Canada in encouraging immigration for the development of natural resources and the increase of production of wealth from these resources."

Sifton, in his most famous sentence, declared that his ideal immigrant was "a stalwart peasant in a sheepskin coat, born to the soil, whose forefathers have been farmers for ten generations, with a stout wife and a half-dozen children." He, his cabinet successors and Laurier stuck rigidly to this ideal. In 1898, Sifton ordered a railway car full of Italian labourers headed to the Prairies to return to New York, not because they were Italian (which he tolerated, so long as they were northern Italians), but because they were too urban.

And there seemed to be plenty of evidence to support this belief. The Wheat Boom was real (at least it was after 1907). Wheat had eclipsed timber as Canada's great export, and with the successful settling of the Prairies in the latter half of the century's first decade, became a truly huge export, turning Canada into the world's breadbasket. But as significant as wheat had become as Canada's chief resource export, it was not the dominant factor in the growth of the Canadian economy—and it was not what was drawing most immigrants to Canada or employing them once they arrived. An even larger change was taking place in Canada, one that had already eclipsed its entire resource economy.

"The . . . rapid economic development of those years was largely a boom in manufacturing," Queen's University economist Marvin McInnis concludes in an analysis of the era's financial flows. "The rapid growth of manufacturing industry and the elaboration of its structure, along with the rapid growth of the economy as a whole, cannot plausibly be explained as a response to or consequence of the Wheat Boom, [which] was not associated with unusually rapid growth of real per capita income. It did not even raise the growth rate of aggregate output of the economy."

What really drove Canada's economic and population growth in those years, McInnis and other economists have concluded, were new industries far removed from the Prairies: the booming steel works in Sydney, Hamilton and Sault Ste. Marie; the hydroelectric generation stations springing up across Canada and the industrial electrification boom they produced; the big business of internal combustion engines; the secondary wood industries such as pulp and paper; the chemical industries (especially aluminum and calcium carbide); the smelting of nonferrous metals such as lead and tin, especially in British Columbia; and the mass production of cheese, butter and bacon in central Canada's cities, mainly for large-scale export to the British market. These industries weren't consequences of the Wheat Boom. Canada's steel mills didn't make railway tracks for the Canadian Pacific Railway (which continued to import them from the United States), and most of those other products were shipped across the Atlantic or the U.S. border, not into the Prairies.

This is borne out in the numbers. About 70 percent of the immigrants who came to Canada between 1900 and 1910 ended up employed in non-agricultural industry or transportation; specifically, 50 percent settled directly in cities and another 30 percent worked in resource or railway companies. In other words, only three in ten of Canada's supposedly purely agrarian immigrants went into farming. On top of this, as Knowles observes, "many of those immigrants who entered the agricultural force as wage labourers soon left it entirely to work elsewhere"—that is, to work in non-agrarian sectors—"but still the government persisted in promoting the immigration of agriculturalists."

The Laurier government was neglecting a key fact about modern agriculture: the more food an area of land is able to produce, the fewer people it needs living on the land to produce it. (Today about 2 percent of Canadians are employed in agriculture, and Canada produces considerably more food than it consumes.) Rural land can support populations or it can produce food; by the nineteenth century, most of Canada's land had switched to productivity. This, after all, was why so many Europeans were seeking to emigrate to Canada in the first place. Their rural villages, after high-productivity agricultural commercialization, no longer had any use for most of the people living in them. Canada needed some farmers, but not as much as it needed almost every other kind of immigrant.

As a consequence, the Laurier government neglected another fairly visible fact: at the turn of the century Canada was experiencing its own, internal, migration boom. Hundreds of thousands of established Canadians were moving from rural areas into cities as Canada's own agriculture modernized and its economies changed. During the Laurier years, Montreal grew by 50 percent, Toronto by 81 percent, Winnipeg by 200 percent, Edmonton (which had barely existed at the era's beginning) by 600 percent and Vancouver by 300 percent. At the beginning of that era, in 1896, two-thirds of Canadians lived in rural areas. By the end of the 1910s, half of Canadians lived in cities. This huge shift (like the one taking place in Asia today) was not simply a matter of immigrants coming to cities; it was a decision made by a great proportion of Canadian families as well.

And contrary to the Laurier government's language, it wasn't simply a case of migrants (both from other countries and from rural Canada) filling jobs in a pre-existing urban and industrial economy. A sizeable proportion of those immigrants were starting their own businesses, usually small at first but often growing into large manufacturing enterprises. The immigrants weren't coming just to participate in employment and economic growth; they were one of the chief causes of it.

The really significant thing that happened to Canada in the 1910s was not that wheat production and British immigration reached peak levels, but that both were eclipsed. For the first time since the War of 1812, most immigrants to Canada weren't British. And for the first time, the majority of Canada's immigration, and population, and economic activity, was not rural. The Laurier wave was not so much an intensification as a shift: it turned Canada into an urban, non-British country.

Politicians dared not mention these changes and often appeared not to comprehend that they were taking place. This was one of the chief reasons why Laurier fell so far short of his population goals. By actively excluding non-rural immigrants, Canada was depriving itself of an even larger population source, and of precisely the sort of people its economy most needed. Canada nevertheless did well: almost as soon as they'd landed, those self-described farmers eagerly turned themselves into mechanics and technicians and merchants, and 200,000 immigrants a year during most of the decade after 1900 was an extraordinary accomplishment. But it's worth keeping in mind that the United States averaged 800,000 immigrants a year during that same decade, and about four out of five of those immigrants settled in cities. A great many of them, given the opportunity, would happily have made their start in a newly optimistic Canada.

The most serious lost opportunity for Canada during that decade, in the long run, was not the exclusion of urbanites. It was the increasing antagonism toward racial and religious minorities, both as prospective immigrants and as existing Canadian citizens. This intolerance would not only reduce Canada's population opportunities during the Laurier years, it would also threaten Laurier's leadership before becoming the dominant form of politics for the next several decades.

It was not as if Canada was an all-white country at the beginning of the twentieth century. Chinese, Japanese and Sikhs had sizeable settlements on the west coast, black Canadians had long been established in Nova Scotia and Ontario, and there were pockets of other racial-minority groups, such as the indigenous Hawaiians known as Kanaka who had arrived with the shipping trade and established a community on Vancouver Island.

The Chinese had been living in Canada in substantial numbers since the late 1860s, drawn and recruited to British Columbia by the railway construction boom and the gold rush; they continued arriving in steady chain migration movements through the early 1900s. Macdonald, who saw them as racially inferior and incompatible with what he called the "Aryan character" of Canada, passed the Chinese Immigration Act of 1885, which imposed a fifty-dollar head tax on each Chinese arrival. He underestimated the determination of Chinese Canadians to reunite their families; thousands continued to save or borrow money to pay the head tax in order to come to Canada.

By the early twentieth century the Chinese and their descendants were well established and integrated Canadians, albeit Canadians subject to considerable discrimination and segregation. Thousands of them lived in the populous towns, urban districts and agricultural regions they had settled. The Japanese began to settle in British Columbia in the earliest years of the twentieth century, often using the shipping industry to gain passage via Hawaii to Vancouver Island. And Sikhs began settling around 1904, shiploads of them arriving from the Punjab to fill gaping labour shortages in the lumber industry; they numbered more than five thousand by 1908 and were well regarded as workers and merchants.

By that time, however, a new political movement was rising in Canada, one whose rallying slogan was "White Canada." Notions of racial superiority had become more or less commonplace by the end of the nineteenth century. But they exploded into Canadian consciousness shortly after the turn of the century, inflamed by settler rivalries in British Columbia, Conservative politicians inflaming passions against Liberal immigration policies, and a wave of dark ideas emerging from Europe.

In 1907, Canadians came out in droves to see a cross-country speaking tour by Rudyard Kipling, who had just won the Nobel Prize in Literature. He received lengthy ovations and admiring coverage in the newspapers as he delivered off-the-cuff advice on stopping Asian immigration to the Canadian West, where he owned land.

"Immigration is what you want in the West," Kipling told his audience in Toronto on October 18. "You must have labourers there. You want immigration, and the best way to keep the yellow man out is to get the white man in. If you keep out the white then you will have the yellow man, for you must have labour. Work must be done, and there is certain work to do which a white man won't do so long as he can get a yellow man to do it. Pump in the immigrants from the Old Country. Pump them in; England has five millions of people to spare." The *New York Times* covered the speech prominently with the headline "Flood Canada with White Men—Kipling."

This was potent stuff, and Robert Borden's Conservatives seized upon it. (In fact, Kipling would later intervene on behalf of Borden in the 1911 federal election, penning an influential front-page editorial denouncing Laurier's open-border policies; some believe it turned the election.)

Kipling had deliberately chosen an explosive moment to demand a whiter Canada. Only six weeks earlier—likely when the author had been on the west coast—Vancouver had endured three days of destructive anti-Asian riots, in which thousands of furious white Vancouverites, whipped up by a group calling itself the Asiatic Exclusion League, had destroyed Chinese and Japanese businesses and homes. The riots of 1907 would prove a turning point in Canadian immigration policy and national politics.

Borden, whose party had slumped through three unsuccessful federal elections, knew an opportunity when he saw it. He raced to Vancouver to join the emerging "White Canada" movement. "British Columbia must remain a British and Canadian province," he declared in a Vancouver speech days after the riots, "inhabited and dominated by men in whose veins runs the blood of those great pioneering races which built up and developed not only Western, but Eastern Canada."

Laurier, who had appeared ambivalent about Asian Canadians before, tried to fight off this new Conservative threat by tightening up immigration laws. He'd raised the Chinese head tax to $100 in 1900, to little effect: as many as five thousand Chinese emigrants a year saved or borrowed enough money to pay this substantial sum. But then, facing pressure from B.C. parliamentarians, he had raised it to a prohibitive $300 in 1904. This temporarily ended Chinese immigration but caused a rise in Japanese and Punjabi arrivals; until 1908 as many as seven thousand Japanese a year were arriving to fill lumber industry labour shortages. (In fact, false rumors of a pending shipload of as many as fifty thousand Japanese had triggered the Vancouver riots.) Laurier commissioned his deputy minister of labour, William Lyon Mackenzie King, to investigate; King declared some Asian groups "wholly unsuited to this country" and recommended stronger restrictions. Laurier negotiated a deal with the Japanese government in which they would restrict their own emigration.

The numbers would immediately fall, though about five hundred Japanese a year would migrate to Canada for the next two decades, until they were banned outright.

Laurier's efforts did little to stop Borden's anti-immigration campaign. During the tumultuous 1908 election, Borden embraced the "White Canada" movement. He sent a telegram to the B.C. Conservatives that ran in the province's newspapers and was repeatedly read at rallies: "Your message received. The Conservative Party stands for a white Canada, the protection of white labour and the absolute exclusion of Asiatics." (Borden would later claim that he had not written the last six words of this message, though not until after the election was done.) It was not enough to win the election, but the Conservatives gained ten seats (a fifth of the House), including a strong majority of seats in British Columbia—a clear signal that the exclusionary messages had worked.

In response, Laurier passed a new immigration law in 1910 that, for the first time, allowed the exclusion of immigrants based on racial or ethnic identity; its Section 38 permitted the cabinet to place bans on "immigrants belonging to any race deemed unsuited to the climate or requirements of Canada." That clause would be applied aggressively in the decades after the First World War. More broadly, the act had the effect of making immigration more difficult and complicated for anyone, immediately placing the Canadian government's immigration bureaucracy in conflict with Canada's almost universally agreed-upon need for more people.

But the new law did not, at first, stop Canada's migratory population growth. If anything, it provoked a sizeable rush among Europeans seeking admission to Canada before the doors slammed shut.

By now, Laurier felt hemmed in on all sides, his maximizing ambitions limited on one hand by the electoral threat of mass anti-immigrant uprisings, and on the other by the high cost of trading with the United States (likely a major reason why a million Canadians had moved to the States during this decade). And then, at an inconvenient moment, he got a break on the second front. William Howard Taft, the newly elected Republican president, used his December 1910 message to Congress to propose a full and comprehensive reciprocity deal with Canada, one that would slash tariffs on manufactured imports to Canada and most Canadian exports to the United States. Taken by surprise, Laurier rushed into negotiations, which produced a deal, the Reciprocity Agreement, by the end of January 1911 that passed through Congress into U.S. law by the end of July. It only needed Canadian approval—and here Laurier ran into trouble.

Anti-American sentiments among Canadians had been mounting through the decade as the United States passed through its age of bellicose imperialism, and a good portion of Laurier's Liberal caucus, plus all the Tories, sided with central Canada's manufacturers, who favoured their protected near-monopoly status over any policies that would lower the costs of living and doing business for Canadians in general. Laurier decided to win a consensus in favour of the deal, which he was sure Canadian voters would support, by calling an election in 1911.

Borden seized the moment. The combination of anti-immigrant whites-only rhetoric in Western Canada with anti-American "no trade or truck with the Yankee" messages in central and eastern Canada was potent. Borden warned voters that Canada would be consumed by the worst American afflictions, including lynchings, alcohol and divorce, if any step were made toward continental integration. His message was, in essence, a more heated version of the minimizing politics of the decades leading up to 1837: a limited mono-ethnic, closed-border, colonial and agrarian Canada. It mattered little that he was delivering this message long after the reality had changed and neither Canada nor the Canadian people fit that image. Borden's vision would successfully defeat a tired fourth-term Liberal government and deliver him a parliamentary majority. Canada's century had ended before its second decade could begin.

Borden, victorious that September night, lauded the return of a little Canada: "Canada has wisely determined that for her there shall be no parting of the ways, but that she will continue in the old path of Canadianism, truly Canadian nationhood and British connection." That election's legacy was better summarized by John Dafoe, the influential editor of the *Manitoba Free Press*: "It was a square stand-up fight, the first in a generation—between two ideals of national development." For the next four decades, a time of two wars, a depression, and considerable periods of growth, the lesser ideal of development would prevail.

Canada's peak year of immigration and growth was 1913, shortly before the country was plunged into a war that would reshape its sense of national independence. Fewer than fifty thousand people a year entered Canada during the war, the great majority of them from the United States. After the war, during which Canada had interned and disenfranchised thousands of Germans, Ukrainians and others because of their ethnicity, the mood of exclusionism did not diminish, so Canada refused to welcome the millions of displaced Europeans seeking a new home. This was exacerbated by depressed postwar economic conditions and the post-1917 Red Scare, which led Canada, in 1919, to impose even tougher immigration restrictions. These rules were aimed at keeping out not just putative communists and anarchists, but any ethnic or national groups believed to be associated with those philosophies (that is, central and eastern Europeans and Jews, but also a good many Americans). In 1923, on a day now remembered by Chinese Canadians as Humiliation Day, a new Chinese Immigration Act was passed that completely barred virtually any Chinese from entering Canada (according to federal statistics, only fifteen Chinese immigrants were permitted into Canada between 1923 and the end of the Second World War).

By devoting itself so singularly to policies of exclusion, Ottawa found itself in a bind when the economy began growing again. In the 1920s, both urban and rural Canada faced gaping labour shortages and sought hundreds of thousands of new workers. But William Lyon Mackenzie King's Liberals inherited the minimizing mindset of Borden's Conservatives and once again sought to populate Canada only with immigrants who were both British and rural. They went to some lengths to attempt this, using numerous grant and promotion programs under the Empire Settlement Act to entice British agriculturalists to come. This effort was an abject failure, in good part because British agriculture was fully developed and profitable: between 1925 and 1931, only 130,000 Britons came to Canada, of whom only 10 percent were farmers. Facing a labour crisis, King cancelled most of the prohibitions on immigration from central and eastern Europe and gave the railways authority to recruit settlers from the East. Those privately recruited Slavs, Poles, Romanians, Yugoslavs, Germans and

Baltic people probably outnumbered the British—but, studies have shown, almost all of them ended up migrating onward to the United States.

In fact, the largest Canadian migration story of the years between Laurier and the end of the Second World War did not involve immigration from abroad but rather emigration to the United States. Once again, but this time at an even greater cost, Canada lost population. Both countries boomed in the 1920s and both had restrictive immigration policies, so both countries hungered for new labour. But the far larger and more entrepreneurial U.S. economy had an outlet valve. With no restrictions on immigration from Canada, it could easily offer higher salaries and living standards to skilled Canadians—and to any British or European immigrants who had recently landed in Canada.

The results were devastating. In the 1920s, when Canada's population was below ten million, more than a million Canadians moved to the United States, only slightly less than the number of immigrants who entered Canada. It would get even worse in the 1930s, when the number of Canadians who departed for the United States greatly exceeded the number of immigrants who came to Canada. This was not just a huge loss of people but also a loss of creative talent. As economic historians Byron Lew and Bruce Cater found in a 2012 analysis, those Canadians who moved to the United States between the wars weren't factory workers and farmers but were typically more educated, highly skilled and "substantially more literate than average." Canada's minimizing policies cost it a generation of inventors, technical geniuses and entrepreneurs.

Quebec's version of the minimizing impulse was even more acute and caused lasting damage to the province's population.

Quebec's clerical and Union Nationale leaders spent the first half the century resisting not just immigration to replace its own population losses but also most immigration into English-speaking provinces. Henri Bourassa, the MP and nationalist pioneer, repeatedly blamed Laurier for populating Western Canada with "foreigners" who shattered what he saw as the natural division of Canada between its two founding races. In his view, which in the 1930s was adopted by the Union Nationale under premier Maurice Duplessis, any expansion of overall Canadian population was a loss to Quebec. This began a half-century during which Quebec's relative population within Canada was considered more important than its absolute population and ability to function economically. And any major expansion of the absolute population of Quebec, which would inevitably be urban in nature, was seen as a threat to the agrarian and Catholic identity of the province, so was actively discouraged.

As a result, Quebec's population share crept downward as its more ambitious citizens continued to depart for New England in the 1920s and '30s. They were doing so for good reasons. As the economist Daniel Parent found in an analysis of U.S. and Quebec statistics, the Québécois who emigrated to New England, and their descendants, ended up with far better educational (and thus income) outcomes for the remainder of the twentieth century than those who stayed in Quebec. This was, in good part, deliberate. For the Unionistes, the prospect of an educated and urban immigrant population was a threat to the small, homogeneous, rural and devout conception of "Quebec" that defined their ideology and underwrote their governing authority. "Nationalists and Church leaders were very concerned with the socio-economic impact of mass immigration" and, in fact, of almost any immigration, the historian

Michael Behiels concludes in his study of the period. "The dual processes of industrialization and urbanization in Quebec, particularly in Montreal, threatened the very fabric of the traditional rural and Catholic French-Canadian society as well as the ability of the francophone professional middle class and clerical leaders to retain effective control over that society."

The extreme minimizing policies of the 1920s, 1930s and 1940s created a large human deficit whose existence and scope would bedevil Canadian politics for decades. Most infamous of these policies was the systematic exclusion of Jews fleeing the Holocaust, including the 1939 turning away of SS *St. Louis* and its cargo of 930, all of whom were rejected by Canada and many of whom were sent back across the Atlantic to face the camps. This was only a tiny part of Canada's near-total ban on European refugees, making the country a uniquely heartless exception among the Western nations that had agreed to share the refugee burden.

Canada's decision to play no role as a place of asylum was rooted in Prime Minister R.B. Bennett's 1931 order-in-council barring the landing of any non-British refugees or immigrants; that policy would be enforced rigidly for the next 16 years (continuing for some time after the war). After aggressive lobbying by governments and humanitarian agencies around the world, only a few small clusters of refugees would officially be admitted to Canada. Quebec newspapers and government leaders were describing Jewish refugees and immigrants as a socialist threat; the result was an often overtly anti-Semitic campaign to prevent their entry. By 1941, when millions of European Jews were seeking resettlement, Montreal's Jewish population had reached only 64,000, or less than 5 percent of the island's total.

This was not just a moral failing, it was yet another missed opportunity. Consider the outsized role that tens of thousands of European wartime refugees—a sizeable part of the educated middle class of Europe—played in the postwar intellectual, artistic, scientific, educational and commercial life of the United States. Imagine, then, Canada in the 1950s and 1960s enriched by even a sliver of that human resource. After the war this human deficit, accumulated over the greater part of a century, would be felt even more acutely. How to account for that shortage, and the vulnerability it produced, would be the dominant Canadian question for decades to come.

PART TWO

A PLURAL NATION

CHAPTER 4

The Battle for 1967

In the spring of 1945, the MV *Britannic*, a White Star ocean liner converted into a troop carrier, made a series of special sailings from Liverpool to Halifax carrying hundreds of British war brides and their soldier husbands. These crossings were among the first immigration voyages after the war's end. One of those immigrants was Pamela Smith, a southern English girl who had joined the Women's Auxiliary Air Force. While serving at a secret radar base, she had met her future husband, Alan, a Royal Canadian Air Force officer. They were processed at Pier 21 and made the cross-country train journey to their new home in Hamilton, Ontario, with their toddler daughter Patricia, my mother.

My maternal grandmother, like my paternal ancestors in the 1830s, also came to Canada from Britain in the aftermath of a war, and also at a moment when Canada was still trying to stay as British as possible. Unlike my father's ancestors, she and my grandfather did not take up arms against their neighbours; in fact, my grandfather was annoyed when officials made him hand over his revolver. They were at the early end of a steady but far from torrential stream of 1940s immigrants escaping the tough and constricted life of postwar Britain. Hamilton, like most industrial Canadian cities, was filling up with newcomers in those years, but by the time my mother was in high school, most of the immigrants she met on the bus and in her night job at Dominion Glass were Italians and eastern Europeans. The notion of Canadians as British subjects, while a reality in her school textbooks and in law, was increasingly at odds with the world around her.

Canada emerged from the Second World War to a slowly dawning realization that the closed, compact and colonial world that had formed its national self-image in 1939 had been obliterated. Once the smoke cleared, it became apparent just how thin and exposed the country had become. The war had made Canada a more confident and independent-minded country, capable of organizing its own forces and speaking in its own voice. It had also turned the United States into the only militarily and financially independent power left in the developed world; for the next decade, every Western country was either deeply indebted to or materially dependent upon the Americans. Britain was a shell of its former self, relying on Washington's funds to bail out its economy. It was incapable of providing its own basic needs (food rationing was more severe in the late 1940s and early 1950s than during the war) and poised to spend the next decade rebuilding its domestic stability by winding down the remains of its former empire.

Still committed to that empire, Canada was caught dancing alone to a song that had long stopped playing. All those decades of reliance on east-west resource trade, restricted immigration, imposed mono-ethnic identity and privileged relations with the mother country suddenly looked, to many, like wasted endeavours and missed opportunities.

While the United States had grown dramatically in size and capacity, Canada had barely budged. During the ninety years between 1851 and 1941, Canada had attracted 6.7 million immigrants but had lost almost 6.3 million people through emigration. As a result, Canada's net population intake during that near-century had averaged only 4,400 people per year. Its population had grown to 12 million by the war's end mainly as a result of its birth rate—which itself had fallen steadily until the war. The United States by this point was home to 145 million people—and they were in many ways a more talented, better equipped group. For during the years when Canada was officially taking only British farmers (and Quebec was resisting almost everyone), the Americans had often welcomed urban, educated immigrants from far-flung places. That included those who had come from Canada. By the late 1940s, more than a million Canadian-born people were living in the United States, and reports indicated that they were overwhelmingly professionals, academics and educated members of the middle class.

Canada's population had become more rural, less industrial and less entrepreneurial during the key decades when the United States grew into the world's nerve centre of invention, export and manufacturing. Historian Ruth Sandwell found, in her work *Canada's Rural Majority*, that the war years marked the highest proportion of rural and resource employment Canada had seen. "In 1941, the number of people working in the rural, resource occupations of agriculture, logging, trapping, and fishing reached their highest levels, outnumbering those employed in all other industries and manufacturing combined," she writes. "It would not be until 1951 that for the first time more people in Canada would be employed in manufacturing than in agriculture"—a threshold the United States crossed shortly before 1920, when its population was approaching the 100-million mark.

It may have been possible for Canadians to maintain this myopic view of their own future before the war, but by the late 1940s it was obvious to everyone that the combination of Canada's tiny market size, the lack of a sustainable transatlantic trading partner, and the extraordinary new economic and cultural power of the United States meant that something had to change. After a couple of years of startled inaction, Canada launched itself into a two-decade debate over the fundamental nature of its economy, its relations with the outside world, and the size and composition of its population. This war of ideas would consume Canada's major political parties, its English and Québécois media, and its intellectuals and scholars, reaching peak intensity on the eve of the Centennial.

Canada's predominantly North American status was, by the late 1940s, hard to deny; the United States was everywhere, on Canada's airwaves and bookshelves and in its supermarkets and car dealerships. The question was whether this posed an existential threat or a challenging opportunity. Was it something to be fought and resisted, by building walls of policy and protection to guard the old, minimal Canada while attempting to rebuild its British cultural identity and trade relations? Or was it something to be met face to face, with an economy and a population robust enough to thrive in the New World and a culture suited to invention and novelty?

A strident opening salvo was fired by Harold Innis, the economic historian whose "staples theory" had provided the defining vocabulary for Canada's resource-extraction identity. He issued, at the end of the 1940s, an essay-length call to arms against the overbearing presence of the United States in Canadian culture, media and daily life, one that reflected the alarm experienced by a great many postwar Canadians. "The impact of commercialism from the United States has been enormously accentuated by war," he began.

> The effects of these developments on Canadian culture have been disastrous. Indeed they threaten Canadian national life. . . . In radio and in television accessibility to American stations means a constant bombardment. . . . The jackals of communication systems are constantly on the alert to destroy every vestige of sentiment toward Great Britain holding it of no advantage if it threatens the omnipotence of American commercialism. This is to strike at the heart of cultural life in Canada. The pride taken in improving our status in the British Commonwealth of Nations has made it difficult for us to realize that our status on the North American continent is on the verge of disappearing. Continentalism assisted in the achievement of autonomy and has consequently become more dangerous. We can only survive by taking persistent action at strategic points against American imperialism in all its attractive guises.

Innis championed the creation and expansion of Canada's cultural-nationalist institutions: the Canadian Broadcasting Corporation, the National Film Board, the large-scale subsidies and protections for book and periodical publishing, the institution that would become the Canada Council, and a strengthened tie to the British Commonwealth (which Innis saw forming a "Third Bloc" in opposition to both U.S. and Soviet influences). On these issues, both federal political parties would broadly agree, at least at first.

Almost as soon as the war was over, stress fractures had begun to tear at the edges of the minimal model of Canada. In 1946, the House of Commons was consumed with debate over the King government's proposal to create a legal Canadian citizenship. Up to this point, Canadians had simply been British subjects who happened to live in Canada; the war had created a sense of national identity that the Liberals felt ought to be recognized in law. The Tories vociferously opposed the idea of Canadians being anything other than British, as did some Liberals. In the end, a compromise was reached: Canadian citizenship became a legal fact on January 1, 1947, but the law that governed it declared, in its main clause, that "a Canadian citizen is a British subject." (This clause would remain in place until 1977.)

The effort to cling to the minimizing impulse had consequences. The notion that French Canadians were a distinct community with their own history and identity escaped the government's notice in the first postwar decade. As did any notion of indigenous citizenship: those living on First Nations reserves could not leave them without government permission, and indigenous peoples would have no voting rights until the 1960s. Likewise, the 1950s saw the peak of the residential-school bureaucracy and the mass program to replace Inuit names with government-assigned numbers printed on "Eskimo identification tags" worn around the neck. As long as the resource-nation vision continued to dominate, Canada's original peoples and its linguistic minorities would continue to be viewed mainly as problems to be managed.

As Canada's population grew and diversified, however, this sort of thinking slowly became untenable. A number of people in Canada's media, political, business and academic communities began to see the benefits of a larger population, a larger market and cities large enough to compete with those in the United States. In 1946 University of British Columbia professor and sometime government official Henry Angus made a popular argument for increased population, which he argued would require an end to immigration restrictions on race and nationality: "Canada has won a position of great importance in the World. Without a very substantial increase in her own population it will be impossible for Canada to retain her relative importance when other nations of equal or greater population rebuild their shattered lives."

This view drew an angry response in 1949 in *Maclean's* magazine, from historian Arthur Lower—who, along with fellow historians Donald Creighton and Innis, was one of the most outspoken defenders of the minimizing model. "Just bring in enough new people, they say, and our population will soar, our cities will double in size, every merchant will increase his business, every manufacturer will sell all his wares at good prices, labor will become abundant, and, in short, Utopia will be here," he wrote. "In my opinion, it won't." In Lower's view, Canada could only be an agrarian and resource-based economy; its economy could not work if there were not at least three acres of arable land per inhabitant (in 1948 there were five). "I, personally, find it hard, for at least the next century, to imagine humanity divorced from the soil," he wrote. The population, he said, should not go much higher than twenty million: "When we get beyond 28 millions here in Canada we begin to worry about our food." And the immigration of non-British people, as occurred in the Laurier years, would be dangerous: "A similar movement today would once more upset our slowly forming national society and postpone indefinitely the formation of a Canadian people with its own way of life."

Regardless of which model of growth Canadians chose, it became obvious, from about 1947 onward, that Canada needed a lot more people. The economy was booming and there weren't nearly enough working-age people to fill most employers' needs. Canada's unemployment rate stayed well below 6 percent (a level more or less equivalent to "full employment") until 1958, and it often fell below 3 percent, indicating that millions more workers were needed. And a huge supply was available: the war had created the largest refugee crisis in history, with millions of Europeans homeless and seeking a new country. Canada waited two years before accepting any significant number of them, and then held heated debates about whether IDPs (internally displaced persons, or refugees) from beyond Britain and Western Europe could ever be suitable for Canada's economy and culture.

Faced with pressure from voters, businesses and his cabinet to open the doors—and pressure from other Western governments to play a larger part in the reconstruction of Europe by settling the continent's refugees—Prime Minister King finally declared to the House of Commons in the spring of 1947 that "the policy of the government is to foster the growth of the population of Canada by the encouragement of immigration." But he made it clear, in the same breath, that this immigration would be highly selective—once again, mainly British and white. Canadians, he said, "do not wish to make a fundamental alteration in the character of their population through mass immigration," and he specifically noted that "any considerable Oriental immigration" would "be certain to give rise to social and economic problems."

Since the restrictionist policies of the prewar Duplessis government in Quebec had left the province with huge labour shortages, it had become somewhat more open to immigration. In 1948, the federal Liberals declared, for the first time since Confederation, that French citizens would have the same largely unrestricted immigration status as British subjects and U.S. citizens. But it would not result in many more immigrants. As historian Reg Whitaker found, the federal bureaucracy and the RCMP rejected most prospective French immigrants out of suspicion that they were either communist sympathizers or former fascists. Over the next five years, despite great numbers wishing to emigrate from France, fewer than five thousand would land in Quebec.

Other non-British ethnic groups fared better. There was a big publicity push, on behalf of federal offices, to get Canadians to recognize eastern and southern Europeans—who had been seen by many Canadians as effectively non-white and incompatible with Canadian values—as admissible members of the Euro-Canadian family. "Hierarchies among European races were . . . rejected," University of Toronto scholar Triadafilos Triadafilopoulos writes in his history of this transition, and replaced with "the notion that Canada was a the product of a 'mixture' of white European nationalities. . . . Thus, Italians, Slavs, Jews, and Greeks, among others, came to be regarded as legitimate Canadians who were officially on a par with their Anglo- and French-Canadian counterparts."

The first non-Western immigrants to be accepted were Poles and other Baltic-region Europeans who had fought with the Allies. By 1952, more than 165,000 of these "displaced persons" had come to Canada. Canada also quietly struck agreements with fellow Commonwealth members India, Pakistan and Ceylon to take South Asian immigrants in small but significant numbers (officially fewer than three hundred per year at first); 1947 also saw the removal of the total ban on Chinese immigration, causing East Asians, albeit in small numbers, to come to Canada for the first time in decades. In 1948, a population of Palestinian refugees was quietly accepted, and after 1955, a new immigration scheme allowed several hundred "coloured" domestic workers per year from the Caribbean. Non-white immigration, while still barred by official policies, was becoming a de facto reality in Canada, and non-Western immigration a significant factor for the first time since the Laurier years. As a result, what would twenty years later be called "multiculturalism" was already becoming a lived experience in Canada's cities.

By the end of the 1940s, there weren't many IDPs left and emigration from depressed postwar Britain, while substantial, fell far short of Canada's needs. The larger resource and manufacturing corporations, along with the railways, were coming to Ottawa with requests for thousands of immigrant workers each. As has always been the case, the push for a greater Canadian population arose not out of policy or ideology but out of practical necessity: Canada could not function without more people. Canada's immigration officials settled on a contract-labour immigration system that became known internally as "bulk orders"—that is, recruiters in Europe and the Commonwealth would respond to employment demands by assembling shiploads of migrant labourers for emigration to Canada.

The bulk orders program, though, did not anticipate that postwar immigration was not simply supplying units of labour, but was also creating entire communities and cohorts of new Canadians. These very quickly became an integral part of the country's civic, business and political life—and their presence, in turn, began to change public perceptions of Canada's identity and future growth.

The first recipients of bulk-order immigration were some five thousand Polish ex-servicemen and their families, and the policy became Canada's chief method of introducing non-Western immigration. The most visible, though, were the Italians, who were by far the largest group to immigrate under this program. During the three decades beginning in 1946, more than 440,000 Italians would arrive in Canada, initially through bulk-order hiring in agriculture and domestic service, and then through large-scale family sponsorship. At first, their recruitment was highly controversial. As historian Franca Iacovetta found in her study of internal government policy discussions, southern Italians in particular and southern European Catholics generally were seen in many official circles as being impossible to integrate.

"The Italian South peasant is not the type we are looking for in Canada," deputy immigration minister Laval Fortier wrote in one memo. "His standard of living, his way of life, even his civilization seems so different that I doubt if he could even become an asset to our country." The Anglican Church, which still had enormous political influence in the 1950s, elaborated on this concern, producing a report to warn the government that Italians were "amenable to the fallacies of dictatorship" and lacking in democratic traditions or beliefs.

Despite such lingering prejudice, the Canadian public was warming to the idea of living and working alongside people of different religions, languages and cultural backgrounds. Nowhere was this more evident than in the 1956 campaign to take tens of thousands of refugees after Hungary was invaded by Soviet forces—the first "refugee crisis" to be known by that name, and the one that set the pattern for all future refugee crises. The Hungarians, including much of Budapest's educated middle class and thousands of members of the defeated democracy movement, had fled for their lives and were overflowing refugee camps in neighbouring Austria. The Liberal government of Louis St. Laurent at first rejected the cry to accept Hungarians. The cabinet and intelligence agencies warned that the refugees' religion, ethnicity and tendency to political extremism were all incompatible with what they saw as Canadian values.

Canada's director of immigration warned, in an internal memo, that the Hungarian refugee population would contain too many "persons who had taken advantage of the situation"—who were, in the director's words, "all of the Hebrew race and were in possession of a considerable amount of funds" and should be deterred. On top of this, Ottawa feared that the refugee group would contain extremists capable of committing violent acts: "Canadian security personnel again warned government that the communists might attempt to infiltrate this refugee movement in order to place secret agents into unsuspecting Western countries, including Canada," explains historian Harold Troper. Similar warnings would be repeated over the coming decades about Vietnamese, Balkan and Syrian refugees.

Ottawa engaged in what Troper (who unearthed the memo years later) calls "bureaucratic inertia." The government faced overwhelming demand from citizen groups, churches and humanitarian organizations to take Hungarians. Thousands of Canadian families volunteered to sponsor Hungarian refugee families, but Ottawa was balking.

In December 1956, the *Globe and Mail* ran an editorial headlined "For Shame," which summarized the growing public sentiment around refugees. It began by expressing dismay at the "unreasoning bigotry" of those in government who would "question and even protest the efforts being made to bring the refugees here," whose "clangorous views" were bringing "discredit to Canada." It then put the tens of thousands of refugees into context:

> The numbers that will come form an infinitesimal portion of the New Canadians who have settled here in the past decade—not, as the critics are trying to make out, a huge mob which will somehow absorb Canada instead of being absorbed. . . . This country's past has been plagued by priggish xenophobia. Let us, for once, live up to the standard of a truly civilized nation and meet the challenge of this glorious opportunity to serve freedom and mankind—as well as ourselves.

The government relented, but the public was already there. Under the newly improvised family sponsorship system (which was, and would continue to be, unique to Canada), more than 37,000 Hungarians were rescued and settled within months. Ottawa's official recommendations to turn away Jews were followed obediently by some officials but were evidently widely disregarded or ignored: at least 15 percent of the Hungarians Canada finally admitted were Jewish. By 1956, in other words, religious intolerance did not always extend down to the front lines. The Hungarians, most of whom settled in and around Toronto, quickly became an integral and highly successful part of Canada's intellectual, civic, culinary and entrepreneurial life, playing a central role in shaping modern Canada. It was a lesson for the future: by taking refugees during crises, Canada found itself turning the most ambitious and creative members of a foreign country's middle class into devoted members of the Canadian project.

The year 1957 would see a record spike in Canadian population growth. On top of the near-peak levels of births caused by the baby boom, that year saw the greatest immigration levels since the Laurier years, with 282,164 people arriving (including the Hungarians). This level would not be experienced again until after 2010, but it caused little controversy among flourishing postwar Canadians. The expansion had begun to change Canada. Entire economic sectors were opening up—petroleum, aerospace—though almost entirely with U.S. investment. Despite its preferential agricultural trade arrangements, Britain had become a small slice of the Canadian economy. Expanding Canada badly needed its North American market. Both King and St. Laurent abandoned plans to pursue free trade with the United States as too politically risky. But their cabinet ministers, especially C.D. Howe and Lester Pearson, opened up North American economic ties and trade relations, using the General Agreement on Tariffs and Trade (the precursor to the World Trade Organization), which had eliminated many tariff barriers between Canada and the United States by the end of the 1950s. It appeared that Canada would spend the rest of the decade growing larger, more diverse, more independent and more entrenched in the North American economy.

John Diefenbaker's election in June 1957 put an abrupt stop to many of those trends. His victory ushered in a full-scale bid for a return to the minimizing Canada: a smaller, more British, more resource-focused vision of Canadian development. For the next ten years, in government and opposition, he would force an overt policy struggle between minimizing and maximizing impulses. He had become convinced, during his years in opposition, that Canada needed to return to the east-west resource-extraction economy championed by John A. Macdonald—and that he should frame himself as the heir to Macdonald's vision. As biographer Denis Smith found, it was economist Merril Menzies, Diefenbaker's adviser and muse, who persuaded him in 1957 to revive and champion a version of Macdonald's National Policy. This vision played a big role in Diefenbaker's 1958 majority, because that colonial vision appealed both to older-generation Canadians who yearned for a return to British Canada and to a traditionally Liberal cohort motivated by rising feelings of anti-Americanism and cultural nationalism. It was a potent political mix, one that would continue, through the Centennial decade, to attract both arch-conservative and left-wing Canadians to a century-old set of ideals.

Diefenbaker's minimizing mission began with a quixotic bid to restore Canada's place in Britain's heart. He tried, from 1957 until he was nearly out of office in 1963, to negotiate a free trade agreement between the Commonwealth and Britain, or between Canada and Britain, continually urging and pressing the idea upon Harold Macmillan, Britain's Conservative prime minister (whose term in office overlapped almost exactly with Diefenbaker's). This was at first bemusing and then increasingly annoying to Macmillan, who was desperately trying to negotiate Britain into the newly created European Economic Community (later to become the European Union), a mission that could only be hurt by more open trade with the far less lucrative Commonwealth. (The United Kingdom already had preferential prices on Canadian agricultural goods, so there was little it could gain.) Britain and Canada were in somewhat similar straits with regard to trade. Both countries were very much in need of more open trading relations with the larger economies adjoining them—but Macmillan recognized this, while Diefenbaker was convinced that a deal with Britain could displace the United States as Canada's key trading partner.

To this end, Diefenbaker spent much of 1957 and 1958 declaring to media and political audiences that Canada would soon have a policy that would "see about 15 percent of Canada's imports from the United States transferred to British suppliers"—a move that would have doubled Canada's trade with Britain and shifted some $625 million (almost $5.5 billion in today's dollars) annually from U.S. to British coffers. How this could be done without contravening the crucial GATT rules that governed Canada-U.S. trade was never explained; in any case, the idea was never taken seriously by Britain. This was more than just a waste of time, however. It meant that during a crucial seven years of Canada's formative growth, economic relations with the United States stagnated—for example, the crucial Auto Pact, which would have benefited the Canadian economy hugely during the economic stagnation of the late 1950s, had to wait until 1965, after Diefenbaker was out of office, to become reality.

Diefenbaker's minimizing approach exerted a centrifugal force on all his policies. As was the case in the 1870s, his British, resource-focused trade approach had an inevitable effect on population, immigration and intercommunal relations. The Diefenbaker government's insistence on a strictly British national identity meant that Quebec was bound to be treated as an afterthought. Diefenbaker scandalized Quebec Tories by neglecting them for cabinet posts and paying little heed to Québécois concerns, triggering a voter rejection of federal Progressive Conservative politics in Quebec that would last until the 1980s. And it left immigration, population and urban development to decline—which they did.

Diefenbaker was not opposed to immigration in principle, though he rarely discussed the subject. And he was a believer in racial equality, at least in theory: he would introduce the Canadian Bill of Rights in 1960. But his National Policy vision meant that immigration would be curtailed sharply as soon as it collided with any of his key agendas. In 1958, when the economy slowed somewhat, the Progressive Conservatives choked off immigration with a number of changes, including a policy that prevented people on temporary visas from taking employment—a key pathway to naturalization. Immigration numbers fell by almost two-thirds, to 106,928 in 1960; in 1961, newspapers reported with alarm that more Canadians had departed for the United States that year than had arrived as immigrants—a return to the prewar pattern.

In spite of this, Diefenbaker found himself wrestling with the emerging reality of the new, growing Canada and a population of Canadians who no longer saw themselves as colonial subjects. That became apparent in 1959, when Ottawa realized Italians were immigrating to Canada in greater numbers than British. In response, the government attempted to cut off Italian immigration with an order-in-council ending most forms of family reunification. The fact that Italians had been sponsoring relatives was actually a strong sign of their successful integration. They were forming tightly entrenched family networks to settle Canada, as the French and British had done before. Diefenbaker's officials were missing the point; Italians and other non-Western Europeans were now a major part of the populations, the consumer markets and the electorates of Canada's major cities. Almost immediately, the government felt the backlash from influential Italian Canadians in the media, the opposition benches and, most importantly, constituency offices. The restriction was quickly repealed—marking what was probably the first time new Canadians had been felt as a political force unto themselves.

While Ottawa was struggling to maintain the illusion of a homogeneous Canadian identity, Canadians themselves were experiencing something very different on the streets of their cities, in their workplaces and especially in their schools. As Robert Vipond discovered in *Making a Global City*, his cultural and political history of a single Toronto public school, many of Canada's institutions had been dealing with a plural, multi-cultural, multi-linguistic reality throughout the 1950s and were becoming increasingly comfortable with it. He found that many Toronto schools in the 1950s had pluralities or even majorities of students who did not yet speak English; the schools and their board improvised an English as a Second Language program in which students were kept in normal classes and encouraged to mix their own cultures and aptitudes with those of the more established students. In an early 1960s report titled "Immigrants and Their Education," the school board concluded that it should be "providing an education for a multi-culture student population" (using a word that was not yet part of the political vocabulary), one built on a system of "mutual accommodation, of give and take, in which both established Canadians and immigrants have the ability—and the responsibility—to adjust their civic lenses." These ideas—of integration rather than assimilation, of newcomers integrating within their cultural communities rather than being stripped of them—would become part of official debates in the 1970s. But as Vipond and Triadafilopoulos have both found, many urban Canadians, schools and government agencies had been living this reality for decades.

That mismatch between Diefenbaker's policy ambitions and many voters' real lives was forcing the Conservative leader to back off his Macdonald-era visions. As the 1960s dawned, fewer Canadians saw their country as a resource-extracting asterisk on the side of the British Empire, even if they still distrusted the United States. That was visible in Diefenbaker's decision, in 1962, to quietly remove the de facto racial restrictions in Canada's immigration policy, ending the "White Canada" policy that had existed since Borden's time.

That change hadn't come about because Diefenbaker's government sought to impose some new society-shaping vision on Canada. On the contrary, it changed because Canadian voters, including many Progressive Conservative voters, no longer saw it reflecting their lived experiences in increasingly plural cities.

As the 1967 anniversary of Confederation approached, Canada became consumed with a struggle for the country's overarching identity. It was a battle over flags and anthems, One Canada and *deux nations*, America and Britain, Diefenbaker and Pearson, unilingualism and bilingualism, established Canadian colonists and new Canadian immigrants. But those political showdowns did not cause Canada to change; rather, for the first time, profound changes that had taken place in Canadians themselves were reflected by their politics. What began in the Centennial decade was official Canada beginning to catch up with the real Canada.

The battle of symbols filled headlines. The replacement of the colonial Red Ensign with the Maple Leaf consumed Parliament's energies from 1963 and continued to simmer for years after it was officially resolved at the end of 1964. The choice of "O Canada" over "God Save the Queen" faced even more resistance from many Canadians, including now–opposition leader Diefenbaker, and would not be fully resolved until an official national anthem was passed into law in 1980.

Something deeper was taking place, involving not just the symbols but the realities they represented. Across Africa, Asia and the Americas, scores of countries were freeing themselves from centuries of control by European masters, and struggling, sometimes violently, to find ways to represent and govern themselves as independent entities. People were learning to think of themselves not as colonial subjects but as autonomous individuals within self-created states. In that light, the swelling of Canada's national pride and symbol creation around 1967 can be seen as the apex of its postcolonial moment. The wars over symbols were one small manifestation of a global shift.

The most dramatic part of that shift in Canada was the awakening of Québécois self-consciousness, nationalism and resistance at the political, cultural, institutional and sometimes violent militant level. This, too, was not a cause but an effect. It was merely the most visible expression of something that had been unfolding in Quebec throughout the postwar years, around a million dinner tables and in thousands of workplaces—a generation who had no patience with either the Catholic authoritarianism that had governed the province for the better part of a century or the British paternalism that had relegated French Canadians to servant-class status. Quebec's transformation in the 1960s was part of the worldwide postwar wave of postcolonial awakenings, but also part of a wave of post-Catholic moments that swept across Europe and the Americas. It was an inevitable consequence of Canada's shedding its closed colonial identity.

The Quiet Revolution is well known and understood—after all, it gave rise to two major political parties and a short-lived violent insurgency, a half-century of constitutional turmoil and Quebec's ascendance as the new centre of gravity in Canadian politics. Less well understood is the identity shift that transformed life in English-speaking Canada. As University of Quebec historian José Igartua points out, a revolution in English-Canadian identity "took place roughly with the same speed and over the same period as Quebec's Quiet Revolution . . . of similar magnitude in the cultural changes it wrought."

In other words, by 1967, the British-subject identity was not just obsolete but completely irrelevant to most English Canadians. "Before 1960," Igartua says, "British referents occupied the same dominant place in definitions of English-Canadian identity as Catholicism did in definitions of Québécois identity; they were an article of faith for most—though, as in Quebec, not for all." But no more: "Within less than 10 years, these dominant referents had been displaced in both collective identities."

It was not a gentle displacement. When Prime Minister Lester Pearson declared in 1967 that Canada is "a nation of two founding peoples" (in French, he used the even stronger word *nations*), he drew a furious rebuke from Diefenbaker, who declared, as he had in the 1950s, that the two-nation concept "would lead to the breakdown of confederation. But Diefenbaker's own party soon broke ranks with him. By 1967, the Progressive Conservatives were passing conference motions declaring, to the outrage of their own leader, that Canada should be seen as a federal state "composed of two founding peoples (*deux nations*), with historic rights, who have been joined by people from many lands." The space between the parties was narrowing.

When Pearson attempted to respond to growing Québécois disenchantment by establishing the largest government inquiry in Canadian history, the 1963 Royal Commission on Bilingualism and Biculturalism, it was widely expected to endorse some version of the "two nations" model, which was controversial enough in first-century Canada. But when, to endless media attention, it released its three reports, starting in 1965, Canadians were surprised to find that the idea of Canada as two peoples and nations was not its most dramatic proposal. It did call for a bilingual country, but that was expected. What was not expected was the very large part of the first report, and of the subsequent reports over the next two years, devoted to what the commission's original mandate had called "other cultural groups." The commission had found a Canada that could no longer be described as having merely one or two or three founding "peoples," "nations" or "races." It was instead becoming a place that could no longer be defined by its colonial origins.

A less famous but equally dramatic indication of Canada's new postcolonial consciousness came from a second blockbuster government report, released in 1967 and also four years in the making. It carried the anodyne-sounding title *A Survey of the Contemporary Indians of Canada*, but its conclusions, organized by anthropologist Harry Hawthorn, were far from academic. The

Hawthorn Report concluded that the residential school experience, having reached peak population in the early 1960s, was "unpleasant, frightening and painful" for some indigenous children. For others it was "not so much adaptive as maladaptive"; in other words, "their motivation to do well in school drops during their stay there. . . . They come to see themselves as failures."

The attempt to turn hundreds of thousands of indigenous kids into "the typical middle-class white child"—a central part of minimal Canada's mono-ethnic sensibility—had stripped indigenous communities of their human and cultural resources and damaged them for generations. Such words had not been heard before in establishment Canada. But they were a reflection of something indigenous Canadians already knew. The Hawthorn Report would set off a cycle of reactions from government and, especially, from First Nations (as they came to call themselves a few years later); it marked a turning point after which indigenous peoples could not so easily be described as obstacles to resource extraction or wards of a paternal state. Because it was no longer necessary to believe in one undifferentiated people, it became possible to notice the horrors that had been inflicted on Canada's original peoples.

Today, we tend to remember this opening of second-century Canada to a non-homogeneous identity as "multiculturalism." There's an assumption that it took place a few years later, imposed from above during the Trudeau years—or that it was an idea produced and foisted on Canada by the new non-European immigrants who came in the 1970s. In fact, the rejection of mono-ethnic English Canada had begun to take place a decade or two before "multiculturalism" became a popular Canadian word. And the change took place in the minds of those British-origin Canadians themselves. What we saw in 1967 was the final death of the old notion of monoculturalism, which by then had lost the support of even those who had been its beneficiaries. Once Canadians adopted an expansionist mindset, a whole circle of illusions dropped away, and everything began to change.

CHAPTER 5

The Dawn of the Maximizing Consensus

Change tends to have a long windup and a quick strike. In the words of the late economist Rudi Dornbusch, the transformation of a society "takes a much longer time coming than you think, and then happens much faster than you would have thought."

That was how it went with Canada's transformation from a closed and colonial society to a plural and expansive country. If you could somehow pay a day-long visit to Canada five years before its Centennial and then five years after, you would come away with the conclusion that you had visited two utterly different countries with only a vague and superficial relationship to each other. The Canada of 1962 was still, in most day-to-day respects, colonial, closed, dependent, paternalistic and pretending to be ethnically homogeneous—a place whose sleepy streets you'd have to leave if you wanted to make something of yourself. The Canada of 1972 was less placid, less innocent, more fraught and confrontational, but also far more exciting, far more expansive and promising. It was a country of self-invention and iconoclasm, a North American place whose several peoples had begun to build something much bigger, more complex, but also more secure and more educated and more urban, something entirely our own.

This wasn't an easy process. In the years after the Centennial, Canadians began to confront seriously the schisms, divisions and gross inequities that had been masked before beneath a colonial patina. The two decades that followed would unleash a cascade of dramatic confrontations and interlinked debates that would drive Canadians apart before creating a fragile new consensus. We would have, over the next fifty years, two secession crises, an all-encompassing political battle over our North American economic identity, three attempts (one successful) to redraw the constitution, and a hard-fought political reawakening of indigenous nations. These were the crucial struggles of becoming a real country, of finding a governing mechanism and a common set of values to bring together those long-disparate peoples—and centrally, to confronting the century-long crisis of underpopulation that had kept the country closed, dependent and in denial.

What emerged in Canada over the years that followed was a set of broadly shared ideas (though far from unanimous or fully realized ideas) about how the country should develop, grow and relate to itself. As with the minimizing-impulse spiral that overtook Canada during key periods of the nineteenth and twentieth centuries, this maximizing impulse produced ideas and policies that tended to follow inevitably from one another. That is, even if a government supported only one or two of the maximizing ideas and officially opposed some of the others (for example, if it attempted to broaden immigration and cultural diversity but opposed more open North American trade), it would sooner or later find itself confronted with the other maximizing elements—and those ideas, once part of the public dialogue, would become harder to oppose. That's because these principles weren't coming from Parliament or the courts; they were becoming embedded in public thought, as the collective results of twenty million lived experiences. They were not isolated policy ideas but the consequences of a postcolonial mentality that had crept into the national ethos. That is, at root, the story of Canada's past half-century. At the heart of the country's major political battles was an attempt to come to terms with the cascade of consequences that flowed from an independent, postcolonial, plural, North American view of nationhood.

These are the key elements of Canada's maximizing impulse:

Pluralism and ethnic heterogeneity. An understanding—always present in some Canadians but by the end of the twentieth century held by a large majority in both English Canada and Quebec—that the country's identity is not linked to a non-optional British and Anglican identity, or to a fixed and primal combination of British and French (and, in some formulations, indigenous) identities. Rather, this view of Canada sees the country's core national values and institutions as being independent of national, ethnic, religious or racial identities (though not independent of linguistic identities, either in Quebec or in the rest of Canada). The goal of the national culture, in this view, is to find common ground and a uniting terrain of language and citizenship that can tie together these disparate identities.

Broad-source immigration aimed at expansion. Immigration is no longer part of an imperial project, tying Canada to a mother country and its dominant ethnic group. Immigration becomes an instrument strictly to foster economic and demographic growth, and to reunite families and communities under the larger umbrella of Canadian culture and institutions, so any ethnic or racial mandate falls away.

A diversified, value-added economy. The mid-century shift away from a predominantly agrarian and natural resource economy coincided with (and was in good part caused by) the shift away from a colonial mentality. This transition of the workforce away from extractive industries and toward manufacturing, and then toward services and the "knowledge economy," was part of the process of becoming an independent-minded country.

Open North American trade and continental integration. The colonial staples model of trade had ceased to be the dominant force in Canada's economy by the Second World War, and after Diefenbaker's last stab it ceased to be even an imaginary policy objective. The emergence of a diversified, urban-centred economy, combined with the unavoidable fact that Canada's main trade pathway was now southward rather than eastward and the slow disappearance of British affinities and loyalties in Canadian culture, meant that a more open southern border would become indispensable.

Indigenous nations as sovereign partners. The closed, colonial view of Canada tended to view indigenous populations not as legitimate occupants of shared territory but rather as problems of a territorial or social nature, to be managed through bureaucratic and homogenizing institutions (with frequently tragic results), to be cleared from territory sought for agrarian or strategic purposes into reserves, or to be confronted or inhibited as potential threats. In a postcolonial, maximizing Canada, the legal and constitutional view of indigenous peoples—as well as, gradually, the public view of indigenous peoples—shifted to a recognition of them as sovereign and constitutional partners with constitutional and legal rights defined in treaties.

A view of society as a collection of individuals. In the minimizing Canada, the individual was a subject—that is, a part of a greater imperial, or British, whole (or, in another popular view, as a member of one of two "founding races," one British and Anglican, the other French and Catholic). Indigenous nations, religious and ethnic minorities, and sometimes Québécois were not recognized as being distinct peoples. This subordinate status manifested itself both in the law and in the English-Canadian consciousness. In postcolonial, autonomous-minded Canada, this view no longer made sense, and the individual, as the holder of rights and obligations, became the primary focus of the law and the state. This meant that the Canadian state and courts could acknowledge the existence of multiple constitutionally recognized "nations" (including Québécois and multiple indigenous nations). This acknowledgement did not threaten the sovereignty of the state, because "nations" in Canada are viewed in the law as self-defined collections of rights-holding individuals (a fact that was acknowledged well before the 1982 Constitution Act codified it).

A growing population. The purpose of population growth, in the minimizing vision, was to fill territory. In the maximizing ideology, the purpose of population growth is to create sufficient concentrations of people to support the institutions, industries, creative endeavours, cities, cultural expressions, fiscal bases and circles of invention and entrepreneurship that a more or less self-sufficient country needs. In both English Canada and (among the leading voices during most periods) in Quebec, population expansion—and the pluralism that came with it—grew to be seen as a crucial facet of nation-building.

By the time we reached the 150th anniversary of Confederation in 2017, the ideas described above had all become part of the Canadian mainstream. Most remain contentious topics of public debate and divisive issues in politics and the media, but the debate is mainly about the details. The ideas themselves, broadly speaking, have been accepted. Surveys show that the core maximizing ideas—ethnic, racial and religious pluralism (popularly known as "multiculturalism"), population growth, immigration, North American free trade, individual rights and indigenous self-government—have come to be accepted by a majority or a large plurality of the public. Those ideas also came to be accepted, more or less, across the conventional political spectrum—that is, they were rarely questioned during the first decades of this century by the mainstream branches of the Liberal and Conservative parties (though tensions began to arise on the right during and after the 2015 federal election), by the mainstream New Democratic Party, by the Quebec Liberals and by significant (though not always dominant) factions of the Parti Québécois and Bloc Québécois. After half a century of pitched battles, there is today among a plurality and possibly a majority of Canadians a fragile but successful maximizing consensus.

Yet many Canadians have little idea how these ideas came to

be so central to our self-understanding. A popular myth holds that they were the creations of political parties, prime ministers, elite officials and courts. Under this often-repeated narrative of modern Canadian history, starting in the late 1960s, a series of political decisions, parliamentary votes, court rulings and royal commissions descended on an unsuspecting Canadian public and forced upon it an awkward jumble of novelties: non-white immigration, bilingualism, multiculturalism, religious and racial diversity, refugees, indigenous nationhood, free trade, individual rights extended to minorities. This story holds that multiculturalism is the product of the 1971 policy by that name introduced by Pierre Trudeau's Liberals, and that Brian Mulroney's Progressive Conservatives launched Canada-U.S. free trade, as a political agenda, into the 1988 election. But Canada was not remade by the political, legal and constitutional actions of the post-1967 decades; it was reflected by them.

It helps to understand the past half-century of Canadian history as a cascading sequence of consequences arising from this new public understanding of Canada's place and role—that is, as a series of maximizing causes and effects in which the political reality of Canada gradually caught up with its existing human reality. The major transformations of this period followed a set of inevitable axioms of Canadian expansionism, which I will examine one by one.

Axiom One: A more autonomous Canada had to recognize its cultural and ethnic diversity. One of the more persistent myths of Canadian history holds that ethnic and racial diversity is a product of government policy—specifically, of Prime Minister Trudeau's 1971 declaration of a policy of official multiculturalism.

In fact, Canada had become multicultural long before there was anything called "multiculturalism." By the 1960s, more than a quarter of Canada's population was not of British, French or indigenous descent. The huge population of Ukrainians, Italians, Chinese, Greeks, eastern European Jews, Indians and Portuguese who increasingly filled the streets of Canada's cities was, by 1970, more numerous than the francophone population of Quebec. These new Canadians were recognized by the Royal Commission on Bilingualism and Biculturalism in 1965 as the crucial "Third Force" of Canadians—a realization that rendered the commission's original mandate, not to mention its name, somewhat beside the point. The allophones of Quebec and the non–Western European populations of the major cities were already an abundant force in Canadian life. Even if Italians and Jews were still, in much of the Canadian media in the 1960s and early 1970s, considered somewhat exotic and "other," their stories and accomplishments had quickly become fixtures in Canada's self-definition.

This illustrated the first inevitable law of Canadian expansionism. Those who sought a coherent postcolonial country with unifying institutions and values were bound to conclude that it would be necessary to allow new polyglot citizens to express their Canadianism through their own language and customs—in other words, that they needed to integrate rather than assimilate.

Historian Peter Henshaw has traced this recognition back as far as John Buchan, the Scotsman who is most famous for having written such thrillers as *The Thirty-Nine Steps* but who also served, under the title Lord Tweedsmuir, as Canada's last British-appointed governor general, from 1935 to 1940. Buchan spent almost all that time formulating and promoting the idea of multiculturalism (without using that word). In Fraserwood, Manitoba, for example, he gave an address to a big crowd of Ukrainian Canadians in September 1936: "You will all be better Canadians for being also good Ukrainians. . . . The strongest nations are those that are made up of different racial elements." He used a Canadian Club address in Toronto to declare that Canada's many ethnic groups "should retain their individuality and each make its contribution to the national character."

By the late 1950s, the challenges of cultural diversity were part of the daily lives of policymakers, educators and front-line officials in Canada's big cities. As Robert Vipond's study found, urban school boards and provincial education departments had developed sophisticated systems and institutions for handling the form of pluralism they had just begun to call "multi-culture," a decade before it became a policy. The first politician known to have used the word "multiculturalism" was Paul Yuzyk, a Progressive Conservative senator of Ukrainian descent, who used his 1963 maiden speech to denounce Pearson's "biculturalism" proposals as being too narrow (in contrast to his own party leader, Diefenbaker, who considered them too expansive). Senator Yuzyk joined a growing group of Tories by declaring in his speech that Canada was a "multicultural nation." Biculturalism, he explained in a subsequent speech, "denies the multicultural character [of Canada], which can only lead to dis-unity. What we need is a firm basis of our nationhood which will unite all elements of society."

The notion of multiculturalism—as a common national identity and set of values shared by people of disparate backgrounds, religions and ethnicities—was not an exotic position by 1963, even if it was hotly debated. These opinions represented, by the 1960s, the views of a significant part of the Tory caucus (the party leader notwithstanding) and likely a majority of the Liberal caucus. For a great many Canadians—including most of the 25 percent of Canadians who weren't British or French (many of whom, such as Senator Yuzyk, had become active in politics) as well as a significant proportion of their Anglo and Québécois neighbours—they were simply common sense.

So when Pierre Trudeau declared a policy of "official multiculturalism" in his 1971 speech, he was not charting new territory. Controversy erupted not because the policy advocated pluralism, but because it seemed to be politically cynical: it was seen as a bid either to undermine Quebec nationalism by widening the "Third Force" or to turn millions of new Canadian families into Liberal loyalists. Both accusations were certainly true—but a third, which holds that official multiculturalism changed Canada, does not have much basis in fact.

Multiculturalism, far from inducing the sort of angry backlash it has elicited in European countries, quickly caught on. Polls show that the idea remains popular among a majority of Canadians, and even among a majority of Tory-voting Canadians. This is in good part because the word, in Canada, has a very different meaning than its name suggests. Nobody in 1963 or 1971 was suggesting that newly arrived Canadians be settled permanently in isolated ethnocultural enclaves. That form of multiculturalism only really existed in the early nineteenth century and in the Laurier years, when central European religious sects were given their own territory, schools and local self-government rights in order to remain unchanged after settling. Nobody in the late twentieth century believed there should be a multiplicity of cultures, if "culture" is defined most widely as a set of common values and core beliefs and loyalties.

Multiculturalism, in Trudeau's formulation, was simply a way to describe the practice of integration. Canada had moved away from what political scientist Will Kymlicka calls the "racially discriminatory and culturally assimilationist approach to ethnic groups," mainly because, through decades of attempts to subsume Québécois, indigenous Canadians and immigrants into a British ethnic identity, it hadn't worked.

Trudeau's official multiculturalism had four elements. First, the government would, in the words of the policy, "assist all Canadian cultural groups that have demonstrated a desire and effort to continue to develop a capacity to grow and contribute to Canada." Second, Canada would "assist members of all cultural groups to overcome cultural barriers to full participation in Canadian society." Third, Ottawa would "promote creative encounters and interchange amongst all Canadian cultural groups in the interest of national unity." And fourth, federal authorities would "assist immigrants to acquire at least one of Canada's official languages in order to become full participants in Canadian society." Official multiculturalism, in other words, was entirely an integration strategy. Multiculturalism did not challenge English or French as the official languages, challenge Catholicism as the only faith entitled to funded schooling, challenge Quebec's linguistically homogeneous policies, or suggest that there could be any exemptions to the core Canadian values that would later be enumerated in the Charter of Rights and Freedoms.

The budget to implement multiculturalism under the Multiculturalism Directorate was never more than a few million dollars, most of it spent on symbolic grants to festivals and self-appointed ethnic organizations and ethnic media. (These grants have been cynically, but to a large extent correctly, described as vote-buying splurges.) In recent decades, much of the budget has gone unspent. Few really believe that Canada became diverse because a government department decreed it. Some scholars, such as Keith Banting and Will Kymlicka, have argued that official multiculturalism had an indirectly persuasive influence on government policy across all departments, especially in education and broadcasting. This influence may have hastened changes to policy. But sooner or later, as the proportion of "Third Force" Canadians multiplied from a quarter of the population in the 1960s to more than half today, it is hard to imagine that provincial education policies would not have embraced a multicultural approach to integration and language education (since this approach is demonstrably more effective) or that ethnic media would not have thrived.

A post-British Canada was going to become multicultural, no matter what party was in power. By the end of the 1970s multiculturalism had been widely embraced by Tories; it was Brian Mulroney's Progressive Conservative government that enshrined it in law with the 1988 Multiculturalism Act. Likewise, in Quebec, the nationalist movement that had exploded in the 1960s quickly became a multicultural movement. René Lévesque made sure that his Parti Québécois was not an ethnic-nationalist party but at least nominally a multi-ethnic nationalist party defined on linguistic and territorial lines—though, despite repeated efforts to recruit political candidates from racial and religious minority backgrounds, the party's caucus has remained overwhelmingly French Canadian.

When a right-wing populist movement—the Reform Party and then the Canadian Alliance—became the controlling force behind the reimagined Conservative Party in 2003, its new leader, Stephen Harper, recognized that in order to win a parliamentary majority it would need to silence its ethnic-nationalist and anti-immigration factions. It did this aggressively during its eight years in government while embracing the language of diversity and working hard to court the votes of racial and religious minorities. This approach paid off in the 2011 election, when for the first time the Tories won more votes from racial-minority Canadians than the Liberals did. Likewise, while Harper broadly shared Diefenbaker's views of a British-focused Canada, he generally kept this a symbolic mission (by, for example, restoring the coat of arms to parliamentary business cards and restoring the word "Royal" to branches of the military). When, in their unsuccessful 2015 election campaign, the Conservatives made some concessions to ethnic nationalists, with restrictive policy proposals aimed at Muslims, they were widely denounced from both within and outside their party.

The connections between growth, prosperity, population expansion, electoral success and ethnic heterogeneity have become difficult for any governing party to ignore, no matter where they sit on the political spectrum. The consensus around immigration and pluralism is strong enough that even those who question it tend to do so within a broadly pro-immigration perspective. "There are immigration critics in Canada," University of Toronto scholar Jeffrey Reitz concludes in a study of public immigration attitudes, "but in the Canadian context, even the critics turn out to be actually pro-immigration by international standards." The deep cuts and restrictions proposed by the harshest critics would still leave Canada with some of the world's highest immigration rates and diversity levels.

Axiom Two: By ending illusions of homogeneity, Canada would need to see indigenous peoples as partners and co-sovereigns. During the first century of Canadian confederation, indigenous nations—"Indian," Metis and Inuit—held a legal and citizenship status not dissimilar to that of wildlife. Until 1960, they were not allowed to vote. Also illegal were land claims, potlatch ceremonies, the wearing of indigenous clothing or performance of dances outside of reserves, living on-reserve if one married a non-indigenous person, the hiring of lawyers to contest government policies, and in many cases even leaving a reserve without the permission of government officials. Indigenous peoples, in other words, were regarded by the law as non-citizens with no autonomous rights, and by Canadian governments largely as a problem to be managed through bureaucratic means. Most of these means were administered, after 1880, by the Department of Indian Affairs, whose functions were more related to policing and regulation than to anything having to do with citizenship.

This near-total subjugation, and the resulting destruction of families, contributed to a crisis of underpopulation within indigenous nations far more severe than elsewhere in Canada. The First Nations and Metis populations had collapsed from an estimated two million in the early nineteenth century to about 150,000 by Laurier's time. That population had risen to only 240,000 by the Centennial. Canada's approach to its original peoples was unapologetically colonial in both method and intent, and rooted in a view of indigenous populations as economic obstacles and racially inferior subjects.

When that colonial view collapsed at the end of Canada's first century, the logic that underpinned the subjugation of indigenous communities ceased to function. The next five decades would bring a political and demographic rejuvenation of indigenous peoples, and a sometimes begrudging but largely inevitable recognition by Canada's institutions of the status that indigenous communities had held before Confederation.

Indigenous nations themselves provoked the change. The 1960s and early 1970s saw a large-scale awakening of political consciousness among "Indian" communities (the term "First Nations" would not be coined until the 1970s) and a large-scale push for civil rights, treaty rights and land-claim recognition. In 1967, around the same time as the Hawthorn Report revealed the horrors of residential schools, many Canadians were shocked to visit the Indians of Canada pavilion at Expo 67; it had been designed by T.R. Kelly, a Haida, and denounced by officials from the Indian Affairs department, which had funded it. Upon entering, visitors were greeted, in the words of the Canadian Press wire service, with "photographs of tattered, unhappy-looking Indian children placed beside pictures of white Canadian children playing in the comfort of suburbia." At the entrance was a sign whose words pithily summarized the history of indigenous–Canadian relations: "When the white man came we welcomed him with love, we sheltered him, fed him and led him through the forest. Many Indians feel our fathers were betrayed."

That sense of betrayal provoked a set of highly effective legal and constitutional challenges. Shortly after this early awakening of 1967, the Nisga'a Nation of British Columbia launched a court challenge, *Calder v British Columbia*, arguing that aboriginal title to traditional lands was an existing fact that had not been extinguished by colonization—that is, that the First Nations had a more or less sovereign right to land title. The Supreme Court recognized this title as existing above and beyond Canadian law.

Once the courts recognized the existence of aboriginal title it became much more difficult for courts, politicians and informed citizens to see indigenous peoples as only subjects of the Canadian state. What emerged over the next decades was recognition of indigenous sovereignty and self-government on a Canadian territory shared between constitutionally recognized parties. This became a full reality in 1982, when the repatriated Constitution Act included Section 35, recognizing "the existing aboriginal and treaty rights of the aboriginal peoples of Canada," and its Charter of Rights and Freedoms, Section 25, recognized that "aboriginal, treaty or other rights or freedoms that pertain to the aboriginal peoples of Canada" are guaranteed, including those recognized in the Royal Proclamation of 1763.

In essence, Canada's postcolonial mentality led it to recognize, and enshrine in its constitution, the precolonial sovereignty and rights of its original peoples. The logic of this recognition would unfold over the coming decades. The 1999 Nunavut Agreement created a new Canadian territory as a self-governing Inuit nation within Canada. The 2000 Nisga'a Treaty recognized that First Nations had their own inherent rights to establish laws and governments within their territories. Canada had come to recognize, in the words of the 1996 Royal Commission on Aboriginal Peoples, that its centuries of treaties are "constitutional documents, designed to embody the enduring features of the law of the country," and that the promises in those treaties are "part of the foundation of Canada, and keeping those promises is a challenge to the honour and legitimacy of Canada."

None of this arose because Canadians suddenly became altruistic and generous; it arose because indigenous communities demanded it, and there was no longer any logical rationale, in a Canada freed from its minimizing mindset, to refuse those demands.

During the five decades following the Centennial, Canada's indigenous peoples became the youngest and fastest-growing population in the country, reaching 1.4 million by 2017. While still suffering grotesque inequities and unresolved legacies of mistreatment, the original peoples of Canada are now poised to seize the maximizing impulse and overcome the legacy of their own crises of underpopulation.

Axiom Three: In an expanding Canada, Quebec had to choose absolute strength over relative influence. Until the 1960s, Quebec governments, of both major parties in the province, were broadly opposed to population growth and immigration. They tended to share English Canada's belief in a citizenship defined by ethnicity and religion, but they also feared that any significant growth in Canada's overall population would reduce Quebec's share of that population and, therefore, its political influence.

For example, in the early 1950s, the Quebec conservative nationalist François-Albert Angers declared that the federal attempts to increase immigration were part of "the great battle between races in which we have been engaged for 200 years." University of Montreal demographer Pierre Dumareau warned in 1952 that Quebec's share of Canada's population was collapsing, from 32 percent to well below 30 percent and further, as Newfoundland joined Confederation and anglophone immigration increased. As historian Michael Behiels observes, these conservative nationalists "feared the decline in Quebec's francophone population would weaken Quebec's political clout in the federal system"— that Quebec would lose not only its cultural role in Canada but also its share of federal parliamentary votes and comparatively high proportion of prime ministers and cabinet ministers.

Starting in the late 1950s, that view was challenged by the neo-nationalists, who saw population expansion as a source of absolute strength. They weren't interested in Quebec's holding a larger relative role in a federal Canada, but rather in possessing greater absolute strength as a quasi-national entity. Canada's postcolonial moment was also Quebec's postcolonial moment—a rejection of the mono-ethnic, Catholic-led politics that had been Quebec's version of the minimizing impulse. Among Québécois, the maximizing impulse produced a number of different responses: For one, a recognition of Quebec's distinct status within a non-monolithic Canadian federation. For another, a rejection of that federation, its colonial origins and its anglophone hegemony, by rising separatist movements. And, more broadly, a desire to expand Quebec, in economic clout and population, in order to break it free of its former bonds.

The influential neo-nationalist writer Jean-Marc Léger argued forcefully that Quebec was making a mistake in opposing immigration: "An effort to absorb within the Francophone community the greatest possible number of immigrants" would have been better for Quebec than the "systematic refusal" of immigrants and immigration of the postwar years. Combined with the exodus of Quebec's population to New England and Ontario, Léger and other neo-nationalists argued, this refusal of immigration would doom Quebec to dependency by keeping its population too small to self-govern.

By the time the neo-nationalists had evolved into the Parti Québécois in 1968, both separatists and Liberals shared the view that Quebec's absolute population needed to grow, and fast, even if that meant that Canada itself grew faster. The collapse of Quebec fertility rates during the Quiet Revolution injected urgency into this argument: by 1973, Quebec was losing more people through emigration than it was gaining in children. The PQ, under René Lévesque, embraced ethnic and racial pluralism as an approach to expanding the francophone population base, and Liberals largely shared this view. It was simply a matter of ensuring that these immigrants either spoke French or would educate their children in the language—a question that would be the subject of three Ottawa-Quebec immigration policy agreements and two highly controversial Quebec language laws during the next decade.

The Quebec approach to pluralism was intended to be more sharply tailored to Quebec's needs than Trudeau's official multiculturalism, but in practice their differences are few. Both approaches are integration policies that tolerate religious and ethnic differences as a means to acculturation. The big difference is that Ottawa's multiculturalism policy is designed to help non-fluent immigrants integrate into their choice of an English- or French-language education system; the Quebec policy, after 1973, permitted only one language of integration (and is less tolerant of first-generation immigrants doing business in a third language). Quebec's 1981 PQ government plan for "cultural communities" (as minority groups were known by then) had three objectives, strikingly similar to Trudeau's four: "To insure the maintenance and the development of the cultural communities and their specificity, to foster increased awareness among francophone Quebecers of the contribution of the cultural communities . . . [and] to favour the integration of the cultural communities into Quebec society." This approach, separatists recognized, was necessary to gain a sufficient majority to win independence, and indeed, a large part of the PQ "yes" campaign in the 1995 referendum on Quebec sovereignty was devoted to wooing and reassuring minority groups.

By the twenty-first century, this Quebec approach had become known as "interculturalism," and it has been broadly supported by both Liberal and PQ provincial administrations. As sociologists Cory Blad and Philippe Couton describe it, Quebec's official "intercultural framework" is "a collection of legislation and policies that simultaneously strengthens the dominant position of the French language while facilitating the accommodation of immigrants commonly referred to as 'neo-Québécois.'" The links between expansion, growth, immigration and diversity became much harder for any of the province's parties to ignore as Quebec pushed its population beyond eight million, using birth rate–boosting policies and immigration. A minimizing vision of Quebec remains popular in some circles; PQ premier Pauline Marois attempted to draw on these sentiments with her Quebec values charter, which proposed to restrict religious-expression rights. While presented as a French-style defence of secularism, the charter was widely seen as a restriction on the rights of minorities, especially Muslims. The decisive defeat of the bill, and of Marois's government, in the 2014 election was seen as a test of ethnic politics in Quebec, much as the federal Tories' proposed "barbaric cultural practices" act turned the 2015 federal election into a national test of symbolically restrictive ethnic politics. The voters roundly rejected both pieces of legislation, and that neither the PQ nor the federal Tories even suggested a serious stance against ethnic pluralism or immigration shows the extent to which Canadian and Quebec political parties had by 2015 reached a consensus around the maximizing principles.

Axiom Four: A more diversified and independent Canada had to become a more North American Canada. The national consensus around trade took longer to reach than a unified view on ethnic plurality and immigration. By the 1960s, resource trade with Britain was only a marginal part of Canada's economic activity, and after Diefenbaker's failed lunge toward Britain, it was not coming back. By the Centennial, it was obvious to any informed observer—or any consumer perusing the shelves—that Canada was embedded in a North American economy.

The 1965 Auto Pact and the loosening of tariff barriers under the General Agreement on Tariffs and Trade had gone partway toward creating a continental economy already, but the relationship remained awkward. Much of the Canadian economy was owned and controlled by Americans, Canadian exporters had a hard time gaining access to the huge market to the south, and Canadian consumers and companies were both hurt by the higher price of imported goods.

Nevertheless, in 1967, and for a decade thereafter, the need for a more open North American economy could not be articulated in politics. The country was consumed with debate about the United States, but the main subject was U.S. control of Canadian cultural and commercial life, the "silent surrender" (the title of a popular 1970 book on the subject) to U.S.-owned branch plants and homogenizing multinational corporations. The post-Centennial decade saw the expansion of nationalist cultural policy to prevent U.S. domination of the media, including a ban on U.S.-only newsmagazines and the subsidy of Canadian titles and the introduction of Canadian-content regulations in radio and TV programming. It also saw the launch, in 1973, of the Foreign Investment Review Agency, designed to restrict the U.S. takeover ~~of strategically important~~ Canadian companies.

A more general anti-Americanism had crept into Canadian life. The Vietnam War, hugely unpopular in Canada (which became home to tens of thousands of well-educated war resisters), and then the military and political excesses of the Nixon era had made closer ties with Washington seem distasteful. The old minimizing view of Canada as defiantly British and non–North American, previously a core facet of Tory ideology, for the first time made inroads into the political left. Religious philosopher George Grant's angry 1965 book *Lament for a Nation*, which denounced Pearson's economically and culturally liberal policies and called for a return to Diefenbaker's closed and British Canada, became an unlikely bestseller among left-leaning Canadians in the late 1960s and 1970s because it offered a nationalist denunciation of the American war machine and its corporate offshoots. North American integration, in this atmosphere, was a non-starter.

The economic horrors of the late 1970s and early 1980s changed the political logic of North American integration. Everyone felt the lack of a secure economic foothold as resource prices decayed and export markets dried up. It was Pierre Trudeau's Liberals, late in their mandate, who first made the case for a more North American economy. Trudeau appointed Donald Macdonald, his finance minister, to produce a mammoth report exploring the best policies to avoid a repeat of the devastating 1981–82 recession; his research brought around the Liberals, and then Mulroney's Tories, to free trade.

The Macdonald Report is worth visiting here. Its 1,900 pages are, at heart, a detailed account of the maximizing impulse and its consequences. Its full set of proposals—which include an elected Senate and a guaranteed basic income—was never implemented, but its argument for free trade became the dominant Canadian idea of the 1980s. The report described the social and economic consequences of Canada's postcolonial independence, then linked those consequences to the economic problems of Canada's limited population:

> We are now on our own. The United Kingdom has receded in importance for Canadians, both practically and psychologically. . . . English-speaking Canada is now multicultural, defined by language rather than by a shared British past. The metropolitan centres of anglophone Canada are home to a diverse population of many cultural backgrounds and various countries of origin. French Canada, too, is now multicultural. . . . That ethnic awareness is evident in the contemporary self-confidence and assertiveness of Canada's aboriginal peoples, who have exchanged their former political obscurity for a high visibility sustained by various political organizations. . . .
>
> Our trade with Britain is much reduced from earlier times: it represented 2.2 per cent of our merchandise exports and 2.5 per cent of our merchandise imports in 1984, well under half of our growing trade with Japan. The United States is now overwhelmingly dominant as our major trading partner. We can no longer judiciously balance ourselves in trade between the United States and Great Britain. . . . Our domestic market is too small for us to look inward for salvation and to reduce the ties of international economic interdependence which already exist. . . . Protectionism is counterproductive and self-defeating. In a world of growing regional trading

blocs, Canada is one of the few industrial countries lacking secure access to a market of over 100 million people. . . . The small size of our domestic market weakens whatever attractions might possibly reside in protectionist measures if we had five times our present population.

This observation—that Canada would not be able to grow successfully as a country until it looked outward for markets—was in 1985 self-evident to many Canadians. But it would take a decade, including an ugly showdown over free trade in the 1988 federal election, for this view to become a national consensus.

The 1980s seemed to experience an odd political inversion, in which the Tories and Liberals reversed the positions they'd held for a century on Canada-U.S. free trade. This was partly an illusion born of political contingency. The big, and historic, change was the Progressive Conservatives' abandonment of the colonial, anti-American view they'd held at least until the end of Diefenbaker's leadership. The Liberals hardly seemed comfortable with their anti-trade posture and would soon abandon it, ratifying the North American Free Trade Agreement and returning to their pro-trade status by the time they formed a majority government in 1993. The NDP spent a decade as virtually a single-issue anti-trade party, a stance that thrust them into the political margins until the 2000s, when it was largely abandoned by leaders Jack Layton and Thomas Mulcair. By 2003, there was a wide political consensus across the mainstream Canadian political spectrum in favour of North American integration—a consensus that appears to be shared by most Canadians.

That more open view of trade and economic relations, along with a widely shared expansionist view of the economy, the role of Quebec and indigenous peoples, the rights of individuals and the plural nature of citizenship and society, means that Canadians—if they can find the political will—are in a position to build an increasingly equal, thriving, ecologically sustainable and socially just country during this century. The major remaining limitation is the increasingly visible price of underpopulation.

PART THREE

OUR COUNTRY'S CAPACITY

CHAPTER 6

The Price of Underpopulation

If you're stuck in traffic on Vancouver's Lions Gate Bridge, shoulder-to-shoulder on the King streetcar in Toronto or trying to find a free seat on a *terrasse* on Montreal's Plateau any summer evening, you might easily be convinced that there are in fact too many Canadians. The country's low population density is not usually something you live and feel. It becomes tangible only when you set out to do certain things that require an audience, a market, or the support of an institution or medium that only a populous country can provide. Then you discover that there's just not enough Canada.

If you're an entrepreneur seeking venture capital, an activist fighting for better public services or a professional searching for the best credentials, then you have probably, at some point, run up against the limits of Canada's population. Same if you're an artist or writer looking for an audience big enough to provide you with a living, an online entrepreneur seeking clicks for your apps, a mayor hoping to cover your city with decent public transit or an environmentalist seeking a big shift to green technology in energy and transportation.

For individual Canadians, the most familiar experience of underpopulation is the discovery, at some point in your career, that you need to leave the country. Whether it's for a couple of years to get an education, sponsorship or big break in a key venue, or a couple of decades to get a contract, a reputation or a patent, or the rest of your life to succeed on a larger stage, it's part of the experience of successful Canadians to discover, at some point, that there aren't enough people at home to give you what you need.

This is a constant theme in the lives of successful Canadians I've met abroad: an appreciation of the opportunities that full-scale countries can offer, but a regret that these opportunities can't all be transferred back home. I once sat down with Frank Gehry in his Santa Monica studio, fifty years after he'd left postwar Toronto for Los Angeles, and asked him why he hadn't stuck around Canada to build his architecture career. He told me, with some dismay, that Canada had not offered the well-supported educational institutions, the critical mass of creative people to produce radical new ideas, or the consumer markets for architecture to support more inventive practices. "I remember reading the final exam for first-year architecture—they had the exams there [in secondary school] so you could see what it was like—and you had to design a traditional little cottage. And I remember thinking, this is just terrible, boring, nothing to it. So based on that, if I had stayed there, I never would have gotten into architecture." Or consider the words of the jazz pianist Paul Bley, who left Montreal's downstairs clubland for the frenetic experimentation of Greenwich Village. There simply wasn't, in any Canadian city, the critical mass of musical inventors or the audiences to support the sort of venues where major things happen. "For us practicing our standards and sitting in and playing 'well' and whatever, it just wasn't the same breed of animal," he told interviewer Bill Smith. "You thought you were playing jazz. . . . But when you heard the amount of wind that came off these stands [in New York], you realized you would have to totally lose your reticent Canadian personality before you could even expect to keep up. That was the shock. That incredible power and confidence."

Those sentiments would be echoed by well-known Canadians from Donald Sutherland to Malcolm Gladwell to Céline Dion to Mark Henry Roswell (who, under the name Dashan, is the most famous comedian in China), and by millions of lesser-known Canadians in less public occupations. They all made a start in the small Canadian market before discovering that it simply did not have the resources to support their ambitions. To have a public and a set of establishments and peers large enough to support them, these Canadians had to move south of the border or to Europe, or sometimes to Asia. Many move back after using more populous reaches to develop themselves (and, if they enter politics, they sometimes face opposition heat for it); many others do not. Almost three million Canadians live abroad—nearly 9 percent of our population. This shouldn't be seen strictly as a net loss for Canada; even in a fully equipped country, it's admirable to use the wider world to expand yourself. The problem, in Canada, is that there's often no other way.

———

On the most basic level, population doesn't matter. Having more people does not by itself make a country more successful. Some of the poorest and most deprived countries in the world have very large populations; some of the most prosperous have tiny populations. Switzerland, Israel, Norway and Singapore all have fewer people than the city of London (though their tiny geographies give them a much higher population density, which, as we'll see, is important). Nor does population have any effect on democracy or quality of governance, one way or another. When we talk about Canadian underpopulation, we are not talking about the absolute number of people. More is not better.

Rather, the issue of population in overly sparse countries such as Canada is one of *capacity*. Do we have the right people, in the right numbers, concentrated closely enough together in the right places, to do the things together that we want and need to do? Given our huge geography, our widely dispersed communities and our wavering dependence on larger, foreign markets, do we have a sufficiently high density of taxpayers, consumers, audiences, inventors, specialists, investors, elders and healers, entrepreneurs, caregivers, scholars, activists and leaders to create the things we need to sustain our standard of living through a potentially difficult future?

Citizens, after all, are not simply figures in a statistical table or a homogeneous lump of population adding up to some national grand total. Their numbers matter insofar as they do things, insofar as they play roles in the civic, economic and cultural life of the country. To determine the effectiveness of our population, we need to examine not the raw totals of people but the ways in which citizens group together to interact with one another and the world.

There are several crucial ways to look at our population. We can look at it as a *market*—that is, as people who will consume the goods and services created by other people, allowing their enterprises to succeed. As *taxpayers*—people of working and therefore taxpaying age who can provide a fiscal base that will support public institutions and infrastructure at a scale needed by a successful country, in great enough numbers to keep their tax rates reasonable. As a *labour force*—people whose skills and strengths can be put to work, in enough numbers to make enterprises function. As an *audience*—people who consume and support the information services, the cultural and media institutions and the online resources of the country. As *clusters of expertise*—groups of skilled and educated people who work closely together, sharing knowledge, enterprise and funding, in order to create new products, services and scientific advances. Finally, as *cities*—pools of people living closely together and sharing resources. A generation of research has shown that high-density cities are disproportionately where economic and creative activity flourishes.

In other words, Canadians together simultaneously form a market, a group of taxpayers, a labour force, an audience for culture and media, clusters of inventors and entrepreneurs, and a set of urban bodies. At the moment, we have enough people to make things work reasonably well. But if we examine each of these population groupings and their ambitions, we start to see the capacity that is missing, the potential that is unavailable, and the shortfall in human activity that leaves Canada vulnerable and leaves us unprepared for a more challenging economic future.

THE PUBLIC COST: A LACK OF CHOICES

When scholars and governments talk about population shortfalls these days, they are most often looking at the demographic and fiscal challenges of a population that is aging fast and growing slowly. This is not Canada's problem alone; many other countries face this demographic crunch, and some, including France and Germany, have already taken aggressive policy action to counter it with population and labour-force policy. It is not the most pressing or the most insoluble problem of underpopulation, and it is largely a medium-term problem, occurring over the next forty or fifty years. But it happens to be one that terrifies governments, economists and investors, because it has the potential to measurably lower our quality of life.

Canadian families today have an average of 1.6 children each, a rate somewhat higher than it was at the turn of the twenty-first century but still below the rate in many other Western countries, and well short of the 2.1 children per family needed to maintain a stable population. As a result, Canada's population growth currently depends entirely on immigration. The national population has been growing, at a modest rate averaging about 1.2 percent each year, but not as fast as the average age of Canadians has been increasing. To put it more bluntly, the number of baby boomers turning sixty-five each year outnumbers the babies and children entering Canada through childbirth and immigration. For the first time in our history, there are now more Canadians over sixty-five than there are Canadians fourteen and younger.

This has a direct impact on Canada's capabilities—that is, on the ability of our governments, agencies and charities to act effectively on things like environment, infrastructure, poverty and justice for indigenous peoples. That's because an aging, slow-growing population means a country that has both fewer fiscal resources and higher costs.

At the moment, 16.1 percent of Canadians are sixty-five and older. By 2035, the proportion of Canadians over sixty-five will have risen by more than half, to 25 percent. By 2026, more than 2.4 million Canadians over sixty-five will require continuing care support (long-term care, seniors' homes and so on)—a 71 percent increase from 2011. By 2046, this number will reach 3.3 million.

The most important figure for governments is the dependency ratio: the number of working-age people (who contribute the lion's share of taxes) compared to the number of retirement-age people (who tend to consume considerably more tax-supported services). In Canada, this ratio is shifting quickly. At the moment, there are four working-age Canadians to support each retirement-age Canadian; by 2031, that will be halved to a two-to-one ratio. For a couple of decades, we will have only about two taxpayers to support each senior.

This will be expensive. According to the Conference Board of Canada, spending on continuing care for seniors will need to increase from $29.3 billion in 2011 to an extraordinary $184.2 billion in 2046. Two-thirds of this spending will be provided by governments, which at the same time will be losing tax revenue because of a lowered workforce ratio. And this estimate is based on Canada's eldercare institutions relying, as they do today, on a significant number of unpaid or poorly paid caregivers and volunteers—a situation that could prove unsustainable or intolerable to a generation of seniors, and their families, who expect better care. Therefore the $184.2 billion estimate may be low.

Long-term care is only part of the puzzle. Healthcare spending by provinces, currently $150 billion a year, will increase from

37 percent of government revenue today to 44 percent by 2042—a huge chunk out of already strained provincial budgets. Likewise, the share of federal tax earnings that will have to be spent on Old Age Security will rise from 16.5 percent today (making OAS the largest single item in the federal budget) to 20 percent by the 2030s. Health and eldercare spending will eventually begin to fall as the baby boom generation passes away, but this won't happen until after 2050.

This means that both federal and provincial governments will face some very difficult choices. After all, healthcare, long-term care and Old Age Security are not items that would be politically or practically easy to cut; quite the contrary, there will be substantial pressure to increase funding for all three. Without additional places to draw revenue from, beyond a slim margin for further tax increases, most of this adjustment will need to come from large-scale reductions to other government departments and programs, including education, transit infrastructure, the social safety net and environmental protection—areas that are otherwise considered central to generating future growth and stability.

At the same time as this is happening, low population growth will also eat into revenues. The proportion of high-tax-contributing working-age people in the population will be decreasing fast, and the demographic realities will cause a slowing of economic growth. According to the Organisation for Economic Co-operation and Development, Canada's economy will grow by an average of only 1.5 percent per year for the rest of the century if current immigration and fertility levels stay the same.

In other words, governments will find their capacity limited—both by rising costs and by falling revenues. If nothing changes,

Canada is headed into a future where it will have to do more with less. Not some catastrophic dystopia, but a frustrating sort of time that Canada has known before: a more difficult and straitened place where a lot of hopes and ambitions will have to be put off until later.

That is not the only possible future. It could be a lot tougher. According to Conference Board forecasts, if immigration were restricted to half its current level in coming decades—for example, if an anti-immigration party of the sort we've seen in Europe and the United States were to hold power for some time—then the decline in population growth rates would cause economic growth to fall to an average of 0.6 percent annually. This would both choke off private-sector investment and limit government capacity.

On the other hand, if a maximizing agenda were pursued—a robust set of family policies to bring fertility rates to 1.7 and a modest increase in immigration, to a rate of 1.3 percent annually (that is, a gradual increase to a peak of 408,000 immigrants per year, or less if birth rates rise more), with the aim of reaching a population of 100 million by 2100—then the dependency ratio would shift. The proportion of Canadians over sixty-five would peak at a markedly lower 23.2 percent, creating considerably more options.

Under this population-growth scenario, provincial healthcare spending would fall from 34.5 percent to 29.2 percent of the budget, a savings equivalent to $21.2 billion in today's dollars annually. Old Age Security would decline to 10 percent of the federal budget. And economic growth would be much stronger: an average of 2.6 percent annually rather than the current 1.5 percent, driven by a larger domestic market with greater retail sales, savings and investment. A more capable government and a more sustainable economy would mutually reinforce one another.

This is, admittedly, not the most exciting case for population growth. There is something a bit bloodless and desperate in governments urging their citizens to pop out more babies and welcome more immigrants simply in order to make their balance sheets add up—even if we are aware, on some level, that those balances have a profound effect on our standard of living and our children's ability to have a better life in Canada.

And a reasonably big slice of the dependency-ratio problem can be dealt with through non-population means. An aging workforce can be expanded as other countries have done, with policies allowing retirees to return to full-time work while still collecting their pensions, and programs such as flexible worktime and expanded childcare making it much easier for women to return to work while raising children. Some European countries that have spent heavily on such policies expect them to take care of as much as a fifth of their dependency-ratio problem, somewhat reducing the need for immigration and fertility policies.

While a larger population will make it possible for Canada to grow and improve its living standards during the decades of aging population, it won't completely erase that problem. In any of these scenarios, the proportion of the population over sixty-five will not return to current levels, and the 2040s will be an expensive time for governments no matter what happens; provincial health-care spending will rise to above 40 percent of the budget for a decade, no matter what we do (though with a larger population, it would fall far more quickly). As a Conference Board analysis commissioned by the Century Initiative concludes, "the increase in the population will not reverse the consequences of an aging population but will significantly help to cushion the economic impact." A population increase will, however, have even more significant impact on the savings, investments and jobs of Canadians, for the impact of underpopulation on our economic lives is profound.

THE PRIVATE COST: INADEQUATE COMPETITION AND INNOVATION

For most of Canada's first century, the price of underpopulation was a near-total dependence on the export of things pulled out of the earth and ocean: timber, grain, fish, minerals, oil, gas. Or to put it the other way around, the price of resource dependency was underpopulation; an agrarian and extractive economy does not require a large concentration of people.

That changed gradually until the 1960s, and then dramatically, with a larger and more urban population increasingly linked to the world economy. Today, if you get a job in Canada, it's most likely to be in a service field, in the public or private sector; construction and manufacturing are also among Canada's large employers. Natural resources account for between 14 and 17 percent of Canada's economic activity, and an even smaller share of employment—although resources have a disproportionate effect on our financial well-being, because the majority of Canada's export earnings (between 50 and 65 percent, depending on commodity prices) come from what one study calls "unprocessed and barely processed materials." This makes the value of the Canadian dollar, and thus of much of the Canadian economy, a reflection of the raw material sectors. Internally, we are economically diverse, but we still often face the world as a source of staples.

Our desire to build a more diversified, innovation-based economy often hits the brick wall of a limited domestic market or runs aground on Canada's comparatively sparse distribution of investors and venture capitalists, top technical minds and skilled specialists. Our existing population is well equipped for the country to become a creative-economy leader: Canadians are now among the most educated people in the world, with 64 percent of adults aged twenty-five to sixty-four having post-secondary education. Canada consistently ranks in the top four countries of the Global Entrepreneurship Index, meaning that it has the right resources and policies for giving inventive new businesses a start. And Canada is a world leader in science and technology innovation, in the top handful of nations in measures of patents, research papers and Nobel Prizes per capita. But anyone in business will tell you that there are real limits to what can be accomplished in Canada's low-density population, and those limits would become prohibitive should levels of globalization decline further and world trade become restricted.

For most Canadians, the relatively small size of the domestic consumer market is not some abstract economic concept; it's a matter of day-to-day experience and occasional exasperation. That's in large part because we live next door to a culturally similar consumer market that happens to be ten times larger. As a result, the limits of underpopulation are often experienced by Canadians as a routine consumer nuisance. Many international products cost considerably more in Canada than they do a few kilometres to the south, because of the higher cost of distributing them across a thinly populated geography. Many others are simply never available in Canada, or aren't available until years later, because the profit margins don't justify the cost of entering such a small market, or in the case of certain books and movies, because the audience doesn't make it worth the time to sell separate Canadian rights. Likewise, the number of retailers offering consumer goods in Canada is much more limited; this lack of competition means that sale prices and discounts are less exciting than they are in the States or in Europe. When we head for American discount malls during our winter vacations, we're living the consequences of underpopulation—albeit in a small, not terribly damaging way.

We also know, from long experience, what it means to be dominated by larger markets—not just consumer markets but also capital and investment markets. We may have moved beyond the days of the 1950s, 1960s and 1970s when controversies over U.S. ownership and the transformation of Canada into a "branch-plant economy" dominated politics and media, but we still run up against the limits of market size. Canadians, after the battles of the 1980s, became less economically nationalist and made an uneasy peace with foreign ownership. We came to see ourselves as a global trading nation, and it also became apparent that for a country with a low population, the only significant available investment is foreign investment.

Still, much of recent Canadian business history has been a series of disappointments. Many of our largest national companies, once they grow big enough to compete in world markets, are suddenly too big to be owned by Canadians. So we have endured the Brazilian purchase of Inco, the Australian purchase of Alcan, the Swiss purchase of Falconbridge, the U.S. purchase of Stelco, the Luxembourgian purchase of Dofasco, the French purchase of Newbridge Networks, the U.S. purchase of Molson Brewery and the Belgian purchase of Labatt. On one level, we know that the nationality of a company's owner isn't really so important—an owner can be a local tyrant or a foreign saint. But we also know that in foreign-owned firms, the top jobs—the innovative and creative side of the company, the most important research and development and engineering—always migrate toward the owner's home country.

Low-population countries can and do thrive as inventors and innovators in a global economy, as any Swiss, Israeli or Singaporean businessperson knows. This is what Canada's successful companies have done: they have leapt almost immediately into the global economy. Technology policy researcher Mark Zachary Taylor, in his work *The Politics of Innovation*, finds that smaller-population countries that have become leaders in science and technology innovation tend to be those with very limited geographies and, thus, populations highly concentrated in a small area. They are also quite often countries that face some sort of threat or extraneous limitation (Taiwan, Israel, Singapore, South Korea), forcing their businesses to innovate internationally rather than to hold steady in a safe harbour. This may be why so many of Canada's most successful international non-resource businesses are headquartered in Quebec: the Québécois population is more concentrated and has a sense of constricted linguistic and cultural identity that provides a stronger incentive to search outside for opportunities.

Over the past twenty years a substantial volume of research has been conducted by economists into the population and demographic factors that allow companies to succeed, generate high employment and achieve "takeoff" into the global economy. Many studies have concluded that size of market is centrally important—not just consumer market but the markets in skills, employees, services, patents and expertise. Consumer markets can be located partly or entirely outside the home country, but markets in skills and ideas often have to be domestic. And even under free trade, international borders are not completely porous; there's a benefit to companies that start in a big domestic market.

In his landmark 2003 study "The Size of Countries," Harvard economist Alberto Alesina found that a state's physical size matters little but that the size of its domestic markets—and their concentration across geographic space—matters a lot. Assuming that a country already has a middle-class industrial economy and successful trade relationships, Alesina identified a set of factors that improve when it has a larger population. First, as noted above, the "per capita costs of many public goods are lower in larger countries where more taxpayers can pay for them." Second, national security is easier to maintain without outside assistance. Third, the size of a country's domestic market allows for greater endogenous growth (that is, growth that is not dependent on trade or outside forces). Fourth, a larger population allows countries to provide insurance to their weaker regions should they suffer a downturn (what Canadians call equalization payments). Fifth, a larger population means that the forces that affect economic growth, the value of the currency and so on tend to be internal, domestic forces (and therefore more controllable) rather than international forces—what Alesina calls "an internalization of externalities." And sixth, the economies of scale provided by a large population make it easier, and more affordable, to combat social inequality through safety-net programs.

Companies can partially compensate for small population size by drawing on international trade, Alesina notes, but this has its limits—and makes them very vulnerable to international economic and political shifts. A larger domestic market does two things an international market cannot: it causes productivity to increase and it allows entrepreneurs and investors to step in, overcome fixed costs, and spur development." International trade will never be as strong a driver as domestic demand. As Alesina notes, "two distant Canadian provinces [British Columbia and Ontario] trade much more with each other than with U.S. states and Canadian provinces bordering each other, even though distance is usually a strong determinant of trade flows. . . . Trade makes borders more open but crossing national borders still has a cost in terms of trade flows."

A limited population hurts a country's innovation and business creativity in another way, one that will particularly affect Canada. An aging and slow-growing population—that is, one without a sufficiently large influx of younger newcomers to compensate—not only produces less consumer demand but is also measurably less able to create new ideas and products.

Swiss economist Stefan Legge, in a 2016 analysis of OECD data across thirty-five countries over thirty-eight years, found that aging populations have a negative effect on innovation. "In an aging population," his research concludes, "a larger fraction of the population does not invest in acquiring new skills. The amount of R&D is reduced as demand for innovative goods falls. Those countries that faced the largest demographic shifts [in average age] experienced the sharpest growth reduction in patent applications."

Many successful Canadian companies have gotten around the population problem by plunging directly into foreign markets, taking a "straight-to-global" or "mini-multinational" approach. Relatively easy access to foreign markets has meant that leading Canadian companies, from Bombardier to Couche-Tard to

BlackBerry to EllisDon, have all but skipped over the Canadian market to go international first. And Canadian businesses are hoping to repeat this trick in a range of medical, information technology, service and energy fields in coming years.

But it is becoming much more difficult, and sometimes impossible, to go global this way. That's because the politics and economics of the global market have changed dramatically, especially since the 2008 financial crisis. Aside from the looming threat of trade protectionism (which has become far more politically palatable, especially in the United States), two other things have changed dramatically since 2008.

First, many of the world's largest markets are giving exclusive access to their own countries' businesses in a way that Canada never could. In 2009, at the peak of the financial crisis, the United States passed the sprawling American Recovery and Reinvestment Act, whose "buy American" provision requires all public projects receiving federal funds to use only materials and manufactured goods produced in the United States. While Canadian companies have been exempt from this program since 2010, its larger effect has been to give U.S. firms a sizeable competitive advantage in the form of guaranteed purchasing agreements from the world's largest government.

And the United States is far from alone. India has pursued a series of official and de facto "buy local" policies, some contested by the World Trade Organization but many still in effect, which together with other restrictions make it very difficult for foreign firms to enter the Indian market. China has implemented aggressive "buy Chinese" policies. These include a formal provision by the National Development and Reform Commission, in place since 2009, requiring any state-funded projects using stimulus funds to buy only from Chinese companies unless no domestic supplier exists, as well as the even more comprehensive "indigenous innovation" policies, in effect since 2006 but greatly amplified after 2010, in which Chinese governments at all levels may purchase technology products only from catalogues that generally exclude suppliers that are foreign-owned or receive foreign investment (even if they are located in China). So, for example, of the 523 products listed in the government of Shanghai's procurement catalogue, according to the *China Business Review*, only two are made by "foreign-invested enterprises," and these are "Chinese-foreign joint ventures with majority Chinese ownership." Western business organizations report that it has become prohibitively difficult—some would say nearly impossible—for foreign firms to enter Chinese consumer or public procurement markets in any significant way. A free-trade agreement between Canada and China would have only a slight effect on these barriers. And a great many other major economies, both in the West and in the larger emerging markets, now have preferential policies that give domestic firms a significant, and sometimes total, advantage. While the European Union forbids such preferential policies, the number of countries whose markets are genuinely open to Canadian firms is dwindling fast.

In a second major change since the downturn of 2008, larger economies now pour huge sums of public money into the research and development budgets of their favoured domestic companies and sectors. Because WTO rules don't restrict government funding of private-sector research, this has become a popular way to give national firms a global competitive advantage through de facto subsidies. A 2016 study of international R&D funding by the OECD found in many countries—notably Germany, Japan and Korea, but also China and the United States—"a tendency among governments to focus more on offering R&D tax incentives to firms than funding R&D in universities and public laboratories," and concluded that this served to help companies enter global markets more than it did to spur important new inventions. A big part of the U.S. Recovery and Reinvestment Act consists of billions in subsidies to corporate R&D.

Of course, Canada can respond in kind. And it does. Initiatives such as Ontario's Green Energy Act have imposed "buy local" restrictions on public spending, and Ottawa and many provinces offer tax credits for private-sector R&D; the federal program funnels more than four billion dollars a year into Canadian corporations. If other countries are boosting their technology, health and energy companies into global markets through procurement and subsidy, why shouldn't Canada do the same?

This, however, is where Canada gets tripped up by its low population. Unlike companies headquartered in larger economies, Canada's businesses can't fall back on a domestic market to build a global standing, because Canada's scale is not large enough to provide enough consumers or state support to give companies a base of activity. This is why almost all of Canada's most successful innovative companies—those that aren't in resource-extraction fields or state-protected sectors such as banking and telecom— have generally taken a "straight to global" approach. For high-development-cost, high-employment industries based in Canada, the global market is the only market. And when that market begins to turn inward and protect its own, Canadian companies are left with nowhere to expand.

This was the conclusion reached by Dan Herman, the founder and director of the Centre for Digital Entrepreneurship and

Economic Performance at the University of Waterloo, who spent several years (before he joined the federal government's division of Innovation Policy and Analysis in 2016) analyzing the prospects for innovation and creative growth in the Canadian economy. He and his colleagues found that population kept getting in the way, as he told me:

> From 2009 onward, we've had this massive upsurge in protectionist measures. We can no longer look outside our country for growth because we're now living in a slow-growth world, so we're now asking ourselves, "What does our market allow us to do internally?" And you think, What does a small economy do in that world? And at 34 million people, we are small; that makes us a trading nation by design and necessity. We don't have a market size that's going to grow firms and allow them to develop with a domestic market of that size.
>
> So we're dependent on the international market. But, wait a minute, the international market is increasingly looking inwards. We have always sought to find another market. But the challenge is that all of those potential replacements, in China and India and the rest of Asia, they've become inward-looking and exceptionally focused on endogenous domestic growth in targeted sectors. And all these countries are looking at the same sectors as us—they all want to build the next platforms in ICT [information and communications technology] and in medical and in energy.
>
> And if everyone else turns inward, there's not much value in Canada also turning inward. That's when you get back to the 34 million and you ask, What can you sell to that

market and actually build big companies? Not much. What can you do for an international company in terms of government contracts? Not much. We don't have the consumer base or the tax base to do it—we can provide some support, but there's a real limitation as to how deep that can be.

Again, Canada's population problem is not simply a matter of raw numbers of people but also of their connection, density and accumulation. We don't have the very large groupings and clusters of talented people that larger countries do. One thing economists and business analysts agree on is that economic success takes place not in countries as a whole but in major cities, subregions and "agglomerations" or "clusters" with high population density. And as Canadians are learning, if cities aren't sufficiently populous, dense and developed, they limit economic success.

In their classic 2003 paper on the subject, Massachusetts Institute of Technology economists Daron Acemoglu and Joshua Linn used data analyses of pharmaceutical companies to show that companies located in larger regional or national markets are measurably more innovative, inventive and, as a result, profitable. Specifically, they found that every 1 percent increase in the size of a market leads to between a 4 and a 4.75 percent increase in the number of patents in that area—and that a greater market size spurs faster innovation and more patents.

In a major meta-analysis of "the geography of innovation," Maryann Feldman of the University of North Carolina and Dieter Kogler of the University of Toronto found that levels of innovation and inventive output (as measured by number of patents registered) are tightly tied to the size and concentration of population in a company's location. As they found, innovation tends to be spatially concentrated in a few key places, but "places are not equal." Locations where large volumes of invention occur tend to be defined by high levels of urbanization and urban population, high levels of localization (that is, related enterprises located near to one another) and high levels of economic diversity.

In his analysis of the factors driving the "Canada-US prosperity gap" (that is, the considerably lower rates of income, economic activity and productivity in Canada as compared to the United States), University of Toronto economic analyst James Milway found that the largest factor holding back Canada's productivity was the comparatively small size of its major cities:

> Canada's lower degree of urbanization hurts our productivity compared to the US. There is a positive relationship between degree of urbanization and the labour productivity of 60 jurisdictions in North America. Urbanization is defined as the percentage of their population living in city areas of greater than 50,000 people. For Canada it includes our 43 largest cities ranging in size from Toronto to Lethbridge.
>
> Our analysis indicates that we have a $3,200 per capita disadvantage against the US. In other words, if the rate of Canadian urbanization matched that of the US and our productivity grew in relation to current North American patterns our GDP per capita would increase by $3,200. This makes low urbanization the largest negative contributor to Canada's productivity gap.

Economic activity at the highest levels won't take place until city regions have grown to a substantial size and density. Milway lists three key reasons. First, because network effects drive innovation (that is, close proximity of firms increases the social and intellectual interactions that forge inventiveness). Second, because economies of scale reduce costs. And third, because "thick" labour markets—that is, places with a large concentration and variety of skilled people—are beneficial both for workers and for companies.

We know that any substantial increase in Canada's population this century will take place mostly in its largest cities. During the past thirty years, almost all of Canada's population growth has occurred in four places: Metropolitan Montreal, the Golden Horseshoe area surrounding Toronto, the Calgary-Edmonton corridor, and the Lower Mainland and surrounding area of British Columbia. Everywhere else, population growth rates have been close to zero. An increase in Canadian population will not pave over large areas of valuable farmland and green space, as it did in previous centuries; if done to create maximum economic benefit, it will instead expand the density, intensity and diversity of Canada's existing cities.

The lion's share of this century's population growth will take place in the economic and creative hubs of southern British Columbia, central Alberta, southern Ontario and western Quebec, and in the population-hungry high-technology and university-focused cities such as Victoria, Lethbridge, Winnipeg, Kitchener-Waterloo, Hamilton, Kingston, Ottawa, Trois-Rivières, Quebec City, Moncton and Halifax. Canada is a highly urbanized country, and both immigration-based and fertility-based population growth tend to take place almost exclusively in its larger cities. While there is certainly an important *Little Mosque on the Prairie* phenomenon in which newcomers take over failing businesses and underutilized farms in small towns and rural areas, it is numerically limited. Almost all growth is urban.

This growth is badly needed, because Canada's large cities currently suffer from a set of challenges rooted in low population density. After decades of poor land-use planning, Canadian cities have spread many people over a fairly sparse area, often at densities too low to support decent (and ecological) levels of public transit, infrastructure and business clustering. This is beginning to change in Vancouver and Toronto as demand drives construction of higher-density apartment housing, but it remains a shortcoming. Canada does not yet have a Silicon Valley, a Manhattan or a "Silicon Roundabout" (the City of London's technology district), because none of our cities have developed to the point where they can create such dense concentrations of networked creativity.

As Montreal economic and urban policy scholar Mario Polèse found in his 2013 study of "agglomeration economies," the Canadian cities that have the potential to develop populations capable of "above-average specialization in knowledge-rich 'metropolitan' functions" are those with more than 500,000 people today. An effect known as the "First Mover Advantage" suggests that the current hierarchy of Canadian cities will remain stable, and the larger ones will scale up in size sharply. Significantly, Polèse found that the most important factor determining where businesses will establish themselves is proximity to one of the five largest cities, as well as the ability to gain easy access to the largest domestic markets and trade corridors. He suggests that densely clustered areas of large and small cities within a two-hour drive of Vancouver, Montreal, Toronto, Ottawa and Calgary are where most business growth and economic development will take place.

THE ECOLOGICAL COST: INEFFICIENT CITIES

Underpopulation harms Canada's climate and ecological prospects in two important ways. It forces us to use inefficient and highly polluting forms of transportation, heating and energy, because our population density is too low to support more energy-efficient technology. And it denies us the critical mass of fiscal and human resources we need to build infrastructure for green-energy generation and alternative low-energy national transportation networks, and to protect us against the effects of climate change. So the growth of Canada's urban population is important for reasons that go beyond the economy. By settling in urban areas—and in numbers large enough to provide a fiscal base for public infrastructure—the next wave of Canadians will be the country's most important ecological asset.

Canada's largest source of greenhouse gas emissions during most years, accounting for a quarter of the carbon we put into the atmosphere, is transportation. Passenger vehicles generate the largest share of these emissions by far, and most of the output is urban. The heating of buildings—especially inefficient single-family homes—accounts for another 12 percent, and the use of inefficient fossil-fuel electrical generation, 11 percent. In other words, half of Canada's atmospheric damage is caused by factors directly rooted in our low population density. We don't have the masses of people needed to replace internal-combustion transportation with efficient public transit and high-speed rail, we rely too much on sprawling single-family dwellings that lack heating efficiency, and we still don't have the population size to pay for rapid replacement of fossil-fuel-based power generation with non-emitting sources (although that change is taking place, slowly).

Toronto and Vancouver are at a particularly frustrating point in their development. Toronto, whose greater metropolitan area contains nearly six million people, and Vancouver, whose Lower Mainland exurb has more than 2.5 million people, were both initially built and planned almost entirely with automobile-based transportation in mind. Both are now large and populated enough that they face a severe need for more high-speed public transit and other crucial transportation infrastructure; their residents suffer from problems of gridlock, isolation, inaccessibility and reduced mobility. But outside their downtown cores, neither metropolitan area has reached the level of population density that can provide the ridership levels to support high-efficiency rapid-transit developments reaching most areas. And neither is quite populous enough yet to have the revenues or voter clout to make such developments happen. Both cities find themselves urgently needing the transportation networks of cities with two or three times their population.

As a result, Toronto and Vancouver are both stuck with wasteful and energy-inefficient transportation and housing models and are struggling to build up enough density to redevelop beyond these models. Or to put it more bluntly, they both face a paradox: they need a lot more population in order to overcome the practical and ecological problems of population.

Larger, denser cities are vastly less ecologically damaging than smaller, looser ones. Luís Bettencourt, a theoretical physicist and professor of complex systems at the Santa Fe Institute, has devoted his career to studying cities as organisms, using huge stores of data involving hundreds of cities over many decades.

He has found a set of consistent patterns that apply in every part of the world and every part of history: as cities scale up in size, they generate more prosperity per person and use much less energy per person. He writes:

> When the size of a city doubles, its material infrastructure—anything from the number of gas stations to the total length of its pipes, roads or electrical wires—does not. Instead these quantities rise more slowly than population size: a city of eight million typically needs 15 percent less of the same infrastructure than do two cities of four million each. This pattern is referred to as sublinear scaling. On average, the bigger the city, the more efficient its use of infrastructure, leading to important savings in materials, energy and emissions.

The ecological benefits of higher density are particularly strong. As Bettencourt's research found, the largest cities in the United States have the country's lowest per capita carbon dioxide emissions. That gain is not a result of pro-green policies but a by-product of "energy-efficient public transportation and simple walking instead of driving, which is almost 10 times more energy-intensive." Green-energy and transit policies are also advisable, of course, and are much easier to implement when a larger urban population provides a substantial fiscal income.

Bettencourt's data are supported by a wider body of research, which finds that the expansion of urban populations reduces the emission of carbon. For example, David Dodman of the International Institute for Environment and Development found, in a large-scale analysis of greenhouse gas emissions inventories, that in most cases "per capita emissions from cities are lower than the average for the countries in which they are located."

In fact, there is strong evidence that the increase in economic activity produced by larger cities is directly related to their decrease in per capita carbon emissions. A number of researchers have identified an "environmental Kuznets curve"—as people move from poverty to low-level incomes, they consume more energy and therefore emit more carbon, up to a certain point. Then the relationship reverses. After they reach a certain level of prosperity, every increase in per capita income produces a sharp reduction in carbon emissions. As people become better off, they become more energy-efficient. While scholars have debated exactly where the Kuznets curve is and isn't found, North American cities are clearly on the downside of the curve. That is, they have reached the point where an increase in urban incomes and density produces a decrease in carbon output. This trend is supported even by research that does not identify a specific Kuznets curve. For example, Australian economists Nektarios Aslanidis and Susana Iranzo examined worldwide carbon-emission data, and while they did not see a curve, they found that the cities of the world are divided into two regimes of carbon emission, "namely a low-income regime where emissions accelerate with economic growth and a middle to high-income regime associated with a deceleration in environmental degradation." Any city in Canada would fit into that high-income regime.

This is all well and good, you might argue, but as much as doubling a city's population from four to eight million reduces the greenhouse gas output per person, isn't it mainly raising carbon levels by adding four million energy-consuming, atmosphere-poisoning people to the population? Surely a higher population means more pollution and degradation.

This is where Canada's role as an immigration nation has an ecological and demographic benefit. The majority of immigrants to Canada, for the past four decades, have come from countries and regions with higher fertility rates—places such as India, which today averages 2.5 children per family, or the Philippines, which averages 3.08. These fertility rates fall sharply when families immigrate to cities (whether within their own country or abroad). It especially happens to immigrant families who come to Canada from anywhere. Within a generation of arriving in this country, the family sizes of the newcomers' offspring have fallen to a rate very close to the Canadian average (which today stands at 1.6). This reduction remains consistent for people who move back to their originating country. Moreover, remittances sent from Canada back home raise prosperity levels, which in turn causes fertility rates to drop. In other words, Canada serves as a population-growth reducer for the world, accelerating the decline in the number of carbon-emitting people. By increasing its own population, Canada will play a major role in cutting worldwide population growth.

A larger population also plays a more direct, and urgent, role in combatting climate change. The coming decades will be extremely expensive if Canada wishes to meet its existing and future commitments to reduce its carbon emissions quickly and also to protect itself against the effects of climate change. Governments will need to build coastal defences against rising sea levels, replace urban infrastructure so that it will be more resistant to volatile weather patterns, participate in a global drive to build carbon-removal technology, take measures to make our extractive industries more carbon-neutral, and shift to non-polluting energy sources. The cost of these shifts, for both the public and private sectors, will be huge. A 2011 research report by the National Round Table on the Environment and the Economy estimated that climate defences alone, even at a modest level, will cost Canadian governments $5 billion per year by 2020 and then rise, by the 2050s, to somewhere between $21 billion and $43 billion per year (with a one-in-twenty chance that those costs could rise as high as $91 billion per year). While those investments will lower climate costs and impacts in the long term, the next few decades will see them take up a very large slice of federal, provincial and municipal budgets. Without a much larger fiscal base provided by considerably more taxpayers, those costs will be paid at the expense of anti-poverty, education, security and international aid programs and will compete with the rising costs of healthcare and eldercare discussed above.

Finally, places with denser and more concentrated populations tend to take greater care of their natural environment. Canadian history has shown that conservation and respect for natural resources rise when populations increase and become more diverse—almost all of Canada's conservation and wildlife protection measures were instituted in the second century of Confederation as a reflection of a more diverse and populous country, where the land and sea are seen as a community asset rather than as an obstacle to expansion or resources to be extracted. The world's most robust conservation programs are found in places with large, dense populations (such as California and France), whereas the world's worst ecological catastrophes (the destruction of the Aral Sea ecosystem and the Fergana Valley and *Exxon Valdez* oil spills) have occurred in sparsely populated places where few eyes are watching and there aren't sufficiently dense communities to press for ecological protection.

A big, active population, if it is concentrated in cities and doesn't sprawl across the landscape, is the best ecological asset Canada could have.

THE STRATEGIC COST: SECURITY AND STABILITY

Underpopulation made Canada a less safe place—not just because it enforced a resource economy that ravaged the land, the atmosphere and the original peoples, but also because a low population is both vulnerable and a danger to itself. We know this from experience. Over the past half-century, as the Canadian population has grown, Canada has become safer. This, on the most basic level, is a direct product of its immigration-led population growth.

Canada is currently experiencing its lowest crime rates in fifty years and, for certain violent crimes such as homicide, rates that may be the lowest in its history. These rates have dropped, in large part, as a direct result of an increase in the proportion of newcomers in the population. It is well established that the foreign-born in North America have considerably lower crime rates than the native-born. And this has been enough to shift the crime rate. As statistical research by Haimin Zhang of the University of British Columbia found in 2014, every 10 percent increase in the number of immigrants in the population (both new immigrants and "established" immigrants) lowers the Canadian crime rate by 2 to 3 percent. This is a direct causal relationship, he found. It takes place because the immigrants commit less crime. And this crime-lowering pattern has been found across types and origins of immigrants. In the United States, figures show that both legal and illegal immigrants have markedly lower violent crime rates than the native-born. A Canadian population increase driven by higher immigration levels is therefore likely to make the country safer, less expensive to keep secure, and more attractive to further visitors and newcomers.

There is another dimension to security, though—one that perhaps depends even more on population. The defence of Canada from international threats—and the ability of Canada to participate in collective defensive actions with it is allies—is directly tied to the population available to serve and the tax base able to pay for the extremely expensive resources and sustained costs a military requires. Before the Second World War, Canada was militarily part of the United Kingdom and relied on the British military for its umbrella of defence. In the seven decades since that war's end, Canada has relied on its membership in the North Atlantic Treaty Organization, which effectively means that it depends on the United States for much of its overarching security.

This has worked well during periods when U.S. and Canadian outlooks and world views have been largely aligned—that is, through much of the postwar era. However, as the Trump presidency demonstrates, there is no guarantee that the United States will serve either Canada's or the world's greater interests through the coming decades. In a number of areas, including security, Canada may need to prepare to go it alone, or at least with a circle of smaller allies.

This is a point examined by Irvin Studin, a University of Toronto scholar and former federal government defence-policy official, in a 2010 essay for his journal *Global Brief*. Studin is the most influential in a school of policy thinkers who see a larger Canadian population as key to building Canada's influence in the world and its strategic and defensive capability; as he argues, "a far larger national population could give Canada greater weight in international affairs." His argument is essentially a variation on the problem, described above, of insufficiently supported institutions—but in this case, the institutions are military, international and strategic:

> First, [a larger population would provide] a far larger demographic base to build strong national institutions and structures (east-west-north-south) across the vast territory of Canada—institutions that, while today often absent or weak, would eventually serve as a bulwark for international strategic influence; and second, a far larger talent pool to populate the strategic arms of the Canadian state—the military, diplomatic, general civil service and political branches of government—as well as connected sectors and organizations (business, cultural, educational, scientific) in Canadian society at large. In the process, the Canada of 100 million, through the force of new domestic structures, coupled with growing international impact (and prestige), undergoes an evolution of the national geist—one arguably appropriate for this new, more complicated, more international century. In short, Canada becomes a serious force to be reckoned with.

This is not necessarily the most popular case for population growth among Canadians. We often prefer to view our country as an impartial "middle power" whose international strength comes precisely from being a moderating influence rather than a "force to be reckoned with." That said, our low population density means that our military, peacekeeping and foreign aid contributions simultaneously are smaller than needed to make a meaningful contribution to our alliances and take up a larger share of our federal budget than they should. Canada has never managed to meet its NATO pledge to devote 2 percent of its gross domestic product to defence (we devote about 1 percent) or its United Nations pledge to devote 0.7 percent to foreign aid spending (in 2015 we devoted 0.24 percent). In the event of a major crisis or threat, we would have a hard time building up our defences quickly enough—something we experienced during our contribution to NATO's International Security Assistance Force mission in Afghanistan, which exhausted our supply of deployable troops for half a decade.

Even that middle-power status is at risk from underpopulation and its effects on economy and institutions. Canada traditionally prefers to wield influence through multilateral organizations such as the G7 and the G20. However, as an analysis by the Century Initiative notes, at current population growth rates (and resulting economic growth rates), Canada would fall, by mid-century, from its current ranking as the eleventh-place world economy to sixteenth—a position "that would barely put Canada in the G20 and outside anything that would qualify it for the G8." If, on the other hand, Canada pursued a policy to bring its population to 100 million by 2100, it would likely outgrow most other G8 countries in population and economic size. (According to one projection, it would be the second-largest member of the current G8.) That would not necessarily turn Canada into a superpower, which is more or less what happened to the United States when it reached the 100-million mark after the First World War. But it would turn Canada into a country that has no trouble exercising the sort of quiet but effective multilateral influence that has long been its ambition.

Robert Kaplan, a former member of Parliament and solicitor general, expressed this idea in a distinctly Canadian way: "We

Canadians believe we stand for something good in the world, that we have some values and some institutions worth promoting in the interests of international social harmony, peace and prosperity. At 100 million, the world audience might be more alert."

THE CULTURAL COST: THINKING FOR OURSELVES

The most tangible day-to-day cost of underpopulation is a lot like loneliness. We are often unable to talk intelligently to each other, not to mention the world, because we just don't have enough people to support the channels of dialogue or the institutions of thought and culture—whether they're national online platforms, magazines, statistical institutes, movie industries, think tanks or publishing houses. Unlike many of the tightly packed countries of Europe, Canada has multiple, dispersed audiences with different regional cultures. We therefore need a larger base population, especially in our cities, in order to support them. Quebec has done a better job than English Canada of maintaining institutions of thought and communication, in part because it's a more geographically concentrated, homogeneous culture with political reasons to underwrite such institutions heavily, and also because it began to recognize the problems of underpopulation two generations earlier. But in both national solitudes, there is a sense of difficulty in getting a message across.

Anyone who has tried to do entertainment, culture, scholarship, or public or political thinking on the national level will recognize the brick wall of underpopulation. There often isn't a large enough audience, or market, to support such institutions at a reasonable level of quality or scope. That's why all of Canada's major book-publishing houses are branches of foreign firms. As the historian Charlotte Gray writes, "publishers grapple with the same challenges that faced their predecessors a century ago: the audience is too small, the distances too vast, the market too flooded with foreign books." It's the reason our TV and movies are either foreign-produced or government-funded and -regulated and offer such a limited selection. It's the reason why such an important institution as *Saturday Night* magazine failed or the publisher McClelland and Stewart was absorbed by a multinational, even after repeated government bailouts and tax protection. It's the reason our only English-language national newsmagazine, *Maclean's*, could survive (and just barely, reducing itself to fewer than two dozen staff in 2017) only because it has received as much as three million dollars a year in federal grants, on top of laws restricting competition from U.S. titles looking to publish separate editions north of the border.

None of the twenty-four-hour news channels in English Canada or Quebec have enough revenue or resources to be fully staffed twenty-four hours or all weekend; if news breaks at inconvenient times, they rely on anchors and clips. Any comparison between the CBC and the BBC, between Radio-Canada and France Télévisions, between CBC Radio and National Public Radio, between the two private national English networks (CTV and Global) and the Big Three U.S. networks, between TVA and TF1, or between the CTV and CBC twenty-four-hour cable news channels and CNN or Sky News reveals a striking lack of potential and resources on the Canadian side. Canadian audiences are too small to justify large-scale advertising expenditures, and the population is too small to provide the taxpayer base or subscription income that might make up for it. So there are a lot of things Canadian broadcasters simply can't offer their audiences. The situation is worse in Quebec, where the market size of media is even smaller than Quebec's share of the population.

In online media, where protectionist policies are less effective, the tiny size of the Canadian audience creates even more dire effects. If your message or product depends on a national audience or market, there usually aren't enough page views or clicks to keep the lights on. If you run an online enterprise dedicated to content that has an inevitably national audience (for example, in sports, politics, news, personal finance, culture or some forms of retail), it will be extremely difficult for advertising views or subscriptions to finance more than a handful of staff; such outlets are constantly prone to failure or takeover. A great many English-Canadian information sites and online channels have only three or four paid staff, leaving them to rely on recycled foreign content or the work of unpaid interns. Even the smallest of their U.S. equivalents, which face an online market twelve times the size (the population difference between English Canada and the United States) and hold more disposable income, are able to support much larger and more sustainable staffing levels.

A public consciousness cannot feed itself on mass media alone—the most important debates and dialogues are often built on an ecology of small informed-specialist publications and online venues that fuel public thought and generate the key ideas and messages that drive conversation. And Canada's institutions of public thought are badly constrained. Canada has always had trouble sustaining anything on the level of U.S. outlets such as the *New Republic* (54,000 subscribers) or the *Weekly Standard* (81,000) and Britain's *Times Literary Supplement* or *Prospect* (both around 40,000), because once you divide those numbers by twelve, you don't have enough subscription revenue to support even a single full-time staff member. Quebec faces even more difficult challenges.

English Canada retains a few important venues of thought and expression, such as the *Walrus* (39,000 paid readers and a charitable revenue model), *Canada's History* (38,000), the *Literary Review of Canada* (6,500 subscribers), and *Canadian Notes & Queries* and *Brick* (below 5,000). But those magazines rely on government grants, charitable donations, volunteers and low freelance rates. Their online equivalents, such as rabble.ca, Canadaland and the Tyee, subsist almost entirely on crowdfunding campaigns and institutional or charitable benefactors, with audiences too small to support more than one or two staff. A large-scale online outlet with dozens of staff, such as Slate, Politico or the Huffington Post, or a world-class weekly like the *New Yorker* or the *Atlantic* (with circulations in the high six figures) would be inconceivable. We're stuck reading someone else's news.

There is a built-in paradox in attempting to be a venue of thought or culture in Canada. It is possible to succeed by following the model pursued successfully by Montreal's *Vice*, which is to avoid any particularly Canadian content or message and aim for a global model focused on U.S. consumers, advertisers and funders—a perfectly valid and sometimes successful approach, but one not open to anyone with nationally oriented content. Or one can use government, charity and university or think-tank support to build an audience within Canada—the problem being that those funders usually demand a high percentage of specifically Canadian themes and content, eliminating any chance of expansion beyond the small national audience. It's the same paradox discovered by people working in film, television and nonfiction books. You can have a big enough audience to pay the rent or a Canadian audience that gets you donations, but rarely can you have both.

A large proportion of a country's public thought—that is, the big ideas, the deep research and discoveries that we debate, discuss and sometimes turn into policy or culture—typically comes from institutions devoted to research and analysis. Think tanks and institutes generate a substantial amount of what citizens know about their country, raising topics that become the focus of government and private-sector action and public conversation. They also serve as the brain centres of political parties, especially when those parties are in repose. Their deep pools of policy thinkers allow parties to offer more than just ideological responses to pressing issues and to develop detailed policy ideas to make government work better. But in Canada, as a direct result of underpopulation, such think tanks and institutes barely exist.

In the United States, volumes of vital research and political development spring from such places as the Urban Institute (with 450 full-time salaried thinkers), the Brookings Institution (250), the Hoover Institution (320), the Center for Strategic and International Studies (220), the American Enterprise Institute (190), the Heritage Foundation (150), the Carter Center (160), the Hudson Institute (125), and the Carnegie Endowment for International Peace and the Council on Foreign Relations (more than 100 each). Canada has only one institute with more than a hundred staff—the Conference Board of Canada. The only political think tank with more than fifty on staff is the right-wing Fraser Institute, with sixty-four, followed by the respected but tiny C.D. Howe Institute, with only twenty-one and a budget of under five million dollars—and then a whole bunch with a handful of people stuffed into a couple of rooms. A lot of the large-scale research projects that have driven U.S. and European policy—projects that involve dozens of researchers tabulating volumes of data compiled from large-scale databases spanning many years—can't be done on that level in Canada.

This lack of capacity may be called a "democratic deficit." Herman Bakvis, a political scientist at the University of Victoria, sees Canada wrestling with what he calls "policy capacity"—the "intellectual dimension of governance, that is, the capacity of the system to think through the challenges it faces." Ottawa, whose limited budgets mean a lack of staff and capacity to think for itself, often relies inordinately on what Bakvis calls the "external policy community"—institutes and think tanks and foundations—but then gets tripped up by the limited size and range of these institutions, and therefore the limited quality and variety of work they produce.

This problem is described somewhat differently by Donald Savoie, a public-administration professor and former senior federal bureaucrat. In his view, Canada's governments are constantly wrestling with a choice between having a staff that understands and develops policy or having a staff that delivers it. Canada is not a big enough country to have both. In some periods (the 1980s and the 2000s), the federal government greatly expanded its "policy, evaluation, and monitoring units"—for example, Ottawa added seventy thousand public servants, mainly in these areas, between 2000 and 2010. But these expansions always come at the expense of "the regional and local offices delivering front-line services," which were not staffed up or rebuilt after the cuts of 1994–97 and 2011. In other words, Ottawa can either think or it can do, but not both. The size of the public service is constrained by the size of the Canadian tax base, which is determined by the size of the Canadian population.

Canada's population places limits on the country's ability to think about itself. And this, paradoxically, means that Canada has not been able to think seriously about its population crisis, about a possible solution to that crisis, and about the very real obstacles that stand in the way of a solution.

CHAPTER 7

The Case against 100 Million

One hundred million has become a fashionable number. In 2016, the federal Liberal government's Advisory Council on Economic Growth issued a report recommending a population growth strategy that would lead to a target population of 100 million by 2100 (mainly through a modest increase in immigration rates). It provoked weeks of debate in the media. In a sign of the new political consensus around population, this proposal wasn't criticized from across the benches; in fact, prominent Conservative Party leadership figures such as Chris Alexander spoke in interviews and speeches in favour of almost the same population increase. Since 2015, an organization of academic, business and multi-party political figures, the Century Initiative, has been campaigning for a 100-million target. In Canada's fifteenth decade, that nine-digit number has become a Canadian symbol as prominent and controversial as the Maple Leaf was fifty years earlier.

Beyond its being simply an appealing round number, there is a history behind 100 million. It is roughly the population we'd have today if Wilfrid Laurier's hopes had been realized. It has been mooted as an ideal Canadian population by numerous politicians (including, possibly apocryphally, Winston Churchill). The 100-million figure seems to be a constantly rediscovered benchmark of Canadian success, as measured by economic analyses. In 1968, a group of scholars, policy advocates and business leaders formed the Mid-Canada Development Corridor Foundation, which argued that for a sustainable and independent economy Canada required a population of at least 100 million. In 1975, a study by Canada's Department of Manpower (as it was then known) found that economies of scale leading to "significant benefits to Canadian industry" would occur only after the population had reached the 100-million mark. I first encountered, and advocated for, that number in 2001 when I quizzed a number of demographers on Canada's ideal sustainable population; their responses, on social and ecological and economic grounds, circled around 100 million.

Given the growing consensus around the benefits of a larger population, it is worth taking a serious look at the case against another tripling of the number of Canadians—that is, we should seriously look at the costs, risks and hazards involved. And if the answers aren't good enough, we should be willing to embrace the case against growth. If Canada is unwilling to make the investments necessary to overcome the obstacles, it is probably better not to pursue a policy of large-scale expansion. Without preparation and planning, the benefits of a more sustainable population could turn into the political and social risk of an unsupported, segregated, unequal and unproductive population.

There seems to be an assumption, among population-growth advocates, that the tripling of Canada's current population will be as easy as the last tripling—which took place between the Second World War and approximately 2015, when Canada grew from 12 million to 35 million. The next seven decades of Canadian population growth are not going to be as easy or as inexpensive. During the period after the Second World War, the Canadian population grew, and for the most part thrived, largely because we happened to have the right sort of cities with the right housing at the right prices and with the right jobs and entrepreneurial opportunities in the right places. Newcomers arrived and new generations were born into situations that were sometimes challenging but in many ways almost ideal. True, there were debates and controversies over immigration. There were considerable outlays and risks involved in building and equipping schools and universities, urban infrastructure and government agencies for an expanding Canada, and in making investments in housing, institutions and services. But these investments were largely made after the fact. We waited until the population growth had created a problem, our municipal, provincial and federal governments reacted with alarm, and eventually money was spent to deal with it.

In crucial areas, Canada simply got lucky. Employment levels for newcomers quickly merged with those of established Canadians because we were lucky enough to experience large-scale industrial growth, then a shift to a service economy, interlaced with several large-scale resource booms and with only relatively short-lived economic downturns in between. Immigrants were able to use home ownership and small business as their main vehicles for success because our postwar cities had experienced automobile-driven sprawl, leaving their dense central districts underpopulated and underpriced; those districts were ideal settings for immigrant business and community building.

In part because of those decades of success, Canada is now a more complex, multilayered, difficult and expensive place. If we expect another 65 million people to become successful Canadians, we need to ask whether we have the ready resources that helped the current 35 million get there. And if those things have gone missing or have become inaccessible or flawed, then we will need to build them or fix them before we can think about becoming that big.

Luck will not sustain us for the coming decades. Canada will have to get skilled. Let's examine some of the challenges we would need to overcome if we want to think about 100 million.

THE CHALLENGE OF EMPLOYMENT AND ENTREPRENEURSHIP

When we say someone becomes Canadian, we mean several things: they move here permanently, settle in a neighbourhood, get involved with their community, obtain an education—but often, before all else, they get to work. It is difficult to become integrated into Canadian cultural or civic life if you can't find a place in the economy.

During the past century, the steady full-time industrial job and the small but thriving local business were crucial instruments of upward mobility and family success for millions of new Canadians. Canada may have been somewhat naive in thinking that its immigrants were simply units of labour to be plugged into job shortages—in fact, twentieth-century immigrants to Canada typically engaged in a complex mixture of labour, agriculture, small trading, entrepreneurship, real estate and cash transactions. But the steady full-time job was nonetheless the default source of income security and often the anchor that kept newcomer families tethered to Canadian success. Likewise, new generations of native-born Canadians could invest in their futures because they knew they would find secure work and business opportunities that paid as much as their parents made or more.

The workforce is changing in ways that could make it less easy for some immigrants to gain a foothold. Those changes also create insecurity for new generations of Canadians entering the job market. So whatever Canada's population is, these challenges need to be confronted.

Most new Canadians still make their start by finding a full-time job. And Canada, compared to other Western countries, currently has a lot of permanent work. Eighty percent of employed Canadians have a full-time job; temporary employment makes up only 11.4 percent of regular work. But there are signs that those secure full-time jobs are becoming harder to find. Between 1997 and 2012, the number of temporary jobs in Canada increased by 57 percent, compared to only 28 percent for all forms of employment. In 2016, Canada's economy saw a net employment increase of 153,300 new part-time positions but only 60,400 full-time jobs. And a number of studies have pointed to increasing job insecurity and precariousness in the workplace.

For people just making their start in the Canadian economy, secure footholds are more difficult to find. Immigrants to Canada are far more educated than before—almost 60 percent arrive with a university degree—and they tend to come with middle-class aspirations. But these aspirations usually cannot be realized in the first generation. According to Statistics Canada, almost a third of immigrants live below the poverty line; among Canadians in general, only one in eight do. And while both immigrant poverty and general Canadian poverty rates fell by a third during the first decade of this century, they fell at the same rate, so immigrants remain 2.6 times more likely to live in poverty than Canadians in general.

There's nothing unusual in that. Immigrants, even those who led middle-class lives in their home country, tend to start off much poorer than average Canadians as they struggle to find their place in a new economy, society and language. But they've generally built incomes and portfolios quickly: until about 1990, immigrant incomes converged with average Canadian incomes within about fifteen years of arrival. That's no longer the case. Today, immigrants who have been in Canada for fifteen years are about twice as likely as Canadians in general to earn after-tax incomes below thirty thousand dollars a year, and almost 1.5 times as likely to live in poverty. From this we can infer that a significant proportion of immigrants, even those with professional qualifications, are forced to wait until their children's generation comes of age to achieve economic integration.

If you look beneath the statistics, you quickly realize that even those immigrants who officially have full-time work need multiple sources of income. Today, "work" means something very different for many new Canadians—and for an increasing number of young Canadians.

In 2013, the Wellesley Institute conducted a detailed study of 453 recent-immigrant families in the east end of Toronto to see how their earned their livings. It found that almost half of those families, 46 percent, earned at least part of their income from the "informal economy," that is, "economic activity outside formal employment relationships, in a more cash-based and sometimes more entrepreneurial economy"—the unofficial cash economy of day jobs, casual buying and selling, truck and barter, most of it in "factory work, restaurants and stores." These cash incomes "most often supplemented other forms of household income" such as poorly paying part-time and full-time jobs and, increasingly, "gig economy" jobs such as driving Uber cars. Only one family in five made more than thirty thousand dollars a year from such cash-based sources, suggesting that these cash incomes are, for many immigrants, just one part of an elaborate collection of formal and informal income sources—what development scholars call "portfolios of the poor."

This should not necessarily be seen as a negative development; a diversity of income sources can create more entry points into the established economy. The Wellesley study noted that "informal businesses"—that is, unlicensed cash-based buy-and-sell enterprises—"are often a stepping stone towards more formalized businesses," in a pattern that should be familiar to anyone who's lived in a recent-immigrant neighbourhood. It's quite normal for immigrants to start out with a hodgepodge of income sources— money borrowed from fellow immigrants and relatives, favours and IOUs, a few hours at someone's shop, a week of construction here and there, a stint driving a cab, some import buy-and-sell opportunities—all of it leading, eventually, to a proper licensed business or, more likely, a proper full-time job.

Those jobs, though, aren't what they used to be. Immigrants may be stuck in the cash-economy netherworld of informal work for years longer. And there's a chance that they will always have to supplement a poor job's earnings with various extra sources, often leaving little time to raise a family.

To understand this, it helps to look at the widening gap between the sorts of jobs available to new Canadians and those that older Canadians used to get. We don't have great data on immigrant jobs, but we do have detailed statistics on incomes earned by younger Canadians, aged twenty-five to twenty-four. Since immigrants tend to be young—the majority in Canada are between twenty-five and forty-four years of age—this data shows the workforce they're entering.

A 2014 study of income-tax records by the Conference Board of Canada found that the income gap between older and younger Canadians has grown wider over the past three decades. In the 1980s, men in their fifties made 53 percent more than men in their twenties; they now make 73 percent more. For women, the gap was 9 percent; now it is 42 percent. This, the report notes, "suggests that income inequality between generations of Canadians has increased significantly." It also shows that neither younger Canadians nor up-and-coming immigrants can expect to have the wages or the job security they would have had a generation ago. The observed trend in intergenerational income inequality could also fuel new social tensions. As the Conference Board concludes,

> The Canadian generation at the top of the income heap today fought long and hard for principles like equal pay for work of equal value, yet some major employers now offer lower wages and reduced pension benefits for new hires, even for the same work. Employers persistently complain about shortages of skilled labour, yet many highly educated young people seem stuck in low-skill and precarious jobs.

A major and growing part of the immigrant job economy is in domestic service and eldercare work—an army of workers tending to the needs of the aging baby boom generation. This is visible in the fact that Canada's largest source country of immigration, for much of the past decade, has been the Philippines, whose emigrants are most likely to make their start in domestic, eldercare or catering jobs. These fields, while better regulated today than before, still contain large pools of informal and cash-only employment, as well as complex webs of side deals and business opportunities (often, at first, on temporary visas that put the immigrants in a vulnerable employment position).

If Canada's population growth, fuelled in good part by immigration, is built on economic growth that is driven by insecure, precarious or informal forms of employment—lives propped up by thin webs of "sharing economy" contracts, haphazardly scheduled part-time shifts, and positions lacking pensions, benefits or salaries capable of putting children through university—then the project might not be worth it. Adding more people, even if we are experiencing labour shortages, will only make the situation worse.

THE CHALLENGE OF HOMES AND CITIES

More than any other factor, what has made immigrants integrate so quickly and successfully in Canada has been a high propensity to buy the houses and apartments they live in, often soon after landing. Throughout the past century, rates of home ownership among immigrants—even poor immigrants—have been comparable to rates among established Canadians. About seven out of ten immigrant families end up owning a dwelling—the same rate as among non-immigrant Canadians.

Buying a house is, in a number of important ways, central to the traditional experience of becoming Canadian. It isn't just a sign of stable income and commitment to stay in Canada. Upward social and economic mobility depends on access to credit, and immigrants have used the equity value in their houses to obtain the funds they need to put their children through university, improve their own professional credentials, and start and expand small businesses—and those businesses are often located in the same building as the home. Immigrants use home ownership to create communities, most often in urban spaces; these communities link into the established city (in what I've called the "arrival city" phenomenon) and foster integration and intergenerational success. A team of Statistics Canada analysts described the way home ownership makes integration happen:

> Home buying not only increases their resemblance with the host society in terms of type of residence, it also provides them with greater access to the amenities (parks, schools, community centres, etc.) that are more likely to be found in neighbourhoods with predominantly owner-occupied dwellings. As such, it is a good indicator of integration into Canadian society.

The traditional new-Canadian practice of buying a home in a lower-cost urban immigrant district, then using its rise in value to finance social and economic mobility, has recently become more difficult. Urban districts have become middle class and prohibitively expensive to many newcomers (a gentrification process whose main beneficiaries were the immigrants who had bought housing in the twentieth century). House prices have risen dramatically in Canadian cities—especially in greater Vancouver and the Greater Toronto Area, the metropolitan areas where more than half of Canada's immigrants settle.

Home ownership remains important enough to new Canadians that immigrants continue to buy houses, despite their comparatively lower incomes, by making greater sacrifices and borrowing much more heavily than earlier generations did. A 2012 Statistics Canada analysis found that within four years of arriving in Canada, more than half of immigrant families owned a home. The proportion varied by place of origin—well over 60 percent for Chinese, Korean and Filipino immigrants, 40 percent for Caribbean Canadians, and less than 30 percent for Arab immigrants—but even the lower figures represent significant rates of home ownership. Notably, even refugees—who arrive with limited economic and cultural resources—were found to move fairly quickly into home ownership.

What has changed are the places where newcomers are able to buy, or rent, homes. During the twentieth century, new Canadians clustered in the inner city—in the Chinatowns and Little Italies and Jewish districts of major cities; the suburbs were largely white and home to established Canadians. In the twenty-first century, immigration has become suburbanized. In Toronto and Vancouver, the great majority of immigrants, and their Canadian-born children, now settle and live in the inner suburbs. (Montreal remains a notable exception: most of the immigrant and allophone districts remain clustered on the island, and the suburbs are mainly, but not exclusively, ethnic Québécois.)

Geographers Heather Smith and David Ley, in a 2008 study, found that immigrants are increasingly being segregated into the lower-density outskirts by housing availability. This is causing most urban poverty, as well as most immigration, to move into the high-rise suburb districts. "The gateway cities of Toronto and Vancouver display an increasing spatial (and statistical) association between immigrant distribution and areas of concentrated poverty," they write. These new arrival-city districts often thrive—nobody could claim that the high-rise districts of Surrey, Richmond, Scarborough and Etobicoke are failed places, despite social tensions—but they lack two important elements that the older downtown immigrant districts possessed.

The first is proximity to established, better-off districts. The downtown neighbourhoods often had even higher poverty rates and greater health problems than the new suburban arrival cities, but they had the advantage of location. If you opened a shop or restaurant, a steady foot traffic of better-off customers would frequent it. If your kids went to local schools, they'd mix with a wide range of other Canadians and newcomers. While the suburban immigrant districts don't totally lack these qualities—there are plenty of strip-mall ethnic retail successes, and suburban schools are far from homogeneous—the newer generation of immigrants do find themselves more isolated. "Established Canadians," Smith and Ley note, "are increasingly distanced both socially and spatially from the plight of impoverished immigrants."

The second is population density. The inner suburbs, originally built with automobile-only, zoning-restricted development in mind, are more spread out. Their apartment buildings have empty, forbidding grassy areas between them, and their neighbourhoods are buffered by big patches of non-residentially zoned land. This lack of density makes it harder for small businesses and networks of mutual assistance to function; it also, crucially, means that these neighbourhoods often don't contain enough people for cities to justify spending on high-speed public transit connections. Increasingly, both poverty and immigration are being shifted to areas that are lower in population density and harder to get in and out of. This can create isolation, and sometimes alienation.

Research by University of Toronto urbanist David Hulchanski has shown that over thirty years Toronto inverted its suburban and urban roles. In downtown Toronto today (that is, in the old pre-amalgamation City of Toronto), despite its diverse appearance, only 28 percent of residents are foreign born and 82 percent are white. Six in ten downtown adults are university educated, and almost 40 percent of families earn more than $100,000 a year. In the inner suburbs, on the other hand, 60 percent are foreign born and 34 percent are white. Three in ten are university educated, and one in ten earns more than $100,000. The non-white, non-wealthy and foreign-born have settled on the disconnected edges.

This polarization can create isolation and resentment. Toronto saw this in its 2010 municipal elections, when Rob Ford, a right-wing populist candidate who campaigned against the privileges of "downtown elites" and employed messages of intolerance, was elected mayor by an electorate almost entirely composed of people living in the largely non-white, non-wealthy, non-home-owning immigrant inner suburbs (a group that continued to back his movement in the 2014 elections). The "Canadian dream" of rapid integration and social mobility driven by home ownership and employment, while still a statistical reality for most newcomers, is being delayed, deferred, frustrated and even lost for enough people to create an angry political backlash. If we want to triple the population of our major cities, we will need to ensure that the right sort of neighbourhoods, with the right sort of density, transit and proximity, come into existence before they get there. Otherwise, the entire enterprise may end up doing more harm than good.

THE CHALLENGE OF HUMAN INVESTMENT

We're no longer importing farmers, fishers, lumberjacks and assembly-line workers. The people who come to Canada tend to be, on average, more talented and knowledgeable than the people who were born here. In 1981, only a quarter of adult males who immigrated to Canada that year had a university degree; by 2006 the figure had risen to nearly 60 percent. (By comparison, 26 percent of Canadian-born men and 34 percent of women had university degrees in 2009.)

That talent is often wasted. The expensively accumulated education of newcomers is, in a majority of cases, disregarded or rejected by employers and professions. It is something of a cliché to say that half the taxi drivers in Toronto have master's degrees; it is also not much of an exaggeration. The Wellesley Institute study found that among the recent immigrants in Toronto who had been employed as professionals in their home country, only 3 percent had found work in their field. Nationally, a 2012 study by the Library of Parliament found that 24 percent of immigrants (including long-term immigrants) in regulated professions who acquired their education outside Canada were working in their trained profession, compared with 62 percent of Canadians.

That's partly because Canada has significant labour shortages in unskilled and semi-skilled fields, which require less linguistic fluency. Freshly arrived in a new country where you barely speak either language, perhaps with family in tow, it's hard to decline a paying job that's immediately available, even if it's not what you're trained to do. But it's also because many foreign professional credentials, licences, advanced degrees and trade experience are not recognized by Canadian professional colleges, licensing boards, government authorities, unions and trade organizations. And while thousands of immigrants every year enrol in community college and university programs to upgrade their credentials to Canadian standards, many more are prohibited by cost, difficulty navigating Canada's underdeveloped credentialing process, and the need to feed their families and prepare for their own children's education.

Even with sufficiently upgraded credentials, many immigrants find it difficult to enter professions in Canada. Some countries—notably Australia and New Zealand—have recognized this problem and streamlined the accreditation recognition and upgrading processes, using centralized national agencies. Canada, despite some effort at improvement, including the creation of a federal Foreign Credentials Referral Office, remains a confusing hodgepodge of systems that are often more interested in protecting their exclusivity than in welcoming highly skilled newcomers. The Canadian Chamber of Commerce expressed alarm at the scope of this problem in a 2011 report:

> There are nearly 500 professional regulatory authorities and numerous credential assessment/accreditation bodies, hundreds of vocational institutions which are involved in assessing foreign credentials in 13 jurisdictions in Canada. At the same time immigrants still encounter difficulties in obtaining transparent, accountable and systematized information about regulatory requirements. . . . Unnecessary barriers to foreign qualification recognition exist in many professions and sectors. . . . By failing to properly recognize foreign qualifications and experience, immigrants will continue to remain unemployed and/or undercontributing members of the Canadian economy—ultimately earning

less income, paying less in taxes, and unable to afford the goods and services necessary to build their new lives in Canada.

The consequences of this negligence are felt by many new Canadian families. Even though six in ten now arrive with degrees, poverty rates of new immigrants remain persistently high. Of immigrants with university degrees who have been in Canada for fifteen years, three in ten men and four in ten women are working in jobs that require high school or less.

Canadians have tended to overlook these effects or chalk them up as inevitable sacrifices made by first-generation immigrants, who have traditionally given up their own hopes and aspirations in order to provide a better education for their children. And the children of immigrants, whether born in Canada or abroad, do succeed in both education and employment, to degrees equal to or greater than those of average Canadians.

But Canada can't afford to waste entire generations of talent as it expands its population. Aside from driving up social services costs and making immigration more expensive, the wasted-generation effect is depriving Canada of the expertise and knowledge it needs immediately. The Conference Board of Canada forecasts that by 2020 Canada will have a skilled labour shortage of close to a million people—that is, there will be a million more skilled jobs than there are Canadians graduating from high school, college and university. The established Canadian population can't fill the gap. Since 2016, the Canadian-born working-age population has been shrinking; the only thing preventing a decline in the workforce size is immigration. The old practice of sacrificing the best abilities of the first generation will defeat much of the economic purpose of an expanded population. There is no point tripling the population if, in the process, we greatly increase the proportion of Canadians in poverty, depending on social assistance or forced to give up their life's ambitions for those of a later generation.

THE CHALLENGE OF POLITICAL BACKLASH

The biggest barrier to expanding the number of new Canadians could be the attitudes of old Canadians: the risk of a large-scale public and political turn against most or all immigration.

Canada has so far avoided the worst of the anti-minority and anti-immigration politics that have struck western Europe, Britain and the United States. Quebec politics have flirted with xenophobic views under the Parti Québécois government of Pauline Marois and the Coalition Avenir Québec of François Legault (albeit in milder form than those proposed by Europe's far-right parties, and couched in the language of secularism).

And while the federal Conservative Party currently contains factions and leadership figures who echo the populist anti-minority politics that overtook the U.S. Republican Party—and some of that language surfaced under Stephen Harper during the 2015 federal election campaign and in Andrew Scheer's 2019 campaign—that stance has not yet won over a significant plurality of Canadian voters. As Harper's eight years largely demonstrated, Canada's federal and provincial right-wing parties have generally prevailed when they have avoided explicitly anti-immigration positions.

That's in large part because Canadians, almost uniquely in the Western world, remain supportive of immigration and its resulting proliferation of skin colours, linguistic backgrounds and religions. Surveys repeatedly show that both immigration and the concept of multiculturalism—whatever it may mean to people—are popular among a majority of Canadians of all mainstream political leanings, including conservatives. That majority appeared to get smaller during the 2010s, however. Perhaps that was due to a sense among some traditional English and French Canadians that minorities are becoming a majority, or perhaps it was because the political rhetoric of the United States has reached north of the border through online and broadcast channels. However, an expansive vision of Canada remains popular, for now, with at least a slim majority.

This is no cause for complacency. Widespread support for immigration and multiculturalism didn't come about because established Canadians were naturally inclined to embrace minorities. (Only two generations ago discrimination against religious and racial minorities was a majority attitude.) It arose because, despite initial misgivings among many, the system has worked. Canadians have watched minority immigrants who arrived as mysterious and distrusted strangers become their palpably Canadian colleagues and neighbours. With few exceptions, second-generation Canadians have become identical to average Canadians in language, education, employment, income, political views, and most measures of values and loyalties. So immigration has become part of the background noise of Canadian life, like the tax system or the census.

The biggest danger is that something will interrupt or block that process. For example, a sharp change in the economy, in the political culture or in the geography of cities could cause a political backlash against Canadians, or prospective Canadians, of different religions, skin colours or national origins. As could a sudden crisis, such as an uncontrolled rush to the U.S. border by a great many refugees, damage the fragile public reputation of the immigration system.

In a study of changing rates of tolerance and inclusion in Canada, political scientists Keith Banting and Will Kymlicka found that there are weak points and tensions in Canada's integration model, but that it is generally more robust, so far, than in other Western countries:

> The Canadian record on integration is relatively strong. The economic integration of recent immigrants is taking longer; some racial minority immigrants and their children feel less confident that they fully belong; and there are important gaps in the representative face of Canadian democracy. In comparison with other Western nations, however, the integrative power of Canadian society for newcomers should not be under-estimated. . . . Canada is certainly not some sort of a multicultural paradise. But despite a variety of stresses and strains, there is little evidence that Canada is facing deep new divisions, pervasive radicalism or an illiberal challenge to its core democratic culture.

There may be some risk of a generalized Canadian turn against immigration. But there is a more plausible possibility of backlash against specific religions, skin colours or nationalities of immigrants and minorities, one that could cause sharp political restrictions on immigration from large regions of the world. Muslim Canadians and black Canadians especially, in recent years, have felt targeted for specific or systemic discrimination by the political right and law enforcement, and sometimes by political parties and sections of the general public. The January 2017 Quebec City mosque shooting, which killed six in an anti-Muslim hate crime inspired by the anti-immigration messages of right-wing political and media figures, shocked many prominent figures in Quebec and English Canada into awareness of widespread anti-Muslim sentiments and conspiracy theories. The emergence of U.S.-modelled Black Lives Matter movements in Canadian cities, especially Toronto, is in large part a response to the well-documented phenomenon of police and judicial authorities giving unfavourable treatment to black Canadians.

The other risk is that integration will stop working for some groups—that second and third generations will emerge, in some communities, who do not fit into the Canadian economy, education system or culture, who form "parallel societies" (to use the European term) that don't appear to embrace the country's core values. That reality, or the perception of that reality, could cause many Canadians—including Canadians from other immigrant and minority groups—to turn against immigration.

There is some justified worry that the increasing suburbanization and de facto segregation of immigrants in major Canadian cities—as described above—could cause such integration failures and "parallel societies" to emerge, if interventions aren't made to better connect these communities. Over the years, some observers, including members of the immigrant communities they chronicle, have expressed fears that, for example, second-generation Punjabi Canadians in Surrey or Brampton, Chinese Canadians in Richmond or Somali Canadians in Etobicoke might become permanently trapped in insular cultures or grey-market economies.

While this should be taken seriously as a risk, there is no evidence that any failed integration is being experienced at the moment—quite the opposite, in fact. There are certainly an increasing number of ethnic enclaves in Canada. One study, by Feng Hou and Garnett Picot at Statistics Canada, found that in 1981 there had been only six "visible minority neighbourhood enclaves"—defined as a census tract with 30 percent or more of the population belonging to a visible minority group. By 2001, there were 254 of them, and the number has likely grown considerably.

Scholars Mohammad Qadeer at Queen's University and Sandeep Agrawal at Ryerson University took a statistical look at such enclaves in Toronto. They found that these enclaves "are not ghettos in the sense that they are not the result of discrimination and poverty . . . they are the product of housing market and opportunities . . . largely concentrations by choice, voluntary." The enclaves, they found, are nowadays almost entirely suburban—and they are popular. In 2006, half of Toronto's Chinese Canadians and South Asian Canadians lived in ethnic enclaves, as did almost a third of Italians, 40 percent of Jews and one in five Portuguese.

But the enclaves are not permanent. In fact, Qadeer and Agrawal's data shows, as integration theories predict, that these enclaves become less commonplace as ethnic groups become enmeshed in the economic, educational and cultural systems of the country and their second and third generations disperse into the general population. Among ethnic groups whose immigrants generally arrived before the 1990s, the enclaves are declining. Between 2001 and 2006, the proportion of Italians who lived in enclaves became 8 percent smaller; among Jews, 14 percent smaller; among Portuguese, 25 percent smaller.

At this point, there is strong evidence that the formation of such arrival-city enclaves is generally helping, rather than hindering, the process of integration. These districts provide platforms for immigrant small business and institutions that link new communities into established ones. They make it much easier to deliver settlement services, including tailored educational, social and health services. They create ethnic economies that attract established Canadians into the district. And they generally improve and enrich the suburbs.

There is no statistical evidence that the people living in arrival-city enclaves are disengaging from Canadian life. Banting and Kymlicka note that 82 percent of recent immigrants currently speak French or English at conversational levels. And immigrants, rather than withdrawing into "closed societies," are meshing with established Canadians at greater levels. The percentage of Canadian married couples of mixed race has risen from 2.6 percent in 1991 to 4.6 percent in 2011, among the highest rates in the Western world. According to Statistics Canada, mixed-race marriages are entered by 79 percent of Japanese Canadians, 48 percent of Latino Canadians, 40 percent of black Canadians, 30 percent of Filipino Canadians, 25 percent of Arab Canadians, 23 percent of Korean Canadians, 19 percent of Chinese Canadians, 13 percent of South Asian Canadians and about 4 percent of "non visible minority"—that is, white—Canadians. The latter figure suggests that minority and newcomer Canadians are much more open to integrating, in the most intimate way, with established Canadians than white non-immigrant Canadians are with newcomers.

But, as Qadeer and Agrawal note, there could be social costs if people find themselves living in ethnic enclaves for multiple generations not by choice but through a lack of economic options, real estate costs causing forced segregation, or a rising sense of racial exclusion and discrimination. They point to the dangers of de facto segregation in schools and "tendencies toward social exclusion" in places where there is an extremely high concentration of a single ethnic group. We've seen media reports of such tensions in places such as Richmond, B.C. (whose population is 49 percent of Chinese ethnicity) and Brampton, Ontario (40 percent of South Asian origin), and political tensions around these ethnic concentrations. But these are still largely first-generation populations, and there are no observable signs of the negative sort of ghettoization taking place there—not yet, anyway.

We shouldn't assume, however, that Canada's cities can keep growing and adding immigrants without some serious investments in the policies, the infrastructure and the institutions that allow them to become connected to the heart of Canadian life. Neglect of education, employment, transportation or housing could easily cause Canada to suffer the political fate of some of its Western allies.

CONSIDERING THE NON-MAXIMIZING OPTION

Given these costs, and given Canada's general stability and prosperity at the moment, it's worth taking seriously the idea of avoiding a maximizing program and making do with what Canada has. Even though the 100-million target would entail only a small increase in immigration beyond the levels Canada has experienced since the early 1990s, the risk of any immigration increase's tipping the balance of Canadian public opinion from tolerance into distrust might make it not worth considering. Indeed, as we've seen, any 100-million plan is probably best rejected if Canada is not prepared to make investments and take precautions in advance to ensure that the system continues to function well.

An expansionist population program would deliver substan-
tive benefits, as outlined in the previous chapter, that would far
exceed any upfront investment costs. But without those fairly
substantial investments—in education, urban and transportation
infrastructure and reforms in housing and zoning, employment,
socia benefit, tax, small business and family policies to create economic security and social mobility in the new economy—a major
population expansion could do more harm than good. If we
attempt once again to rely on luck, we are likely to find that circumstances are not as well situated for another 65 million people,
and the results could produce instability and division. It would be
wise, before proceeding with a population-growth plan, to hold a
large-scale inquiry into the investments needed at national, pro-
vincial/territorial and municipal levels to prepare Canada for its
next tripling.

Then again, it would be wise to proceed with such an inquiry
even if Canada doesn't pursue a 100-million population strategy.
The challenges described in this chapter are inevitable under
almost any realistic immigration scenario. Even if Canada lowered
its current immigration rate back to early-1980s numbers, Statistics
Canada estimates that the population could reach 51 million by
2063 and will therefore likely double current its level by 2100.

The only way Canada could avoid substantial population
growth is if a long-term shift to extreme politics caused a
near-complete halt to immigration for a period of decades. In that
case, Canada would, by the 2030s, experience the economically
devastating effects of population shrinkage combined with the
overwhelming costs of caring for a very elderly population, which
would require a very different set of policy interventions (without
the benefit of growing fiscal revenues to pay for them).

Indeed, most of the challenges listed in this chapter are being experienced now and will be growing problems regardless of Canada's population policy. The changes in the structure of the workforce, in the cost and accessibility of housing, in the geographic isolation of major cities; the lack of credential recognition and lost educational opportunities; and the risk of political backlash—these are all threats and barriers that need to be confronted by Canadians and their governments today. They will require intervention no matter what happens to Canada. These problems are created by technological, institutional, geographic, policy and planning forces, not by population itself. With or without a tripling of population, we will need to eliminate those barriers to equality and social mobility, and this will be part of any future political agenda.

It is therefore worth asking: if Canada is badly in need of a period of institutional reform, infrastructure expansion and policy reassessment anyway, why shouldn't we also have a population commensurate with those resources? The changes we need to make to maintain and empower a Canada of 35 million will be far easier to bring about, and yield far greater benefits, if they're applied to a population that is slowly growing to a larger and more self-sufficient scale by the end of the century. Canada will need to start acting like a larger country, even if it is not yet one. We should therefore take a close look at what it will take to make Canada larger and more open, in a way that benefits everyone.

CHAPTER 8

Staying Open Late: A Canada That Sticks Around

What does a sustainable population look like? It is enough people, in the right concentrations, to overcome the barriers of under-population in the long term. It is enough clusters of people, across multiple generations, with the right skills and capacities to support the public institutions and forms of expression and markets that befit a leading nation, to expand minority and indigenous nations to be strong and self-sufficient, to shift further from resource extraction to a more sustainable value-added economy, to become more self-supporting should any of its major trading partners become unreliable. It means having a large enough base and density of population by the end of the twenty-first century to support the creation of institutions, econ-omies and ecological solutions that will support Canada through the more difficult demographic period when world populations start shrinking, which predictions suggest will take place during Canada's third century.

Solving underpopulation, however, does not mean simply filling the country with people. A larger population, by itself, does not make a better, stronger or more prosperous country. A sustainable population does not mean spreading people across the land, as we did in our first century. It means creating places where important things happen: where strong and tight-knit urban communities flourish, where towns participate in clusters of knowledge and innovation, where thriving centres of higher learning, technology and specialization take shape, and where smart growth provides better stewardship and protection, and even expansion, of wild and agricultural lands.

A specific number doesn't mean that much. Some informed observers have settled on 100 million—about three times the current Canadian population—as a useful symbolic goal. But it could very well be 85 million or 130 million and yield the same desired effects. There is no ideal number, and in fact there is no real number, because the population will never stay at 100 million or any other level. Human populations have no homeostatic balance; they must always grow or shrink.

Yet 100 million does offer some specific attractions. It was around the 100-million mark, reached shortly before 1920, that the United States was first able to assert itself economically as a fully independent force and to master and export its own forms of culture. This figure would lead to cities and transportation networks of sufficient size to be fully supported with green infrastructure. It would allow Canada's francophone populations to experience enough growth in absolute numbers to overcome problems of dependence and isolation. It would reshape the population pyramid sufficiently to allow Canada to prosper through the challenging decades that the middle of this century will bring.

And yet it is not so large that Canada would be significantly different in culture and way of life from what it is now.

Another reason 100 million keeps popping up is because it is easily attainable. Even if Canada changed nothing and stayed with its current immigration levels and fertility rate, it would still be approaching 90 million people by 2100.

This is not an especially large number. If the tiny strip of land upon which the great majority of Canadians live—less than a tenth of Canada's land mass—were to develop the population density of the Netherlands (a dense European state, but one with plenty of open spaces and parklands), then Canada would have 400 million people. A population one-quarter this dense, concentrated as it would be in existing cities and towns, would leave Canada's natural spaces untouched and probably better protected. It would give the narrow southern strip of Canada the population density of Spain or Romania, two countries noted for their unspoiled tracts of nature.

If Canadians are willing to triple their numbers, we must make a commitment to overcome the obstacles described in the previous chapter. And we simultaneously need to embark, carefully, on a program to increase our current rate of population expansion.

Solving Canada's underpopulation problem is not simply, or even mainly, a matter of bringing in more immigrants. In fact, a large part of the problem can be solved by bringing new Canadians into the world the more familiar way.

Canadians currently don't have as many children as they'd like. Statisticians call this the "fertility gap." They ask couples in their twenties how many children they'd like to have, then they ask couples in their forties how many children they were able to have; the difference is the fertility gap. In Canada, a 2010 Ipsos Reid study found that on average, couples say they'd ideally have 2.4 children—a number well above the 2.1 children per family needed to have a non-shrinking population. In their forties, 40 percent of Canadian women and 32 percent of men say they've had fewer children than they desired (only 9 percent say they had more than planned).

On average, Canadians end up having 1.6 children per couple—which, subtracted from the 2.4 they'd wanted to have, leaves a fertility gap of 0.8 children per family. If that gap were magically filled and every existing family in Canada suddenly had the wished-for average of 2.4 children, there would instantly be 7.5 million more Canadians. Of course it's not that easy. Some of the fertility gap is explained by couples developing health problems, discovering reproductive limitations, facing marital crises or just changing their minds. But a big part of it can be addressed directly: Ipsos Reid found that 72 percent of couples identified "finances" as a barrier. That may mean they can't afford to add an extra room onto their house for a third kid. More often it means they depend on two incomes but can't afford childcare, which currently costs an average of $14,700 a year in Vancouver, $16,800 a year in St. John's, and $20,832 a year in Toronto. Even with more generous federal tax credits for childcare introduced in 2017, that can still be prohibitively expensive.

We do know, from Canadian experience, that readily available and affordable childcare programs measurably increase the fertility rate, and thus the population. In 1997, Quebec introduced a low-cost universal childcare program that offered spaces for preschoolers at five dollars a day (the price was later raised to seven dollars). By 2011, the program was serving 215,000 preschoolers, almost half the province's children of that age, and allowing 70,000 additional women to enter or return to the workforce. And it narrowed the fertility gap. In the 1990s, Quebec's fertility rate had plummeted to a Canadian low of 1.35 children per family; the new childcare scheme plus better parental leave programs pushed the rate above the Canadian average—to 1.7 children per family by 2010. This was followed by a gradual decline after 2010 to more or less the Canadian average of 1.6 children, still a considerable population boost.

And the program paid for itself. A team of Quebec economists found that the program produced an increase of 3.8 percent in female employment, which raised Quebec's gross domestic product by 1.7 percent, producing new tax income that exceeded the cost of the program.

It's also worth studying the even more robust childcare, family leave and flexible work programs in France, Germany and Scandinavia. In France, a focused and expensive set of programs raised the fertility rate from 1.7 to more than 2 children per family. Sweden boosted its rate from 1.5 to 1.9 with an equally shared parental leave program, and a complex range of new programs in Germany is designed to raise its extremely low fertility rate while putting more women into the workforce. Any program to build a sustainable population in Canada should start with family policy, which produces population growth and economic growth at the same time while easing the frustrations of millions of families.

———

A maximum Canada would not entail a Laurier-era large-scale[1] immigration drive or a noticeably increased flow of newcomers at a pace likely to disrupt the social balance. It would mean a slow increase in annual immigration levels to just above today's approximately 330,000 people. Since the early 1990s, immigration has been steadily near 0.7 to 0.8 percent (that is, 7 or 8 new immigrants for every 1,000 existing Canadians). Increases instituted by the Trudeau Liberal government would see that annual total rise to 350,000 by late 2021, about 10 immigrants per year for every 1,000 Canadians. For a substantial population increase, this rate would need to increase by a few tenths of a percentage point, to perhaps 1.2 per cent. It would not entail a year-to-year increase in immigration numbers beyond the modest changes Canadians are used to. Canada's immigration intake increased several times during the Mulroney years—notably by 50,000 between 1986 and 1987 (from 99,000 back to the 1976 level of 152,000)—and then fell by 40,000 in the Chrétien years, from 216,000 to 174,000 in 1997, and then jumped again by 40,000 in 2000, to 230,000. In 2016, it saw another increase of 40,000, from 260,000 to a target of 300,000.

Most scenarios for population growth call for similar gradual changes in immigration intake. One proposal, by the Advisory Council on Economic Growth, outlines a plan that would see a gradual rise in immigration numbers, with annual increases between 15,000 and 45,000 immigrants each year (to avoid a sudden strain on our education, transportation and health systems) until 2021. At that point Canada would be taking in 75,000 additional primary immigrants (those admitted through the points system) and an equal number of family members (those who come as relatives of the "points" immigrants), for a total annual immigration intake of 450,000 per year and an annual population growth of 1.2 percent—an immigration level considerably lower than, for example, Switzerland's (1.9 per cent) and similar to the rates in New Zealand, Ireland and Norway. The plan would focus exclusively on high-skill and postsecondary student immigration to minimize cost and maximize economic benefit (as well as a predicted sharp decrease in refugee numbers, which tend to spike only during crises every few decades). This would not produce a very noticeable increase in the number of newcomers in Canadian streets and schools; it is less than a third of the proportion of immigration Canada experienced every year in the 1910s. The plan would allow institutions and infrastructure to expand in an organic and managed way, so that cities could plan for growth and phase in transportation, housing and schools as the newcomers' economic participation provided the new tax revenues to pay for them.

The Advisory Council's immigration numbers are on the high side: they assume no change in birth rates. If investments in family policy and childcare deliver a fertility-rate increase, then the immigration numbers could be considerably lower. The effect will be the same either way: more Canadians, and a considerably younger population. This, as Chapter 6 showed, would make the mid-century demographic crunch much more manageable. The price of managing an aging generation would not eat up a third of national and provincial budgets, thereby leaving resources for climate policy, infrastructure and younger generations.

This increase would not come free of cost. If it is to work, it will require upfront investments. First, a considerably larger department of Immigration, Refugees and Citizenship, both in sending countries (to select and pre-integrate the most suitable families) and, more importantly, in Canada (to speed up current processing times). A more efficient system will soon be crucial: almost every sending country will experience population shrinkage rather than growth by mid-century, so we are on the verge of an era of "peak people" in which countries compete for a dwindling supply of migrants rather than trying to control their entry. Canada has considerable advantages in this competition, but it can't afford a sluggish or overburdened immigration bureaucracy, especially at these higher rates. Even more importantly, investments need to be made in urban infrastructure, transportation, housing and workplace policy.

Today, more than 60 percent of immigrants settle in the metropolitan areas of Vancouver, Toronto and Montreal. During the next three decades of growth, that percentage is likely to fall as the high housing prices of those cities encourage a greater proportion of new Canadians to settle in Canada's other large and medium-sized cities and surrounding areas. Still, the largest single slice of population growth will continue to occur in the three big metropolitan areas. This is an opportunity. As we've seen, all three cities have reached a frustrating point in their development. They have become sprawling and expansive enough to outgrow their current transportation and infrastructure, but they do not yet have enough population, or sufficient population density, to support the solutions to those problems. There aren't enough people to fill these cities in and justify rapid and ecological infrastructure development in all their districts, or to provide sufficient tax base and consumer markets to make such new services and infrastructure fiscally sensible. All three metropolitan areas could easily double or triple their populations without extending their current boundaries—in fact, in many ways their existing problems of urban sprawl and "leapfrog development" are products of earlier underpopulation and its property-market effects. The presence of more people will give priority to better use of existing space and more tight-knit, functional mixed-use communities, as long as growth is kept within current urban envelopes.

All three cities need to increase density, prevent further sprawl and protect rural areas from urban development. They need to build new inter-municipality transit links and improve the capacity of their rapid-transit networks. These cities need to increase mixed-use developments and plan new developments, especially in transit-corridor areas, to ensure a mix of forms of tenure (rental, freehold, condominium, cooperative and public housing, ideally with pathways between them) and income levels. And they need to add low-rise apartment and laneway housing to low-density residential neighbourhoods, build up green infrastructure and reduce travel distances to work.

Metropolitan Vancouver needs to keep its growth within the Urban Containment Boundary and to build up population density, mixed-use development, and infill, laneway and apartment housing in sparse and single-family areas of eastern Surrey and Langley, Coquitlam, Lonsdale, Maple Ridge, Metrotown, New Westminster and Richmond, and surrounding towns. The area needs better fast transit links connecting it to the Fraser Valley and Squamish-Lillooet regions, and more capacity on existing rapid-transit routes.

Greater Montreal's eighty-two municipalities need to protect the Agricultural Zone by enforcing the 2031 Metropolitan Boundary and to replace suburban sprawl with infill housing in central neighbourhoods, as well as building up population density and mixed-use and brownfield developments in the Island of

Montreal and Longueuil municipalities and in the central parts of the North Shore, Laval and the South Shore. Fast rail transit routes are needed along east-west corridors across the island and into the North and South Shores, including the Champlain Bridge, and better north-south Metro service is needed if the population is to double.

The lack of density is especially acute in its inner suburbs of Scarborough, Etobicoke and North York and the area planners call the "yellow belt"—the crescent of single-family housing neighbour-hoods, where planning laws permit only one dwelling per lot. Half of Toronto's neighbourhoods are losing population. This decline, of half a million people since 2001, is concentrated in these ineffi-cient single-family detached-home neighourhoods, where a third of households contain only one person. These districts need to add higher-density apartment housing to create a tighter-knit civic life, increase the housing supply and support more mass transit.

The largest receiving areas for new immigrants in Canada, Peel and York Regions (which include the major gateway cities of Mississauga, Brampton, Markham and Vaughan), need to con-tinue their evolution into denser and more urban-minded places, greatly expand their public transit networks, and keep their growth strictly within the Green Belt for both ecological and quality-of-life reasons. This new density needs to support a large-scale expansion of the city's mass transit in central, inner suburban and wider regional corridors. Ideally, Peel and York Regions should become politically integrated into Toronto's municipal governance bodies, much as the outer boroughs of New York City and London became part of an integrated municipal political and fiscal system as they passed the 8- to 10-million mark in the twentieth century.

As important as those three big metropolises and the other big population-growth cities of Calgary, Edmonton, Winnipeg, Ottawa and Quebec City will be medium-sized cities with universities— places such as Lethbridge, London, Kitchener-Waterloo, Hamilton, Kingston, Trois-Rivières, Moncton, Halifax and St. John's. Research by geographer Margaret Walton-Roberts of the Balsillie School of International Affairs at Wilfrid Laurier University found that the mid-sized cities that will attract and keep immigrants are the ones with significant universities, colleges or teaching hospitals. Many new immigrants are either postsecondary students or professionals seeking credential-upgrading diplomas and degrees, and these cities offer more affordable housing in increasingly cosmopolitan and well-serviced surroundings.

Most of these cities are already eagerly seeking immigrants in order to fill the fiscal and housing holes left by aging post-industrial populations. But Canada must also invest in these cities and prepare them for larger populations. They need rapid-transit links to larger centres, higher-density housing in mixed-use neighbourhoods with space for small business, and education and infrastructure investments that will allow them to become larger centres later in this century.

If the immigrant-integration success that made the previous tripling of the Canadian population so successful is to continue during this one, we need to make sure immigrants continue to have access to the tools they use most often to integrate themselves: home ownership, small business and employment. We are entering a new era of housing and work, and Canada needs to provide new handholds to allow both immigrants and new-generation Canadians to climb into the middle class.

Making home ownership accessible to the new generation of Canadians requires not just significant expansions in housing supply and supporting infrastructure; it also requires new financial instruments and supports to ensure access. We have faced similar challenges before. Immediately after the Second World War, hundreds of thousands of Canadians sought housing they could not afford; this led to the creation of the Canada Mortgage and Housing Corporation and its system of government-guaranteed home loans. We need an equally dramatic intervention for this new challenge, one that creates new, long-term and shared instruments of financing and support to allow people to enter the housing market more securely. We also need expansion of supports for rental and social housing, and schemes that allow people to move easily from one to the other, sometimes in the same dwelling.

The changing world of work requires a significant revamp of institutions and services to guarantee that employment and entrepreneurship will continue to provide social mobility. Given the complex portfolios of employment, self-employment, small-business and service incomes that many Canadians now juggle, benefits—housing, employment, health and pension—need to be made more flexible, accessible to people with mixed income sources, and portable across provincial and occupational boundaries. A modernization of the employment insurance system to serve informal, "gig economy" and non-standard workers better as they move between income sources—without penalty—is also urgently needed.

And we need changes in the systems that allow people to work: a system of strong incentives for employers to develop in-house childcare, flexible-hours work plans and family leave programs. A national flexible work and shared work initiative.

A more flexible postsecondary education system that breaks with the traditional four-year degree program to accommodate family members caught in the fragmented labour force, and more part-time, work-integrated learning and co-op programs suited to the needs of new Canadians. A set of schemes to develop and provide credentials for the "soft skills" required in the digital economy that allows newcomers to become recognized in new-economy employment networks.

Most of these reforms to cities, housing and work are changes Canada ought to be making no matter what our population goals. That is one of the lessons of our history. When we have set out to prepare the ground for newcomers, the effort has always made things better for everyone. Just contemplating a larger Canadian population forces us to confront the flaws and stress points in our country. We have learned, over the past half-century, to appreciate Canada as a country of newcomers, as a place of self-invention and mutual assistance. We have overcome most of the barriers and limitations imposed by our constricted history; today we are left only with a deficit of scale, and occasionally a deficit of imagination.

Imagine the Canada in which my grandmother landed: a place with one-third the population, a huge reserve of hope and a narrow range of opportunities. Her artistic and creative ambitions were shunted aside for decades until she found outlets in her expansive private life. She spent her final days, seven decades after she and her family arrived in Canada, in a place whose growth in population, industry, urbanization, diversity and international trade hadn't made it more crowded or chaotic or fractious or incoherent, despite the warnings of those 1940s population pessimists. Quite the contrary: she and her great-grandchildren found themselves sharing gleeful appreciation of a country that had come to feel more intimate, more connected and more secure by tripling its population. Her adopted country had caught up with her.

Imagine a larger Canada. The places that feel crowded and jam-packed today would feel less claustrophobic and more spacious in a maximum Canada, because they would gain the transportation networks and public spaces only a larger population can support. The places that feel isolated, alienating, dark and frightening will feel like tight-knit neighbourhoods, with people on the street and a sense of hope, in a maximum Canada, because they'll have become connected and populated, part of cities that no longer sprawl but rather fill up. The fragile northern spaces, wilderness areas, open skies and ocean shores that feel threatened and polluted today will be more protected and sustainable in a maximum Canada, because there will be far greater resources for ecological care with the sort of population that can drive a large-scale shift to green and zero-carbon sources of energy and travel. A maximum Canada won't be a utopia any more than today's Canada is, but it will be a place with the tools and resources to do many things better, more fairly, more cleanly and more cooperatively: a more fully realized version of the Canadian way.

The coming century of growth won't change anything about the nature or feeling of Canada. But it will make it feel a lot more like home.

A Note on Sources

A comprehensive history of Canadian population has yet to be written. For larger perspectives on Canadian population and policy that inform this book's historical chapters, I am indebted to the two existing wide-scale histories of immigration to Canada—Valerie Knowles's substantial and often-updated *Strangers at Our Gates* and Ninette Kelley and Michael Trebilcock's *The Making of the Mosaic*—and to two comprehensive histories of Canadian economics and trade, Michael Hart's *A Trading Nation: Canadian Trade Policy from Colonialism to Globalization* and Kenneth Norrie and Douglas Owram's *A History of the Canadian Economy*.

PART ONE

The correspondence from Catherine Lloyd-Jones, along with her genealogy, was assembled by the extended Luard family and passed to me by my father, R.J. Luard Saunders. I was able to corroborate it, and extend its context, with the help of the books *The Early Political and Military History of Burford* (Maj. R. Cuthbertson Muir, 1913), *The History of the County of Brant, Ontario* (J.H. Beers & Co., 1883), and

William Scott and His Extended Family (Marie Voisin, 2009), along with *Burke's Landed Gentry*.

On the politics surrounding the 1837 rebellions and the quarter-century of de facto civil war in Upper and Lower Canada that preceded them: Gerald Craig's *Upper Canada: The Formative Years, 1784–1841*; John Little's *Loyalties in Conflict: A Canadian Borderland in War and Rebellion, 1812–1840*; Colin Read's *The Rebellion of 1837 in Upper Canada*; and John Howison's 1822 travelogue *Sketches of Upper Canada*.

On Champlain, the politics of New France and indigenous relations in early Canada: David Hackett Fischer's *Champlain's Dream*; Alan Greer's *The People of New France*; Josée Ouimet's *Jean Talon: Intendant en Nouvelle-France;* Terry Fenge and Jim Aldridge's *Keeping Promises: The Royal Proclamation of 1763, Aboriginal Rights, and Treaties in Canada*; Mathieu d'Avignon's paper "Samuel de Champlain et les alliances franco-amérindiennes: Une diplomatie interculturelle" and his essay with Denys Delâge "We Shall Be One People: Quebec"; and John Ralston Saul's *A Fair Country: Telling Truths about Canada*. Canada's population growth in the eighteenth century is chronicled in Adam Lillie's *Canada: Physical, Economic and Social* (Maclear & Co., 1855).

On Canadian population policy after the American Revolution, Lord Shelburne and the establishment of British North America's mercantile role: Gerald S. Graham's *British Policy and Canada, 1774–1791: A Study in Eighteenth Century Trade Policy* and Charles R. Ritcheson's *Aftermath of the Revolution: British Policy Toward the United States, 1783–1795*. On Simcoe's ambitions: Mary Beacock Fryer and Christopher Dracott's *John Graves Simcoe, 1752–1806: A Biography*.

On the War of 1812 and the formation of Upper and Lower Canada's populations: Alan Taylor's *The Civil War of 1812: American Citizens, British Subjects, Irish Rebels and Indian Allies*; Carl Benn's *The War of 1812* and *The Iroquois in the War of 1812*; and Mark Zuehlke's *For Honour's Sake: The War of 1812 and the Brokering of an Uneasy Peace*.

On the economics and politics of the 1830s and 1840s: Jim Rees's *Surplus People: From Wicklow to Canada*; Marvin McInnis's paper

"Canadian Economic Development in the Wheat Boom Era:
A Reassessment"; Donald G. Paterson and Ronald A. Shearer's paper
"Wheat, Railways and Cycles: The 1840s Reassessed"; and Gerald M.
Craig's edition of *Lord Durham's Report*.

On the loss of Canadian population in the nineteenth century:
the work of Laurent Martel and Jonathan Chagnon in Statistics
Canada's Demography Division, especially their paper "Population
Growth in Canada: From 1851 to 2061"; Roderic Beaujot and
Muhammad Munib Raza's chapter "Population and Immigration
Policy" in Patrick James and Mark Kasoff, editors, *Canadian Studies
in the New Millennium*; David Verbeeten's paper "The Past and
Future of Immigration to Canada"; Marvin McInnis's chapter
"The Population History of Canada in the Nineteenth Century"
in M.R. Hains and R.H. Steckel's book *A Population History of North
America*; and Damien-Claude Bélanger and Claude Bélanger's paper
"French Canadian Emigration to the United States, 1840–1930."

On the often different experiences of the United States during
these decades: Desmond King's *Making Americans: Immigration, Race,
and the Origins of the Diverse Democracy* and George J. Borjas's *We
Wanted Workers: Unraveling the Immigration Narrative*.

On Britain's view of Canada's purpose and the British role in
Canadian Confederation and trade relations: Ged Martin's *Britain
and the Origins of Canadian Confederation, 1837–67*; and Michael S.
Cross's *Free Trade, Annexation and Reciprocity, 1846–1854*. On
Gladstone's positions on Canada: Erich Eyck's biography *Gladstone*;
and Ian St. John's *Gladstone and the Logic of Victorian Politics*.

On John A. Macdonald's policies: Joseph Pope's *The Day of Sir
John Macdonald: A Chronicle of the First Prime Minister of the Dominion*;
and Richard Gwyn's two-volume biography *The Life and Times of
John A. Macdonald*. On the indigenous tragedies and losses resulting
from prairie population policy: James Daschuk's *Clearing the Plains:
Disease, Politics of Starvation, and the Loss of Aboriginal Life*.

On the Laurier era: Oscar Skelton's *The Day of Sir Wilfrid Laurier:
A Chronicle of Our Own Time*; Robert Craig Brown and Ramsay

Cook's *Canada, 1896–1921: A Nation Transformed*, J. W. Dafoe's *~~~~ A Study in Canadian Politics*; Marvin McInnis's paper "Canadian Economic Development in the Wheat Boom: A Reassessment"; Julie F. Gilmour's *Trouble on Main Street: Mackenzie King, Reason, Race and the 1907 Vancouver Riots*; and Patrice Dutil and David MacKenzie's *Canada 1911: The Decisive Election That Shaped the Country*.

On the decades of immigration restriction prior to 1945: Martin Thornton's *Sir Robert Borden: Canada*; Byron Lew and Bruce Cater's paper "Canadian Emigration to the U.S., 1900–1930: Characterizing Movers and Stayers, and the Differential Impact of Immigration Policy on the Mobility of French and English Canadians"; Louis Rosenberg's *Canada's Jews: A Social and Economic Study of Jews in Canada in the 1930s*; Michael D. Behiels's *Quebec and the Question of Immigration: From Ethnocentrism to Ethnic Pluralism, 1900–1985*; Lisa Rose Mar's *Brokering Belonging: Chinese in Canada's Exclusion Era, 1885–1945*; and Irving Abella and Harold Troper's *None Is Too Many: Canada and the Jews of Europe, 1933–1948*.

PART TWO

Details of my mother's and my maternal grandmother's immigration to Canada (and my grandfather's return) are from conversations with Patricia Saunders and the late Pamela Smith, and documented in Alan Smith's mimeographed memoir.

On Canada's postwar population and immigration policies and debates: G.A. Rawlyk's paper "Canada's Immigration Policy, 1945–1962"; Ruth Sandwell's *Canada's Rural Majority: Households, Environments, and Economies, 1870–1940*; Harold Innis's *The Strategy of Culture*; H.F. Angus's 1946 paper "The Future of Immigration into Canada"; Arthur Lower's article "The Myth of Mass Immigration" from the May 15, 1949, *Maclean's*; Donald Creighton's *The Forked Road: Canada, 1939–1957*; Franca Iacovetta's paper "Ordering in Bulk: Canada's Postwar Immigration Policy and the Recruitment of Contract Workers from Italy" and her book *Gatekeepers: Reshaping Immigrant Lives in Cold War Canada*; Yolande Pottie-Sherman and

Rima Wilkes's paper "Anti-immigrant Sentiment in Canada"; Peter S. Li's paper "Cultural Diversity in Canada: The Social Construction of Racial Differences"; and Denis Smith's *Rogue Tory: The Life and Legend of John G. Diefenbaker.*

On the transformations in policy and attitudes that took place around the Centennial decade: Triadafilos Triadafilopoulos's chapter "Dismantling White Canada: Race, Rights, and the Origins of the Points System" from his book *Wanted and Welcome? Policies for Highly Skilled Immigrants in Comparative Perspective*; Jack Granatstein's *Canada, 1957–1967: The Years of Uncertainty and Innovation;* Robert Vipond's *Making a Global City: How One Toronto School Embraced Diversity*; and José E. Igartua's *The Other Quiet Revolution: National Identities in English Canada, 1945–71.*

On the transformations in Quebec immigration and diversity policy: Cory Blad and Philippe Couton's paper "The Rise of an Intercultural Nation: Immigration, Diversity and Nationhood in Quebec"; Michael D. Behiels's *Quebec and the Question of Immigration: From Ethnocentrism to Ethnic Pluralism, 1900–1985;* Louise Fontaine's paper "Immigration and Cultural Politics: A Bone of Contention between the Province of Quebec and the Canadian Federal Government"; and Chris Kostov's paper "Canada-Quebec Immigration Agreements (1971–1991) and Their Impact on Federalism."

On the emergence of multiculturalism, both official and popular, in Canada after 1967: Keith Banting and Will Kymlicka's paper "Canadian Multiculturalism: Global Anxieties and Local Debates"; Will Kymlicka's books *Multicultural Citizenship: A Liberal Theory of Minority Rights* and *Finding Our Way: Rethinking Ethnocultural Relations in Canada*; Lee Blanding's dissertation "Re-branding Canada: The Origins of Canadian Multiculturalism Policy, 1945–1974"; Peter Henshaw's chapter "John Buchan and the British Imperial Origins of Canadian Multiculturalism" in Norman Hillmer's edited collection *Canadas of the Mind: The Making and Unmaking of Canadian Nationalisms in the Twentieth Century*; Kenneth McRoberts's *Misconceiving Canada: The Struggle for National Unity*; and Jeffrey Reitz's paper "Economic Opportunity, Multiculturalism, and the Roots of Popular Support for High Immigration in Canada."

On the emerging recognition of indigenous peoples as constitutional partners: Hamar Foster and Heather Raven's *Let Right Be Done: Aboriginal Title, the Calder Case, and the Future of Indigenous Rights*; P.G. McHugh's *Aboriginal Title: The Modern Jurisprudence of Tribal Land Rights*; John Borrows's *Canada's Indigenous Constitution*; and Olive Patricia Dickason and David T. McNab's *Canada's First Nations: A History of Founding Peoples from Earliest Times*.

PART THREE

On the need to leave Canada: my article "Gehry's Lament" in the September 29, 2001, *Globe and Mail* and Bill Smith's article "Interview with Paul Bley" in the April 1979 issue of *Coda*.

On the public cost of underpopulation: the Office of the Parliamentary Budget Officer's *Fiscal Sustainability Report 2016*; Stefan Legge's paper "Innovation in an Aging Population"; the Conference Board of Canada's reports *A Long-Term View of Canada's Changing Demographics: Are Higher Immigration Levels an Appropriate Response to Canada's Aging Population?* and *Future Care for Canadian Seniors: A Status Quo Forecast*; the OECD report *Looking to 2060: Long-Term Global Growth Prospects*; Robin Banerjee and William Robson's paper "Faster, Younger, Richer? The Fond Hope and Sobering Reality of Immigration's Impact on Canada's Demographic and Economic Future"; the Century Initiative's December 2016 quarterly report; John Gerring and Dominic Zarecki's paper "Size and Democracy Revisited"; and B. Guy Peters's paper "The Policy Capacity of Government."

On the private cost: Statistics Canada's report *Natural Resources, the Terms of Trade, and Real Income Growth in Canada: 1870 to 2010*; the Canadian Centre for Policy Alternatives' report *The Bitumen Cliff: Lessons and Challenges of Bitumen Mega-developments for Canada's Economy in an Age of Climate Change*; Mark Zachary Taylor's *The Politics of Innovation*; Alberto Alesina's paper "The Size of Countries:

Does It Matter?"; Stefan Legge's paper "Innovation in an Aging Population"; the *China Business Review* article "Domestic Innovation and Government Procurement Policies"; the *OECD Science, Technology and Innovation Outlook 2016*; Daron Acemoglu and Joshua Linn's paper "Market Size in Innovation: Theory and Evidence from the Pharmaceutical Industry"; Daron Acemoglu's paper "Technical Change, Inequality, and the Labour Market"; Alberto Alesina, Johann Harnoss and Hillel Rapoport's paper "Birthplace Diversity and Economic Prosperity"; Jeffrey R. Campbell and Hugo A. Hopenhayn's paper "Market Size Matters"; Gilles Duranton and Diego Puga's paper "Nursery Cities: Urban Diversity, Process Innovation, and the Life-cycle of Products"; Maryann P. Feldman and Dieter F. Kogler's paper "Stylized Facts in the Geography of Innovation"; James Milway's paper "Assessing the Drivers of the Canada-U.S. Prosperity Gap"; Marco Guerzoni's paper "The Impact of Market Size and Users' Sophistication on Innovation: The Patterns of Demand"; Diego Puga's paper "The Magnitude and Causes of Agglomeration Economies"; the Canadian Chamber of Commerce report *Stimulating Canadian Innovation: How to Boost Canada's Venture Capital Industry*; the Deloitte report *Age of Disruption: Are Canadian Firms Prepared?*; Mario Polèse's paper "On the Growth Dynamics of Cities and Regions—Seven Lessons: A Canadian Perspective with Thoughts on Regional Australia"; and Mario Polèse and Jonathan Denis-Jacob's paper "Changes at the Top: A Cross-Country Examination over the 20th Century of the Rise (and Fall) in Rank of the Top Cities in National Urban Hierarchies."

On the ecological cost: Luís M.A. Bettencourt's paper "The Origins of Scaling in Cities"; Luís M.A. Bettencourt and Geoffrey B. West's article "Bigger Cities Do More with Less"; David Dodman's paper "Blaming Cities for Climate Change? An Analysis of Urban Greenhouse Gas Emissions Inventories"; Nektarios Aslanidis and Susana Iranzo's paper "Environment and Development: Is There a Kuznets Curve for CO_2 Emissions?"; David I. Stern's paper "The Rise and Fall of the Environmental Kuznets Curve"; the National Round

Table on the Environment and the Economy's report *Paying the Price: The Economic Impacts of Climate Change for Canada*; José Lobo, Luís M.A. Bettencourt, Deborah Strumsky and Geoffrey B. West's paper "Urban Scaling and the Production Function for Cities"; Luís M.A. Bettencourt, José Lobo, Dirk Helbing, Christian Kuhnert and Geoffrey B. West's paper "Growth, Innovation, Scaling, and the Pace of Life in Cities"; the OECD report *Cities, Climate Change and Multilevel Governance*; and Stéphane Hallegatte and Jan Corfee-Morlot's paper "Understanding Climate Change Impacts, Vulnerability and Adaptation at City Scale: An Introduction."

On the strategic cost: Haimin Zhang's paper "Immigration and Crime: Evidence from Canada"; Irvin Studin's article in *Global Brief*, "Canada—Population 100 Million"; Andrew Richter's paper "Sharing the Burden? U.S. Allies, Defense Spending, and the Future of NATO"; the Century Initiative September 2016 quarterly report; and Robert Kaplan's *Globe and Mail* article "Fulfilling Laurier's Vision: A Canada of 100 Million."

On the cultural cost: Charlotte Gray's *The Promise of Canada*; Donald E. Abelson's paper "Do Think Tanks Matter? Opportunities, Constraints and Incentives for Think Tanks in Canada and the United States"; Donald E. Abelson's books *Northern Lights: Exploring Canada's Think Tank Landscape* and *Do Think Tanks Matter? Assessing the Impact of Public Policy Institutes*; Herman Bakvis's paper "Rebuilding Policy Capacity in the Era of the Fiscal Dividend: A Report From Canada"; Alberto Alesina and Paola Giuliano's paper "Culture and Institutions"; Michael E. Porter's paper "Clusters and the New Economics of Competition"; Edward L. Glaeser, Rafael La Porta, Florencio Lopez-de-Silanes and Andrei Shleifer's paper "Do Institutions Cause Growth?"; and Donald Savoie's *Whatever Happened to the Music Teacher? How Government Decides and Why*. I explore the cultural cost in greater detail in my chapter "Public Thought and Canada's Crisis of Underpopulation" in Nelson Wiseman's edited volume *The Public Intellectual in Canada*.

On the history of 100 million: the Advisory Council on Economic Growth report *Attracting the Talent Canada Needs through Immigration*; the Mid-Canada Development Corridor Foundation report *Mid-Canada Development Corridor: A Concept*; and the Manpower Canada report cited in Richard Gwyn's January 4, 1975, syndicated article "Just What Kind of Country Would You Like Canada to Be?" I have previously written on the history of this idea, in my March 31, 2001, *Globe and Mail* article "Why Canada Needs 100 Million People."

On the challenge of employment and entrepreneurship: the Statistics Canada 2014 report *Immigration, Low Income and Income Inequality in Canada: What's New in the 2000s?*; the Wellesley Institute report *Shadow Economies: Economic Survival Strategies of Toronto Immigrant Communities*; the Conference Board of Canada report *The Bucks Stop Here: Trends in Income Inequality between Generations*; the Employment and Social Development Canada report *The Changing Nature of Work: Labour Market Backgrounder*; Sunil Johal and Noah Zon's Mowat Centre report *Policymaking for the Sharing Economy: Beyond Whack-a-Mole*; and the MaRS Solutions Lab report *Shifting Perspectives: Redesigning Regulation for the Sharing Economy.*

On the challenge of homes and cities: the Statistics Canada report *The Housing Experiences of New Canadians: Insights from the Longitudinal Survey of Immigrants to Canada*; Heather Smith and David Ley's paper "Even in Canada? The Multiscalar Construction and Experience of Concentrated Immigrant Poverty in Gateway Cities"; J. David Hulchanski's study *The Three Cities within Toronto: Income Polarization among Toronto's Neighbourhoods, 1970–2005*; and Zack Taylor's paper "Who Elected Rob Ford, and Why? An Ecological Analysis of the 2010 Toronto Election."

On the challenge of human investment: the Library of Parliament background paper "Recognition of the Foreign Qualifications of Immigrants"; the Forum of Labour Market Ministers report *A Pan-Canadian Framework for the Assessment and Recognition of Foreign Qualifications*; the Conference Board of Canada's article "A Labour Market Shortage of 1 Million by 2020?

Where We Stand Today"; the McKinsey Global Institute report *Global Growth: Can Productivity Save the Day in an Aging World?*; the Wellesley Institute report *Shadow Economies: Economic Survival Strategies of Toronto Immigrant Communities*; and the Canadian Chamber of Commerce report *Improving Canada's Immigration Processes*.

On the challenge of political backlash: Keith Banting and Will Kymlicka's paper "Canadian Multiculturalism: Global Anxieties and Local Debates"; Feng Hou and Garnett Picot's Statistics Canada study "Visible Minority Neighbourhood Enclaves and Labour Market Outcomes of Immigrants"; Mohammad Qadeer and Sandeep Agrawal's report "Ethnic Enclaves in the Toronto Area and Social Integration: The City as Common Ground"; the Statistics Canada studies "Mixed Unions in Canada" and "A Portrait of Couples in Mixed Unions"; the Statistics Canada report "Population Projections for Canada (2013 to 2063)."

On family policy, childcare and fertility gaps: Shannon Proudfoot's 2010 Postmedia News series on the Ipsos Reid study of Canada's fertility gap; Jennifer Robson's Institute for Research on Public Policy (IRPP) study *Parental Benefits in Canada: Which Way Forward?*; Pierre Lefebvre, Philip Merrigan and Matthieu Verstraete's paper "Dynamic Labour Supply Effects of Childcare Subsidies: Evidence from a Canadian Natural Experiment on Low-Fee Universal Child Care"; Pierre Fortin, Luc Godbout and Suzie St.-Cerny's paper "Impact of Quebec's Universal Low-Fee Childcare Program on Female Labour Force Participation, Domestic Income, and Government Budgets"; the IRPP report *New Evidence about Child Care in Canada: Use Patterns, Affordability and Quality*; Pierre Lefebvre and Philip Merrigan's report "The Quebec Experiment of $5 per Day per Child Childcare Policy and Mother's Labour Supply: Evidence Based on the Five Cycles of the NLSCY"; Pierre Lefebvre, Philip Merrigan and Francis Roy-Desrosiers's paper "Quebec's Childcare Universal Low Fees Policy 10 Years After: Effects, Costs and Benefits"; and Michael Baker, Jonathan Gruber and Kevin Milligan's paper "Universal Childcare, Maternal Labour Supply and Family Well-Being."

On immigrant benefits: Kathy Georgiades, M.H. Boyle and K.A. Fife's paper "Emotional and Behavioral Problems among Adolescent Students: The Role of Immigrant, Racial/Ethnic Congruence and Belongingness in Schools"; Michael Boyle, Kathy Georgiades et al.'s Offord Centre for Child Studies *2014 School Mental Health Surveys*; and Dominique Fleury's Human Resources and Social Development Canada report *A Study of Poverty and Working Poverty among Recent Immigrants to Canada*.

On preparing cities for growth: the Greater Vancouver Regional District Board's regional growth strategy *Metro Vancouver 2040: Shaping Our Future*; the Resonance Consulting report *Future of B.C. Housing: A Study of Buyer and Renter Sentiment in British Columbia*; Communauté métropolitaine de Montréal's *Metropolitan Economic Development Plan 2015–2020* and *An Attractive, Competitive and Sustainable Greater Montreal*; Toronto City Planning's *Toronto Official Plan*; Ontario Land Use Planning Review's *Proposed Growth Plan for the Greater Golden Horseshoe, 2016*; and Margaret W. Walton-Roberts's papers "Immigration, the University and the Welcoming Second Tier City" and "Immigrant Settlement and Retention in Second Tier and Small Urban Regions: A Case Study of Kitchener-Waterloo, Ontario, Canada."

Acknowledgements

Living abroad for an extended period often provides a clearer perspective on the wonders, peculiarities and shortcomings of home. This book's ideas have their roots in a series of essays about Canada, its history and its demography I wrote from the *Globe and Mail* between 2001 and 2012—that is, during the decade and a half when I was generally living in the United States and in Britain. I am grateful to a series of editors who encouraged me, as a foreign correspondent, to turn my eyes homeward. I am especially grateful to my current editors, Natasha Hassan and David Walmsley, for giving me the latitude, the resources and the encouragement to write at length on this subject.

While living in England, I was invited by Margaret MacMillan to come to Oxford University and deliver the Canada Seminar at Lady Margaret Hall. Among the people I met there was a Canadian graduate student, Scott Young, who shared my interest in, but had a far broader knowledge of, topics in population, migration and cities. Scott enthusiastically agreed to work as a researcher on this book, connecting me with a wide range of new avenues in policy, demographics, history, statistics and scholarship. Scott and I share a similar Canadian story: one side of our families came to Canada in the nineteenth century and the other after the Second World War. But because his father's family immigrated from China to Vancouver in the nineteenth century and his mother's from Korea in the 1970s, his roots would produce a different sort of book about Canada, one that ought to be written.

This book is built on the enduring partnerships that have supported and enriched my writing for many years. Above all I am indebted to my partner in life and writing, Elizabeth Renzetti (who also has a family with one branch that arrived in the nineteenth century and one in the twentieth, in this case one from the United States as loyalists, and the other from Abruzzo, Italy, as bricklayers). Anne Collins, the publisher at Knopf Random Canada, encouraged me to write about Canada after having guided and edited me through two international books with characteristic grace and patience. She connected me with this book's editor, Craig Pyette, whose superb editing sense and broad perspective benefited this book's prose and arguments enormously. And John Pearce has continued to help me as a critical-minded agent blessed with great editorial acumen.

As a generalist, I draw on the intelligence of genuine experts and more knowledgeable people, whose work ideally I help bring to greater popular attention and at worst turn into an over-simplification. In hopes that I have done more of the former, I want to acknowledge fruitful dialogues, conversations, interviews, email exchanges and collaborations with people who include, but are not limited to, Roderic Beaujot, Zenaida Ravanera and the scholars involved in the Population Change and Lifecourse

Strategic Knowledge Cluster; Vasiliki Bednar; Michael Behiels; Jean Charest; Adrienne Clarkson; Miles Corak; Peter Henshaw; Randall Hansen; Dan Herman; David Hulchanski; William and Molly Anne Macdonald; Jeffrey Reitz; John Ralston Saul; John Stackhouse; Kate Subak, Yohana Mebrahtu and their colleagues at the Century Initiative; Stephen Toope; Morton Weinfeld.

And as this was uniquely a book about the place in history occupied by my own family, I am indebted to them for sharing the stories of their arrival and place in Canada. Lengthy conversations with my late maternal grandparents, Pamela Smith and Alan Smith, with my mother, Patricia Saunders and my father, Luard Saunders, and correspondences, gleanings and occasional meetings with the extended Saunders–Luard clan provided this book with both its starting point and its narrative frame, as well as much of its human scale. Having brought another pair of foreign-born immigrants to Canada in their childhood, I have a great appreciation for the far greater challenges endured, and higher stakes faced, by my predecessors.

Index

© Greg Tjepkema

DOUG SAUNDERS is the international affairs columnist for the *Globe and Mail*, where he has served previously as bureau chief in London and Los Angeles. He is the author of two previous best-selling books, *Arrival City: The Final Migration and Our Next World* (2010) and *The Myth of the Muslim Tide: Do Immigrants Threaten the West?* (2012), which have been nominated for the Gelber and Shaughnessy Cohen Prizes and won the Donner Prize, the Schelling Prize for Architectural Theory and the National Library of China Wenjin Book Award. He lives in Toronto.